Praise for *Every Hill a Burial Place*

"Peter Reid's account of the 1966 Tanzanian murder trial of Peace Corps volunteer Bill Kinsey is suspenseful and gripping. It is also a careful, judicial examination of the difficulties the Peace Corps faced in balancing its responsibilities to the deceased, to the accused, and to US relations with Tanzania. Both the research and presentation are masterful."
—John Hamilton, former US ambassador to Peru and Guatemala

"Peter Reid transforms the gripping story of a Peace Corps volunteer death and the acquittal of her husband into an epic study of the Peace Corps from its first days during the Kennedy administration to the present. And the fact that he successfully places this human tragedy within the complicated and troublesome days of the Cold War and after makes the book a stunning achievement. It is an amazing, suspenseful report about two young American volunteers in Tanzania that also deepens our understanding of the Peace Corps, America, and their entangled history for the last six decades."—David Rudenstine, dean emeritus of the Benjamin N. Cardozo School of Law at Yeshiva University and author of *The Day the Presses Stopped* and *The Age of Deference*

"Every Peace Corps volunteer has a story to tell. Few, however, are as surprising and suspenseful as this one."—John Coyne, novelist and former Peace Corps staff (Ethiopia)

"The violent death of a Peace Corps teacher in Tanzania has shocked, saddened, and perplexed the Peace Corps community for more than fifty years. Was Peppy Kinsey's death a horrific accident, or did her husband, Bill, batter her to death, as some African witnesses claimed? Exhaustive, coherent, thoughtful, and suspenseful, Reid's account of the Kinsey murder trial and its aftermath could well be the final word on this dark event—unless, of course, this remarkable book triggers new revelations."—Richard Lipez, author of the *Donald Strachey* series and former Peace Corps teacher (Ethiopia, 1962–1964)

"Peter Reid has written a meticulously researched and fascinating true story about the ambiguous death of a Peace Corps volunteer in Tanzania in the 1960s and the subsequent prosecution of her husband, a fellow Peace Corps volunteer, for murder. Equally compelling is the backstory about a range of issues receiving intense local and worldwide attention, including calls to 'send in the Marines' to rescue the accused, an apparent lack of concern about justice for the deceased, and the perception of special treatment for a white American in a newly independent African nation."—Skip McGinty, 1960s Peace Corps Africa Volunteer and Peace Corps Country Director, Oman

Every Hill a Burial Place

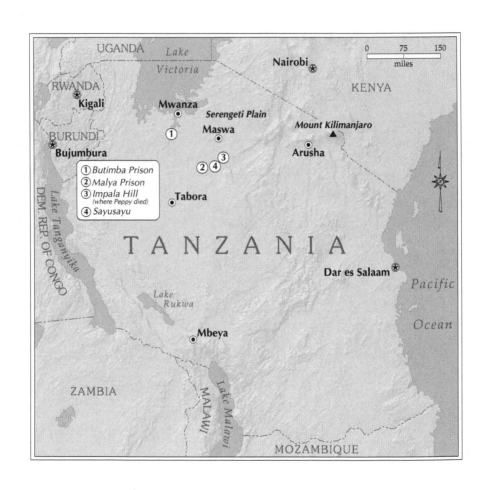

Every Hill a Burial Place

*The Peace Corps Murder Trial
in East Africa*

Peter H. Reid

UNIVERSITY PRESS OF KENTUCKY

Editorial and Sales Offices: The University Press of Kentucky
663 South Limestone Street, Lexington, Kentucky 40508-4008
www.kentuckypress.com

Map by Dick Gilbreath

Library of Congress Cataloging-in-Publication Data

Names: Reid, Peter H., 1942– author.
Title: Every hill a burial place : the Peace Corps murder trial in East Africa /
    Peter H. Reid.
Description: Lexington, Kentucky : The University Press of Kentucky, 2020. |
    Includes bibliographical references and index.
Identifiers: LCCN 2020017972 | ISBN 9780813179988 (hardcover) |
    ISBN 9780813180007 (pdf) | ISBN 9780813180014 (epub)
Subjects: LCSH: Kinsey, Bill Haywood–Trials, litigation, etc. |
    Trials (Murder)–Tanzania. | Peace Corps (U.S.)–Officials and employees–
    Legal status, laws, etc.–Tanzania. | Volunteer workers in social service–
    Legal status, laws, etc.–Tanzania.
Classification: LCC KTT3.7 K56 R45 2020 | DDC 345.67802523—dc23
LC record available at https://lccn.loc.gov/2020017972

This book is printed on acid-free paper meeting the requirements
of the American National Standard for Permanence in Paper
for Printed Library Materials.

Manufactured in the United States of America.

Member of the Association
of University Presses

*For Barbara, whose sense of humor, support, and kindness
keep me going, and for Ada, Brian, Hadleigh,
and Paul, who are the joys of my life*

Contents

Photos follow page 136

Abbreviations

AASF	African American Student Foundation
AMO	assistant medical officer
CID	Criminal Investigation Department
DEO	district education officer
FOIA	Freedom of Information Act
LAPD	Los Angeles Police Department
PCDC	Peace Corps in Washington, D.C.
PCDSM	Peace Corps in Dar es Salaam
PI	preliminary inquiry
REO	regional education officer
RMO	regional medical officer
TANU	Tanganyika African National Union
TEA	Teachers for East Africa
UTP	United Tanganyika Party

Prologue

In December 1964, Bill Kinsey and Peppy Dennett were married in an Episcopal ceremony at Peppy's home in Riverside, Connecticut. The wedding took place three days before they left to serve as Peace Corps volunteers in East Africa. The Kinseys had met and begun dating only a few months earlier during Peace Corps training in Syracuse, New York. The proposed marriage came as a huge surprise to Peppy's family; her mother was unhappy about their short relationship, but in the end the Kinseys married without a hitch.[1] Sixteen months later in the small town in Tanzania where they taught, Peppy would die, and Bill would be charged with her murder.

Introduction

I once shared a house in Africa, nestled among the giant boulders along the shores of Lake Victoria (with apologies to Isak Dinesen and the powerful sense of place evoked by the opening lines of *Out of Africa*). My housemate and I were Peace Corps volunteers teaching in a secondary school in Tanzania; both of us had graduated from college in 1964, John Oliver from the University of North Carolina, I from Stanford. We began Peace Corps training in the fall of that year at Columbia University in New York and arrived in Tanzania in December.

The Tanzania Ministry of Education had assigned us to Bwiru Boys Secondary School, five miles from the cotton-producing town of Mwanza. Bwiru was a boarding school with students from all over Tanzania, although the majority came from nearby areas. It had been established when the British governed Tanzania (then called Tanganyika) and was modeled on the British school system. Grade levels were called "forms," and there were four forms at the school—forms 1, 2, 3, and 4, roughly corresponding to ninth through twelfth grades in the American system. The faculty at Bwiru included teachers from Tanzania, Pakistan, India, Scotland, Denmark, Ireland, England, and America. The mix of cultures often led to interesting, exotic discussions and observations in the faculty room. Religion, politics, and social values were common topics of debate.

On March 30, 1966, well into our second year at Bwiru, John Oliver took his third-form English class on a field trip to visit the court in Mwanza, the nearby town and seat of regional government. While John and the students were sitting in the courtroom, John was startled to hear the clerk announce the case *Republic*

1

v. Bill Haywood Kinsey, a case that involved a charge of murder. Bill Kinsey, a fellow Peace Corps volunteer, was charged with murdering his wife, Peverley (Peppy), on the previous Sunday near their school in Maswa, Tanzania. Peppy was a vivacious, energetic graduate of Mount Holyoke College in South Hadley, Massachusetts, where she was a history major who loved modern dance. Her friends said her nickname captured her—she was enthusiastic and peppy, always ready to try something new. Bill was an honors graduate of Washington and Lee University in Lexington, Virginia, with a long list of activities by his name in the college yearbook. John and I had met the Kinseys at dinners and other social occasions in Mwanza. Although Peppy had died three days earlier, neither John nor I had heard anything about the possibility that her death was designated a murder. Communications in Africa at the time were impossibly slow, at least for Americans, although Tanzanians seemed to get their information with impressive speed.

Bill was the first Peace Corps volunteer ever to be accused of murder. A hearing was held to consider bail for the accused, with Judge Harold Platt presiding. Mr. Gurbachan Singh from the local law firm of Singh and Parekh in Mwanza appeared on Bill's behalf. Singh requested bail for his client on medical grounds; the doctors who had examined Bill found he was suffering from shock and pneumonia-like symptoms. Although the state attorney argued that bail in such a case was unprecedented, the judge granted it on medical grounds, in the amount of 30,000 Tanzania shillings (about U.S.$4,200), but also required the surrender of Bill's passport.[1]

Although bail was granted on medical grounds, Bill was soon transferred to Butimba Prison in Mwanza, where medical care was available, so his release on bail was withdrawn. The state attorney was apparently heard to complain that a white judge (Platt) had granted bail to a white man (Kinsey) even though it was unprecedented to grant bail in Tanzania when a murder charge was involved. Attorney Singh and the Peace Corps felt it was important to reduce the tension in the community on this issue, so after the transfer to Butimba Prison they did not pursue the bail issue further. Paul Sack, the Peace Corps Tanzania director, soon wrote a memo, after consultation with several doctors, that it was important for Bill to remain in Butimba Prison under these circumstances. The doctors recommended this out of fear of his mental state and the possibility of suicide; it was therefore crucial that he remain in prison, where he could be carefully monitored.[2] It is not clear that Bill was ever consulted on this issue.

In 1966, the Peace Corps was still in its infancy and so far had faced few major problems involving the volunteers. There had been an incident in Nigeria when a volunteer sent a postcard home describing the "primitive conditions" in the City of Ibadan. The postcard was intercepted, published widely in Nigeria, and picked up by news agencies in other countries. Nigerians were incensed by her description. Although the young woman apologized and tried to explain her intention, she eventually resigned and returned to America.[3] A possible murder involving Peace Corps volunteers was an issue of significantly greater magnitude and presented the Peace Corps with its first serious controversy.

By 1966, John F. Kennedy had been dead for three years. However, the mythology that has since then grown up around Kennedy and the "New Frontier" was already well on its way to making Kennedy the most publicly admired president of the twentieth century. Professor Larry Sabato reports in his book *The Kennedy Half Century* on a public-opinion poll conducted for his book just prior to 2013. The results of the poll showed the following approval ratings for certain presidents on a scale of 1 to 10: Kennedy, 7.6; Reagan, 6.9; Eisenhower, 6.8; Clinton, 6.7; Ford, 5.0; H. W. Bush, 4.9; Johnson, 4.9; Carter 4.6; and Nixon, 3.7.[4]

The Kennedy legacy has generated hundreds of articles, books, and movies, and as the years pass, the interest may diminish, but an examination of the few successful aspects of his program remains important to our understanding of that legacy.

The Kennedy administration made many important recommendations, but the most controversial of them needed more time to be realized. Arthur Schlesinger provides a list of modest but important legislative achievements in the first two years of the Kennedy "New Frontier":

> 1961: Peace Corps; Alliance for Progress; Arms Control and Disarmament Administration; area redevelopment; general housing act; extension of Unemployment compensation; aid to dependent children of unemployed . . .
>
> 1962: Trade expansion Act; UN bond issue; tax bill; investment tax credit; communications satellite; manpower development and training; accelerated public works; drug labeling; restraints on conflict of interest[5]

It is not by accident that Schlesinger's list begins with the Peace Corps. The Peace Corps was not only one of the very first programs established by Kennedy but also the one that has lasted the longest.

Although Kennedy was in office for only three years, his short list of programs was substantially expanded through efforts by his successor, Lyndon B. Johnson. Johnson purposefully carried forward many of Kennedy's most significant proposals, and while Johnson's legendary skills in dealing with Congress played a vital role in his successes, he was immeasurably aided by a powerful sense of need generated by Kennedy's death. Professor Robert Dallek describes the transition as follows: "None of Kennedy's major reform initiatives—the tax cuts, federal aid to education, Medicare, and civil rights—became law during his time in office. . . . yet all his significant reform proposals . . . came to fruition under Lyndon Johnson."[6]

Among the initiatives and proposals that actually came about during Kennedy's few years in office, it is the Peace Corps that commentators and historians describe as the most important and enduring:

Harris Wofford: "Of all the social inventions of the sixties, the Peace Corps has been the most successful. It is John Kennedy's most affirmative legacy."[7]

Arthur Schlesinger: "But the part of the aid effort which best expressed the distinctive spirit of the New Frontier was the Peace Corps."[8]

Robert Dallek: "The Peace Corps proved to be one of the enduring legacies of Kennedy's presidency. As with some American domestic institutions like Social Security and Medicare, the Peace Corps became a fixture that Democratic and Republican administrations alike would continue to finance it."[9]

Harris Wofford: "From the moment Kennedy called on Americans to 'ask not what your country can do for you—ask what you can do for your country,' the Peace Corps became identified with him."[10]

Brookings Institution: "The Peace Corps is a gem, but a small one in a big world."[11]

John F. Kennedy Library: "After almost five decades of service, the Peace Corps is more vital than ever and still growing."[12]

The Peace Corps not only has been a success in providing assistance to other countries but also has had a profound effect on politics, culture, education, business, and many other aspects of American life. As Stanley Meisler points out in his history of the first fifty years of the Peace Corps,

> One aspect of the story astounded me as I studied the Peace Corps after so many years away: the impressive array of talent among former Volunteers. The alumni roster includes two U.S. Senators, nine members of the House of Representatives, two governors, three

mayors, twenty ambassadors, a host of university presidents, the board chairs of Levi Strauss and the Chicago Bears, and the founders of the Nature Company and Netflix. Novelist Paul Theroux, television news anchor Chris Matthews, and New Yorker writer George Packer are also former Volunteers. It is obvious that the United States itself has benefitted a great deal from the Peace Corps.[13]

Given its place as the primary successful program in the JFK legacy and its impact on so much of American life, it is informative to examine an incident early on in the Peace Corps' existence that could easily have led to its destruction.

When Peppy Kinsey died and her husband was charged with murder, nothing like this had yet occurred in the Peace Corps. The handling of the case could well have a fateful impact on the future of the Peace Corps. Similarly, the very young country of Tanzania faced a potential international disaster, depending on how it handled this complex legal situation. How should the U.S. administration respond? What would be the response of the Tanzania government and its courts? How would the American people and legislators view the situation? These and many other questions are at the heart of this book.

In 1966, the United States was ramping up its role in the Vietnam War. The recent history of the United States contained many examples—Cuba, Chile, Iran, the Congo—of intervention in foreign countries. The Peace Corps would be under intense pressure to do something about a young American on trial in a very young African country. Tanzanians feared that the U.S. Marines would be sent in to spirit Bill out of the country. America's fraught history of racial antagonism became a part of the discussion. The question of legal representation for Bill became a thorny issue because it was unclear how to obtain a lawyer and who would pay for his defense. Even the disposition of Peppy's remains raised questions because overseas it is normally the next of kin who decides what to do, but here the next of kin faced a charge of murder.

This account concerns a major phase of American history and international relations during an intense period of the Cold War. It examines the confluence of a complex personal and family drama, with fascinating characters who exemplify the mindset and cultural assumptions of the early Peace Corps generation. It portrays an era of arrogant idealism; scrutinizes the risk that a possibly innocent American volunteer could be sacrificed to the American government's pragmatism; and recounts the pressures and turmoil in the lives of Peace Corps volunteers as they tried to sustain a normal marital life in a very challenging international context. Woven through the narrative is an examination of the lack of appreciation for the care and pride with which a somewhat untried legal system (albeit one that shared in Anglo-American common law but with local variations) could adjudicate a highly charged criminal case with distinctive rules and procedures.

One of the most serious issues the Peace Corps faced early on was what its position should be on the fundamental issue of Bill's guilt or innocence. Of course, the Tanzania legal system shared with the American system the principle that a person is innocent until proven guilty. However, what would this mean for the activities of Peace Corps staff? Should they do everything they could to help prove Bill's innocence? Or did they have an obligation to Peppy to do everything they could to show her death was not an accident?

In the end, the Peace Corps would walk a fine line in trying to present a neutral face to the Tanzania government, even while in the background it may not have been so neutral.

The stakes were high for the future of the Peace Corps, and decisions made in Washington, D.C., and in Dar es Salaam by relatively inexperienced government officials might very well determine whether the Peace Corps would survive or end in a disaster for all the parties involved.

Although we now know that both the Peace Corps and Tanzania survived, the path to that result had many obstacles.

1

A Volunteer Is Dead

Every hill is a burial place.
—East African proverb

On Monday, March 28, 1966, Jack McPhee, regional director of the Peace Corps in Mwanza, was at work in his office in downtown Mwanza. At about 11:30 a.m., Charlotte Lyles, a Peace Corps volunteer secretary, walked into his office to tell him that a volunteer nurse at Mwanza Hospital had called reporting that she had heard that the wife of a volunteer had died in an accident in Maswa.[1]

McPhee and his wife, Sandy, had arrived in Tanzania in 1965 and resided on the road to Bwiru School outside Mwanza. McPhee had been a member of the Tanganyika I Peace Corps group, which in 1961 was the second Peace Corps group to arrive overseas. He and his colleagues were road engineers who had been requested by Tanganyikan president Julius Nyerere. McPhee grew up in Portland, Oregon, and graduated from the University of Portland with a BS in physics. He worked for RCA's satellite division before joining the Peace Corps in 1961. He served as a road surveyor in Dodoma, Tanzania, where he met Judge Harold Platt, who later would be the trial judge in the Kinsey case. When McPhee returned to the United States, he obtained an MA in African studies at the University of California at Los Angeles, married, and went back to Tanzania to become the regional Peace Corps director in Mwanza.[2] Despite being young and relatively inexperienced, McPhee kept a detailed log of the important events that would take place over the next several days. His foresight not only ensured that the details would not be forgotten but also offered him a measure of protection should his actions be challenged later.

Following his conversation with Lyles, McPhee went to the hospital to talk to the Peace Corps volunteer nurse. He arrived there fifteen minutes after hearing about the death and found the nurse, Nancy Churchill, who told him that Dr. Datar had told her of the accident. They located Dr. Datar, and, when asked, he said that "someone had come in from Maswa the night before and said that the wife of a [volunteer] had fallen from some rocks and had been killed." McPhee said, "Were any names given?" Datar responded, "No, but they were both teachers." McPhee mused, "That could only be the Kinseys."

Mwanza Hospital was a small, well-equipped medical facility where I had recently spent several days suffering from malaria-like symptoms. When the Mwanza doctors were unable to diagnose my illness and to bring down my fever, I was flown to Queen Elizabeth Hospital in Nairobi, where I eventually recovered and then returned to my teaching duties at Bwiru School.

McPhee went back to his office and called the town council to see about a casket that had been requested earlier as a contingency measure. (Telephones were somewhat of a rarity in Tanzania at that time and generally unreliable. Today cell phones are ubiquitous in Africa because most countries there never established a comprehensive land-line system, instead moving directly to cell phones.) The deputy town clerk said, "I am not sure it is ready." McPhee asked the clerk to check and let him know as soon as possible. In the meantime, a telegram arrived at the Peace Corps office in Mwanza from Father Robert Lefebvre, a priest stationed near Maswa. "Mrs. Kinsey died suddenly STOP what are your instructions STOP expect you at Sayusayu Mission STOP."

McPhee quickly returned to the town council office and saw both the town clerk and the deputy town clerk, telling them that he needed the casket immediately. They said it was ready and that it was lead-lined. McPhee waited fifteen or twenty minutes for the storekeeper to return with the keys to the storeroom, but when he opened the room and the casket was found, it turned out not to be lead-lined. McPhee went back to his office and called the town clerk to ask for a lead-lined one, which was essential because of the high heat and humidity in Tanzania and the need for protection of the body on a potentially lengthy flight to America.

Activities in Dar es Salaam

Meanwhile in Dar es Salaam, the Peace Corps country director Paul Sack, Peace Corps doctor Tom McHugh, and other officials were at the U.S. ambassador's home having lunch with Jack Vaughn, who had been appointed overall director of the Peace Corps (succeeding Sargent Shriver) only a few months earlier. While there, Sack had received a call from Charlotte Lyles reporting Peppy's death. At this point, it was known only that a terrible accident had occurred, that a Peace Corps volunteer had died, and that the Peace Corps would handle what was a sad and unpleasant situation. Little did Sack or, on being informed, Vaughn know what a new and enormous issue was about to surface for the Peace Corps. Although it was not unheard of for volunteers to die while in service—in fact, in the first year of its existence, three volunteers had died—a murder charge against a volunteer represented a whole new dilemma.[3] After discussion of what was then known, Vaughn told Dr. McHugh and Sack to do whatever was necessary to take care of Bill as well as of Peppy's remains.[4] Paul Sack had been a successful real estate developer in the San Francisco Bay Area when he applied for an administrative position with the Peace Corps; he was hired and sent to Tanzania in 1966.[5]

When McPhee returned to the Peace Corps office in Mwanza, Charlotte Lyles told him she had "talked with Paul Sack and told him you are making arrangements to go to Sayusayu Mission with the casket to get Bill Kinsey and the body." In the meantime, McPhee had sent the Peace Corps driver to collect the casket. Doctor McHugh called McPhee from Dar es Salaam: "Please try to get a lead-lined casket, embalming preparations ready, and contact Dr. McMahon, a British internist long serving in Tanzania, at Mwanza Hospital. Make sure Mwanza Hospital is ready to receive the body and to take care of Bill Kinsey." McPhee responded, "I expect to have the body and Bill Kinsey on a charter flight to Dar es Salaam [in the] morning. I will try to get the embalming done in Mwanza." Dr. McHugh said, "Please have someone, possibly Dr. McMahon, accompany Bill on the plane."

In 1966, Tom McHugh was the Peace Corps doctor for the Mwanza District, an area that included the town of Maswa. McHugh had graduated from Wesleyan University in 1960 and from the Albany Medical College in 1964. He had then served a one-year internship at the University of Chicago Hospital. In 1965, the Peace Corps hired him as a doctor (or, technically, an employee of the U.S. Public Health Service), and he arrived in Tanzania in July 1965. He spent six weeks in orientation in Dar es Salaam and took up his post in Mwanza that September.[6] McHugh was a tall, slender, athletic man with close-cropped hair. His medical professionalism was immediately apparent to anyone meeting him. During his time in Tanzania, he was known for his impressive basketball and squash skills as well as for coaching a young Tanzania woman who would go on to represent Tanzania in the javelin event at the Olympics.

Once the officials in Peace Corps Dar es Salaam (hereafter PCDSM) heard from McPhee, Norm Hummon, deputy director, cabled the Peace Corps in Washington, D.C. (hereafter PCDC) about the "accident," Peppy's death, and the plans to send her body back to the United States.[7] PCDC cabled back the same day with instructions for the disposition of the body, travel to the United States, and Dr. McHugh and Bill Kinsey's expected arrival time in New York. Peppy's and Bill's parents had been informed. At this point, officials were unaware of potential criminal charges, so they assumed there had been an accident and that normal procedures for a death in a foreign country would be followed.[8]

McPhee Travels to Maswa

At 1:00 p.m., McPhee went home, ate a quick lunch, gathered a coat, a sweater, a flashlight, and other necessary items for the vehicle and went back to his office. At the office, he received a call from the Tanzania regional education officer (REO) for the Shinyanga Region, which included Maswa. Since the Kinseys were teachers, their work was under the jurisdiction of the REO. The REO reported receiving a telegram stating that Mrs. Kinsey died suddenly by falling from a rock while climbing during a picnic on Sunday. The REO went on to say that Mr. Kinsey and the body were in Maswa and that the police were continuing to investigate the incident. McPhee was taken aback since this was the first mention of police involvement, but he assumed it was routine. The conversation was partially in English and partially in Swahili (the lingua franca for Tanzania), in which McPhee was fluent.

At about 2:00 p.m., McPhee left for Sayusayu Mission in the Peace Corps Land Rover with one of the Peace Corps drivers. When McPhee reached Sayusayu around 4:00, one of the brothers from the mission told him that Father Lefebvre, Bill, and the body were in Maswa and that there were indications from the police that what happened to Peppy had not been an accident. McPhee drove on to Maswa, arriving at the hospital about twenty minutes later. There he asked the administrator where the body was. The administrator said, "It is in the hospital morgue, and a postmortem has been performed." McPhee then asked where Bill Kinsey was. The administrator told him, "Go to the Maryknoll Mission in Maswa [a separate facility from the mission at Sayusayu]. He will be there."

10

McPhee went to the Maryknoll Mission and was greeted by Father Charles Liberatore, who said, "Mr. Kinsey has been charged with murder. The police have an iron bar and rocks with blood and hair on them as evidence." Father Charles told McPhee that the REO, the district education officer (DEO), Father Lefebvre, and Vance Barron, a volunteer from nearby Malampaka, were in the next room. McPhee was ushered into the room. During the discussion that ensued, McPhee was told that witnesses had seen Kinsey struggling with Peppy. McPhee was also told that the assistant medical officer (AMO) in Maswa had performed a postmortem exam and had found lacerations on Peppy's head that could be matched up with the stones and the bar. McPhee also learned that witnesses claimed to have seen Bill beating Peppy with these objects. The REO told McPhee that the police were through with the body and that it was up to McPhee to decide what to do with it.

McPhee decided to try to locate Philip Mganga (interestingly, *mganga* is the Swahili word for "doctor"), the AMO in question, and set off. Along the way, McPhee met Martin Kifunta, the Shinyanga Criminal Investigation Division (CID) inspector for Maswa who was investigating the case. Kifunta joined McPhee in the search for the AMO. They went to Mganga's house, but he wasn't there. When they found him in town, McPhee asked him, "Is it still possible to embalm the body?" The AMO said he thought it was. Because of the postmortem, the heat, and the time elapsed, there was a concern about completing a successful embalming. McPhee asked, "Are you through with the body, and can I take it to Mwanza?" The AMO said, "Yes, I am finished with the examination." McPhee and the AMO agreed that McPhee could pick up the body at 5:45 p.m.

Father Robert Lefebvre (Father Bob) was a Maryknoll priest assigned to the Sayusayu Mission, a few miles southwest of Maswa. Bill and Peppy taught at Binza School, a few miles away in Maswa. The Sayusayu Mission had a clinic staffed with Maryknoll sisters, but there were no doctors. Sayusayu also provided an elementary school for grades K through 8. Marianne Dunn, who later would testify in the Kinsey trial, was a Peace Corps volunteer teacher at the elementary school. There was no telephone at the mission, so anyone wanting to make a call needed to go into Maswa to the government office (*boma*).

While Father Bob was in Tanzania, he became fluent in Sukuma, the language of the dominant tribe in the Mwanza District, but never in Swahili. Shortly after the Kinseys had arrived at Binza School, Father Bob met them through Marianne Dunn. The Kinseys often came to dinner at the mission, so Father Bob had gotten to know them and thought them a happy young couple.

On March 28, 1966, two Sukuma men came to see Father Bob to tell him that Bill Kinsey was in jail. Father Bob immediately drove to the jail in Maswa to see Bill, finding him very calm but noticing that he didn't talk about Peppy's death at all. Father Bob became worried about Bill being alone in the jail because the local people might react angrily to what had happened at the picnic. He found the conditions in the jail in Maswa to be very bad, so he also worried about Bill's health and safety. As soon as he could, he went to the telegraph office and wired the Peace Corps office in Mwanza to alert the staff there to the situation.

Father Bob was born in Manchester, New Hampshire. After his parents moved to Connecticut, he attended school there until he went to Maryknoll College in Chicago, after which he was ordained in the Maryknoll order in 1952, followed by his first assignment in East Africa. He worked around Shinyanga District in Tanganyika for a number of years before being assigned to the Sayusayu Mission, where he remained until 1973, when he was transferred to the Maryknoll operation in Indonesia. He became secretary to the Papal Nuncio in Indonesia until he was eventually required to leave by the Indonesian government. In 2011, when I spoke with him, Father Bob was eighty-one years old and retired at the Maryknoll facility in Maryknoll, New York.[9]

Meanwhile, McPhee, after his discussion with AMO Mganga, went alone to the Maswa jail to see Bill Kinsey. At the jail, McPhee was ushered into a cell where Bill was waiting.

McPHEE: "How are you doing?"
KINSEY: "Everyone has been very helpful, especially Father Lefebvre and Mr. Kifunta."

McPhee observed that Bill seemed very relieved to see him. Bill was dressed in clean clothes and seemed to be making a great effort to control himself when he spoke.

McPHEE: "What would you like to do with Peppy's body? Would you like her buried in the States or in Maswa?"
KINSEY: "I would like her buried in Sayusayu, if she is to be buried in Tanzania."

Thinking it would be best for the burial to take place as soon as possible because of the heat and humidity, McPhee suggested it take place the next day at Sayusayu.

KINSEY: "That would be fine, and I would like Father Lefebvre to perform the service."

KINSEY: "Did Dr. McHugh come with you?"

McPHEE: "He's in Dar es Salaam."

KINSEY: "I would like Dr. McHugh to examine the body."

McPHEE: "I will bring McHugh out tomorrow so it can be done before the burial. We will also get you a lawyer."

McPhee left the jail and arranged with Father Bob to perform the burial. He also spoke with Inspector Kifunta and told him he wished to bring a Peace Corps physician to examine the body before burial.

KIFUNTA: "That would be acceptable."

McPHEE: "May we move the body from the morgue then?"

KIFUNTA: "No, it would be better if the AMO and the Peace Corps physician examine the body together."

McPHEE: "I plan to bring a lawyer also."

KIFUNTA: "I have no objection."

McPhee had arranged to meet with the REO and DEO, but by 6:00 p.m. they still had not arrived, so he left for Mwanza in the Land Rover. It wasn't until the afternoon on March 28 that Jack McPhee learned that Bill Kinsey had been arrested and charged with the murder of Peppy Kinsey. With no reliable telephone service in Maswa, he was not able to call the PCDSM until around 8:00 that night to tell the staff of the new development—that Bill Kinsey was being charged with murder. The two Peace Corps doctors in the Peace Corps office in Dar es Salaam, Tom McHugh and Jim Morrissey, discussed this development with McPhee and told him they would call him back shortly after consulting with PCDSM. They asked him to go to Dr. McMahon's house and said they would call him there.[10]

Tanzania Medical Officer Performs a Postmortem

In the morning on Monday, March 28, Inspector Kifunta and Father Charles Liberatore, another Catholic missionary in Maswa, collected Philip Mganga,

the AMO, and took him to the Maswa Hospital morgue, where Father Liberatore identified the body there as that of Peverley Dennett Kinsey. Mganga then
performed the postmortem.

Although Mganga was the AMO and in charge of the government hospital in Maswa, he had not attended medical school but (as he later stated at the
trial) had been enrolled in the medical assistant's course at the Sewa Haji Hospital in Dar es Salaam from January 1946 to December 1948 and then had
served as a medical assistant for seven years with various medical departments
of Tanganyika. In 1955, he was promoted to senior medical assistant and continued in that category until 1961, when he completed the AMO course. He
had studied pathology and medical jurisprudence and had been doing medicolegal work since 1961.

During the postmortem, Mganga dictated notes to his medical assistant,
who wrote them down while Mganga carried out the examination. Mganga's
official government report indicated that death was due to cerebral hemorrhage resulting from fractures of the skull. He found eight lacerated wounds
on the head, a fracture of the right frontal bone, a depressed fracture of the
right temporal bone, and a "fissured fracture" of the left temporal and occipital
bones. He also detected a large blood clot between the cranium and the dura
(the membrane covering the brain) as well as a hemorrhage below the dura on
the right side of the brain. In his report, Mganga also noted several wounds on
the surface of the head. He stated for the record that he had reviewed the notes
and found them to be accurate, and so he signed and dated the report on Tuesday, March 29.[11]

Peace Corps Officials in Dar es Salaam Learn of Criminal Charge

Later in the day on March 28, around 5:00 p.m., Peace Corps officials Norm
Hummon, Leon Parker, and Dr. Tom McHugh drove to the U.S. embassy in
Dar es Salaam to compose a cable for PCDC. While they were there, Dr. Datar,
the regional medical officer (RMO) in Mwanza, called. Datar reported that he
understood a postmortem had been performed in Maswa because of some
"questionable incidents" surrounding Peppy's death.

At this point, Dr. Morrissey, the Peace Corps doctor in the Dar es Salaam
region, telephoned the RMO in Shinyanga in an effort to obtain more information. The RMO told Morrissey that the regional head of the Shinyanga CID

had been called early in the morning, and he had gone to Maswa to investigate the possible murder of Peppy Kinsey. Peace Corps officials then called a local doctor to explore suitable facilities for an appropriate embalming procedure. They were given the name of a doctor based at the University of Dar es Salaam Medical School as the only person with adequate experience to perform the procedure.[12]

At about 9:00 p.m. on March 28, Jack McPhee called Morrissey at home and reported to him and Dr. McHugh that the situation in Maswa was "extremely critical." He reported that Bill Kinsey was being held on suspicion of murder and the police felt that "it was an open and shut case of murder, that several Africans were witnesses to the fact and they had evidence from a camera tripod consisting of blood and hair, and imprints on the skull which matched the shape of the tripod."

Tanzania Peace Corps director Paul Sack was a short, sandy-haired, former real estate developer with a businesslike, no-nonsense approach to his role as director. When Sack learned that Bill was being charged with murder, he was incensed and planned to rush off to Mwanza to protect Bill from what he believed must be an obvious mistake. In the meantime, however, he happened to meet David Kadane, an attorney and Peace Corps volunteer who had come to Tanzania to work in the Ministry of Commerce and Cooperatives.

Kadane was a bright, experienced attorney, graduate of Harvard Law School, former assistant counsel to the U.S. Senate Committee on Interstate Commerce, and former assistant director of the Securities and Exchange Commission. From 1946 to 1970, he was general counsel for the Long Island Lighting Company but was taking leave from 1964 to 1966 to serve as a Peace Corps volunteer. Sack had great respect for Kadane, and when Kadane urged him to proceed with caution because Bill might be guilty, Sack took the advice to heart. This advice and decision seemed to be the beginning of the Peace Corps public policy of caution and neutrality in the case. Sack received no formal directive from PCDC in the matter, but soon, somewhat by default, the policy of neutrality was firmly established in Washington, D.C., and in Tanzania.[13] However, as we will see, the policy was often avoided or ignored in support of Bill in the murder case.

At about 9:30 p.m., Peace Corps staff met at Paul Sack's house in Dar es Salaam. They first tried to reach an attorney for legal advice, but no one was available. Sack and Norm Hummon then drove to the U.S. ambassador's house to discuss the next steps. While at the ambassador's, Sack called his friend the president of the Tanzania Bar Association to seek advice about legal representation for Bill. When Sack finally reached him at about 11:30, this friend recommended the firm of Singh and Parekh in Mwanza and volunteered to help with any further need.

At 10:00 p.m., Dr. McHugh called McPhee at Dr. McMahon's house in Mwanza. McHugh told McPhee that he and Paul Sack would fly to Mwanza in the morning. He also mentioned that a lead-lined coffin would arrive in Mwanza by charter plane in the morning. They discussed the legal situation and agreed that it would be important to find a lawyer to get involved in the case. McHugh said they would investigate the possibilities in Dar es Salaam. He was then unaware of the progress Sack had already made.

Later that night McPhee called PCDSM, again with Dr. McMahon's suggestion that the Peace Corps engage a professional pathologist, if possible, to perform a postmortem with him. The message was passed along to the Dar es Salaam staff, who had gathered to make plans. The consular officer at the U.S. embassy was immediately contacted to get recommendations for possible lawyers and pathologists. After many calls back and forth between the Peace Corps and the embassy, the Tanzania Bar Association, and the Tanzania Medical Society, an attorney in Mwanza was located, and Mr. Parekh (first name unknown), law partner of Singh and Parekh, agreed to assist in the legal proceedings.[14] A pathologist was as yet unknown when McHugh and Sack boarded their plane for the three-and-a-half-hour flight to Mwanza.

Bill Kinsey Appears before the Justice of the Peace

On March 29, 1966, at 8:45 a.m., two days after Peppy's death, Bill Kinsey was brought by the police before A. S. Swai, justice of the peace assigned to the District Court in Maswa. The police informed Swai that the prisoner was charged with murder and that he wished to make a statement. Swai told the police to leave, then carefully questioned Bill about his desire to make a statement. Swai told him that such a statement could later be used against him. Bill confirmed that he would make the statement voluntarily and without any coercion. Swai then asked him, "Do you wish to make a statement?" Bill proceeded with his account of what happened on March 27, 1966, on Impala Hill (see chapter 3) near Maswa. Once the statement was concluded, Bill signed it, and Justice of the Peace Swai signed below Bill's signature, adding that he believed the statement was voluntarily made.

Bill's statement may be summarized as follows:

On Sunday morning, March 27, 1966, my wife and I marked examination papers and wrote some letters. I took the letters to town to mail and bought some bread. We packed our baskets and set off on our bicycles for a picnic nearby. The baskets contained food, camera equipment, and two beers. Before leaving, we decided to eat the food at home, so we took the food and camera equipment out of the baskets. We left on our bicycles about 2:30 p.m. for a nearby hill. At the base of the hill, we walked around looking for a place to sit. We found a spot and removed the remaining items from the basket. I found a pipe in the basket that I had been using to make a tripod. I thought I had removed it at the house. We drank the beer and climbed to the top of the rocks for a view. While I was looking around, I heard the sound of glass breaking. I turned around, and my wife was not there. I crawled to the edge of the rocks and saw her lying below. I ran down to the spot and found her standing. I ran toward her, but she fell down before I reached her. She struggled, calling my name. I tried to calm her and hold her down to keep her from further hurting herself. To keep her from moving, I sat on her. I put a towel under her head and ran for help. I saw an old woman and shouted at her in Swahili to help. [It is unlikely that these Sukuma farmers would understand Swahili.] I went back to my wife, tried to pick her up and carry her, but I fell. I left her again and ran to my bicycle to ride for help. Some men came, I thought to help me, but they stopped me. I asked them to go for help. Finally, the headmaster and the police came, and we returned to where my wife lay.[15]

What may have been a hasty decision by Bill to make this statement without an attorney present would later prove providential in supporting his case. He gave his story several times with little variance, and the consistency proved very persuasive in support of his claim of innocence.

Bill also appeared before District Magistrate D. J. Gumbo, before whom the charge of murder was read and the case received its formal designation: *Republic v. Bill Haywood Kinsey,* Criminal Case no. 85 (1966).

2

A Lovely, Creative Woman and an All-American Boy from the South

Peverley (Peppy) Dennett Kinsey came from Riverside, Connecticut. She spent her high school years at Greenwich Academy, a prestigious girls' school founded in 1827 in Greenwich, Connecticut. In her senior year, Peppy served as vice president of the student body. Among the academy's alumnae are Ethel Kennedy and Jane Fonda. It was recently listed among the most expensive private schools in America.[1] In 1964, Peppy graduated from Mount Holyoke College in South Hadley, Massachusetts, where she majored in European history.

Mount Holyoke was founded as a college for women in 1837 at a time when educating women in college was a revolutionary idea. Mount Holyoke was the first of the "Seven Sisters" colleges, which paralleled the male colleges of the Ivy League. Although some of the Seven Sisters colleges now admit male students, Mount Holyoke remains exclusively for women.[2] Peppy often spent summers working in camps, where she was an effective and popular counselor with children and where she obtained certification as a Red Cross water-safety instructor. Her primary extracurricular activity at Mount Holyoke was her involvement in Dance Club. As described at the time in the Mount Holyoke yearbook, the *Llamarada,* Dance Club was "composed of members . . . who have successfully passed an audition. . . . Its primary purpose is to provide opportunities for those interested in concert dance to participate . . . in the planning and production of programs." During the summer of 1963, before

18

her senior year, she worked at Hickox Secretarial School, providing general office work.[3]

Peppy's ancestors were members of some of the most distinguished families on the East Coast. Her paternal grandfather, Tyler Dennett, was descended from a long line of New Englanders, including his father, a Baptist minister. Tyler held diplomas from Williams College, Union Theological Seminary, and Johns Hopkins University (a Ph.D. in 1925). In 1934, he received a Pulitzer Prize for his biography of John Hay. Dennett taught at Williams College, Columbia University, and Princeton University and served as president of Williams College.

Tyler's wife, Peppy's grandmother, May Belle Raymond, was descended from the Pilgrims and was a member of the Daughters of the America Revolution until she resigned when that organization refused to allow the great African American opera singer Marian Anderson to use their concert hall.

Peppy's father, Raymond Dennett, attended Philips Academy Andover, one of the most prestigious secondary schools for boys in America; among the notable alumni are Samuel F. B. Morse, Henry Stimpson, Humphrey Bogart, and George H. W. Bush. Dennett graduated Phi Beta Kappa from Harvard. He was director of the World Peace Foundation and president of the American-Scandinavian Foundation until he resigned because of ill health a few years before he died at the young age of forty-seven in 1961.

On the maternal side, Peppy had an equally distinguished family based in Maryland. The family farm was invaded by the British during the War of 1812, and Peppy's great-great-grandfather, Andrew Woodall, was the wealthiest man in Kent County, Maryland. When he died in 1906, his son, Peppy's great-grandfather James, was a prominent businessman and director of the Kent Mutual Fire Insurance Company. Charlotte Woodall Dennett, Peppy's mother, attended St. Mary's Hall in New Jersey, founded in 1837, the first all-girls boarding school in the United States; Wilson College, founded in 1869 as a college for women; and Drexel University.[4] Charlotte would later testify at Bill Kinsey's trial.

The Peace Corps assessment of Peppy at the time she was considered for acceptance described her as follows:

> Wants very much to go to Latin America, particularly Chile. This may be linked to male volunteer in Chile who writes a reference for her describing himself as a "close companion." Applicant notes that

she visited a volunteer in a Chile training program, summer 1963. Was invited to non-specific (assignment) in January 1964, declined because "circumstance . . . make it impossible for me to decide right now whether I want to commit myself for the next two years." Wished to be considered in one year. In June 1964 she changed her availability to August 1964. Address for summer 1964 listed as Connecticut College School of Dance.

The assessment went on to describe her, based on several references, "as quite satisfactory as a student," "athletically inclined," "friendly and a happy dispositioned person. . . . sensitive and considerate of others."[5]

Peppy's sister, Charlotte, remembers Peppy as the adventurous one in the family. She was always game to play aggressively with the boys, climbing trees and even falling out of them without significant injury.[6]

Victoria (Vicki) Ferenbach, née Simons, knew Peppy while they were growing up in Riverside, Connecticut, although they attended different high schools. When they entered Mount Holyoke, they asked to be roommates, and the college officials agreed. They remained roommates throughout their college years. During their freshman year, they met a group of women with whom they remained close friends for the four years despite sometimes living in separate dormitories. In their senior year, they all were able to live together in the same dorm.

Victoria remembers that Peppy had been dating a student at Amherst and believes that he was the Peace Corps volunteer in Chile who had written a recommendation for Peppy and was the inspiration for her original desire to serve in South America. Peppy's sister, Charlotte, remembers that when she visited Peppy in college, she seemed very popular and was generally surrounded by boys.

Vicki Ferenbach described Peppy as an all-American girl, serious about studies but also liking to have fun. She was engaging, vivacious, and pretty—not beautiful but with an infectious smile, a twinkle in her eye, and an outgoing personality. She was well liked. Vicki recalled that another classmate remembered Peppy's "wonderful spirit, bright eyes, sense of fun, intelligence."[7]

Bill Kinsey came from Washington, North Carolina, located on the Pamlico and Tar Rivers in the inland coastal region of the state, approximately one hundred miles east of Raleigh. He was a graduate of Randolph-Macon Academy, a prep school in Front Royal, Virginia, which at the time enrolled only male students, and of Washington and Lee University, located in Lexington, Virginia. The current website for Randolph-Macon Academy describes it as "one of the top Air Force ROTC units in the U.S." and "one of the premier college-prep military schools in the nation."[8] Robert E. Lee is buried on the campus of Washington and Lee University. Publicity for the school asserts the following claim: "Perhaps the most distinguishing characteristic of the University is its student run Honor System, and the environment that it creates on campus and in Lexington. Students at W & L enjoy unparalleled academic and social freedom. Undergraduates typically schedule their own final examinations, all students take their exams unsupervised, personal property is generally safe on campus, most University buildings remain open twenty-four hours per day, and a student's word is accepted and respected both on campus and in the community."[9]

Washington and Lee was founded in 1749 for male students only, which remained unchanged until 1985, when women were admitted. In 1796, George Washington donated $20,000 to the school, which allowed it to survive at a time when it was struggling financially. Robert E. Lee was named college president in 1865, which he remained until his death in 1870.[10] In July 2014, the *New York Times* reported that Washington and Lee "was removing its Confederate battle flags from the Lee Chapel on its Lexington campus and will continue to study its historical involvement with slavery."[11]

Although perhaps not as distinguished as Peppy's family, Bill's family had deep roots in North Carolina and was well educated. His father, Bill Sr., was a graduate of Wake Forest University and prepared for his veterinary practice at Auburn University.

Bill graduated in 1964 with a BA in English and as a member of the Dean's List. His yearbook listing at Washington and Lee was one of the most extensive in his class and included his participation in a great many organizations and activities—for example, Washington Literary Society; *Ariel*; track; Rifle Team; University Christian Association; International Relations Club; Radio Washington & Lee; and Kappa Sigma fraternity.[12] In his biography for the Peace Corps, Kinsey noted that he had practice-taught military science and tactics at a prep school and had worked at a YMCA camp.[13]

3

A Tale of Three Cities

Mwanza

In 1966, Mwanza was the third-largest town in Tanzania, with a population of about 25,000, divided into 20,000 Africans, 4,800 Asians, and 200 Europeans. Today it contains a population of more than 700,000. Mwanza sits at the southern end of Lake Victoria, the second-largest lake in the world (209 miles long, 155 miles wide). To the south of Mwanza lies the Sukuma Plain, home to the most populous tribe in Tanzania, the Sukuma. In the 1960s, the Sukuma were known as hard-working farmers who produced most of the cotton grown in Tanzania. The cotton industry at the time featured a very sophisticated and productive cooperative movement. The Victoria Federation of Cooperative Unions was the center for all the cooperatives in the area. It contained nineteen affiliated unions, owned eight ginneries, and had a monopoly on the marketing of cotton, rice, and sisal grown in the region. The cooperative movement had substantially improved the area's economy and led to increasing use of tractors and ploughs.

At the time of the Kinsey trial, Mwanza was also the political center of the region and the regional center for four distinct districts—Mwanza, Geita, Ukerewe, and Kwimba. The four districts focused primarily on agriculture, although the famous Geita Gold Mine, south and west of Mwanza along Lake Victoria, produced a considerable amount of gold. Fishing was also an important industry, particularly among the communities along the lake and on the islands near the shore. The Nile Perch (tilapia) had become a prime catch for export.

Mwanza has a surprisingly mild climate for an area just south of the equator. Most of the area is between 3,500 and 4,000 feet above sea level, which, along with the lake's proximity, leads to a mean monthly maximum temperature of between 80 and 82 degrees Fahrenheit. The average rainfall, between 30 and 50 inches, is a major contributor to the success of farming in the region.

In 1966, Mwanza was home to the East African Institute for Medical Research, which focused on tuberculosis, malaria, and bilharzia. The presence of the research facility accounted for a large number of European doctors and medical researchers in the area and made for a very active medical community at a time when there were few African doctors in Tanzania.

Although Mwanza had a small-town feel, it provided significant services and amenities for the region. Lake steamers and cargo ships stopped at Mwanza port on their way around the lake, stopping at Bukoba and Musoma in Tanzania and at ports in Kenya and Uganda. Lake Victoria was a major economic driver for the entire region. Regular train service connected Mwanza with the capital, Dar es Salaam, some 700 miles away. Stops were made at major towns such as Tabora, Dodoma, and Morogoro as well as at many smaller towns. Train service was complemented by bus service not only to Dar es Salaam but also to other areas of Tanzania such as Arusha, Tanga, Mbeya, and Kigoma on Lake Tanganyika.

As a regional center, Manzwa was home to a number of banks, car dealerships, insurance companies, a hardware store, a pharmacy, and agriculture supply stores. There were two large general stores, which sold not only groceries but also wines and spirits, cutlery, medicine, ladies and children's shoes, sports equipment, and photographic equipment. In the center of town, a large, open-air market sold vegetables, meat, fruit, clothes, and shoes. Although most of the city streets were paved, tarmac on the roads usually ended a few miles out of town. Open sewers ran along most streets. Several tall buildings, including the town hall, had been left by the British Colonial Administration, and the Victoria Federation of Cooperative Unions had recently built a five-story building as its headquarters. The city government was in the middle of constructing a new five-hundred-bed hospital as well.[1]

Maswa

The Maswa District lies to the east of Mwanza, immediately west of the famous Serengeti National Park, and abuts an area largely populated by the Masai people. The entire sweep of land from Mwanza through Maswa and on into the Serengeti is known for its interesting geologic features, including many kopjes or inselbergs arising from the plains to form small hills. The kopjes are made up of huge granite boulders that have been thrust up over the centuries and piled on top of each other, sometimes standing 30 to 40 feet high. Particularly in the Serengeti, they were and continue to be popular resting places for lions and other wild animals. Despite the potential to come face to face with a lion, in the Mwanza and Maswa Districts the kopjes were and continue to be popular spots for picnicking and viewing because they often offer 360-degree views of the surrounding countryside. Impala Hill, where Peppy died, is one of these kopjes. Aside from the kopjes, the terrain in the Maswa area is open bush—that is, wide-open space interrupted by areas of shrub. The average rainfall of between 20 and 30 inches per year in the 1960s offered quite good prospects for agriculture.[2]

Maswa town is about 80 miles from Mwanza town and 40 miles south of Lake Victoria. In 1966, it was a small town with few amenities, although it was the seat of government for the Maswa District. The main facilities were a few stores (*dukas*), a health facility, a Catholic church, a telegraph office, a government office (*boma*), and schools. One of the best-known big-game hunters in Tanzania was based in Maswa.[3]

Dar es Salaam

Dar es Salaam, the capital of Tanzania in the 1960s, was the site of the U.S. embassy and the PCDSM headquarters as well as the prime commercial and marine center of Tanzania. Communications between Tanzania and PCDC originated in Dar es Salaam, which is on the coast facing Zanzibar and the Indian Ocean and has a natural harbor with many lovely, sandy beaches. Because of the coastal setting and proximity to the equator, the weather in Dar es Salaam tends to be very hot and humid. The city was not only an important government center but also home to the only university in Tanzania. The University of Dar es Salaam was founded in 1961 as an affiliate of the University of London. In 1963, it became a part of the University of East Africa, and in 1970 it was split into three separate schools: Makere University in Uganda, the University of Kenya, and the University of Dar es Salaam. During the decade after independence, the three East African countries strove to maintain several joint programs—for instance, a Common Services Organization, East African

Airways, and the combined universities. By the beginning of the 1970s, however, intercountry differences were such that the joint programs could not be maintained.

The name "Dar es Salaam" means "Haven of Peace" in Arabic. In the late 1800s, the German East Africa Colonial Administration established its headquarters there. When the British took control of Tanganyika at the end of World War I, they made Dar es Salaam the headquarters for the government, and it remained the capital until 1973, when Dodoma, in the center of the country, became the capital. In 1966, the population of Dar es Salaam was a little more than 100,000; today it exceeds two million.[4]

4

Government Officials Clarify the Situation

Autopsies Are Performed

We presume murder routinely here in a violent death.
—C. F. Ijumba

On Tuesday, March 29, 1966, PCDSM cabled PCDC with the developing news that the police were holding Bill Kinsey on a charge of homicide. The cable went on to describe eyewitness accounts of a beating and a rod with blood and hair on it. The cable also reported a conversation between Peace Corps officials Norm Hummon and John Hohl and the deputy director of the CID in Dar es Salaam, C. F. Ijumba. The deputy director told them, "We presume murder routinely here in violent death."

Director Ijumba went on to describe the facts of the incident as he understood them at the time. He said his reports indicated that the Kinsey couple were seen walking on the rocks, and people were suddenly attracted to the situation by someone screaming. The man appeared to be beating the woman; the woman disappeared; the man made some quick movements and then also disappeared. The witnesses said they were afraid to go to the scene lest the man be armed, so they sent for the police. When the police arrived, they found the body of the dead woman and the man in a confused state. They also found some "instruments" hidden nearby. The husband was taken into custody, and the body taken to a medical facility.

During the meeting, Ijumba told Hummon that the case seemed to call for an autopsy by the government chief pathologist in Dar es Salaam, so he had ordered the body taken there and delivered to the chief pathologist. However, it appears that such an autopsy was never performed. Had it been done, it is likely, depending on the findings by a qualified government pathologist (as opposed to an autopsy by a medical officer with few qualifications), that either the case against Bill might have been dropped or the prosecution case substantially strengthened. Why such an autopsy was never performed or why Ijumba's orders were ignored is unclear.

Ijumba then mused on how cases develop. A case can start out with much evidence, but as the case proceeds, it fizzles out. Or a case can begin with little and then proceed slowly until there is a big break, and a clear-cut case is developed. He said he hoped the case would turn out to be like the former. Ijumba also observed that most cases beginning with a charge of murder turn out not to be so after further inquiry. As to publicity, Ijumba said the relationship of the police with the press was quite good. The CID did not want to sensationalize the situation, so a press release would be issued routinely the next day, and the incident would be played down. He didn't expect the names of those involved would be mentioned, but the release would likely state that the deceased was a Peace Corps volunteer.[1]

Meanwhile, in Dar es Salaam Dr. Morrissey was dealing with some unexpected medical issues. Apparently, the plane chartered from Nairobi left for Mwanza without the lead-lined casket, so he made arrangements for the lead-lined casket to be sent directly to Dar es Salaam, and a regular casket would be used to transport the body from Mwanza to Dar es Salaam. About noon, McPhee called Morrissey asking that a private pathologist be obtained. Because the only private pathologists appeared to be in Kenya, Morrissey worried that they might not be officially recognized in Tanzania. A conversation with a doctor at the Ministry of Health in Dar es Salaam reassured them that if McPhee and Morrissey contacted Doctor Timms, the chief pathologist in Kenya, he could identify a pathologist who would be acceptable to the Tanzania government. Morrissey then contacted Peace Corps officials in Nairobi and asked them to find a qualified pathologist.[2]

At 10:55 a.m. on Tuesday, March 29, Paul Sack and Tom McHugh arrived in Mwanza on an East African Airways flight. At about the same time, the charter flight from Nairobi arrived in Mwanza, but without the requested coffin. Mr. Parekh of Singh and Parekh met Sack and McHugh at the airport. The group reviewed what had happened, what they knew, and what needed to be done, and they decided that Parekh, Sack, and McHugh would fly to Maswa. At about noon, they left for Maswa on the charter plane. McHugh vividly remembers that once the plane landed in Maswa and was taxiing , the pilot noticed that someone had plowed a ditch across the runway. The pilot ignored it, and the plane hopped over the ditch. Later, leaving Maswa, the pilot employed the same maneuver to take his plane aloft.[3]

At Maswa, Sack and McHugh were met by Father Bob Lefebvre, who took them to police headquarters, where they found Bill Kinsey in Inspector Kifunta's office. McHugh later dictated a report on his observation of Bill:

> His immediate reaction upon seeing me was one of great relief, and considerable emotion. We shook hands and he continued to hold onto my hand. I noted that he had red eyelids and was near to tears. He was unshaven and his hands trembled continuously. He was obviously expending great effort to maintain some control of his emotions. While talking, he was unable to maintain conversation for more than approximately a minute without breaking off into a period of silence, during which, he would stare at the floor, tremble, and occasionally sob. Mr. Kinsey related to me that from the time of his wife's death, he had had no food, except several cups of coffee, and almost no sleep in the two nights which had followed the death. The first night he spent at the Nyalikungu Maryknoll Mission with Father Lefebvre. The second night was spent in Maswa Prison, where it was necessary that he lay on the ground in an attempt to sleep, due to the total lack of bedding for prisoners. . . .
>
> My feeling at the time of first seeing Mr. Kinsey was that he was suffering from a gross stress reaction and that his responses and reactions to events occurring around him affected by his poor mental condition were not normal and could not be expected to be normal. Though I felt that he was in need of sedation, I elected to give none until he had had an opportunity to talk with his counsel, Mr. Parekh. I was satisfied that he was not in danger of harming himself as a result of his condition, but I cautioned that he not be left alone under any circumstances.[4]

While in Maswa, Sack met with Inspector Kifunta. Sack explained to him that Mr. Parekh was there representing Bill Kinsey and not the Peace Corps. At this point, the Peace Corps was beginning its effort to demonstrate neutrality in the case, at least for the benefit of the Tanzania government. While Mr. Singh and Mr. Parekh were in Maswa, Parekh appeared before the local magistrate, where he requested bail for Bill, but it was denied. He did secure an order releasing the body for a postmortem by Dr. McHugh and by an unnamed specialist. He also obtained an order allowing Dr. McHugh to examine Bill. Without these orders, it is doubtful that the testimony by McHugh and the "unnamed specialist" could have been used in court.[5]

McPhee, who was back in his office, tried to call Peace Corps Nairobi several times to request help in finding a pathologist but was unable to get through. Finally, he called the PCDSM and asked that office to contact Nairobi, which it had already done.

Bob Poole, Peace Corps director in Kenya, called McPhee in the afternoon and reported that Dr. Gerald Dockeray, a private pathologist from Nairobi, would arrive by plane about 5:15 p.m. Dockeray was a pilot and had his own plane. At about 4:00, the charter plane returned from Maswa, carrying Peppy's body and a policeman from Maswa CID. McPhee met the plane and took the body to the Mwanza Hospital morgue. He was met there by the Peace Corps volunteer nurse Nancy Churchill, who had arranged for use of the morgue.[6]

Meanwhile, back in Maswa in the early afternoon on March 29, after obtaining the order from the Maswa magistrate, McHugh performed a superficial examination of Peverley Kinsey in the morgue of the Maswa Government Hospital. Father Bob assisted with the examination and took notes on McHugh's observations. Two nurses from the Maswa Government Hospital were also present. McHugh had earlier tried to contact Dr. Mganga, the AMO who had performed the initial postmortem, but Mganga was out of town, and his written report was locked in his office.[7]

McHugh found the body of Peppy Kinsey—now almost forty-eight hours from the time of her death, identified to McHugh by Father Bob and a nun but also recognized by McHugh—lying on a concrete table. Peppy was still wearing her clothes, but they were covered by a green, bloodstained towel. McHugh noted a blue sleeveless blouse with considerable blood on the back and a vertical, approximately 8-inch tear in the right back side. He noted smears of blood on the face and the front of the chest and considerable blood in the hair and on the table where she lay. There were bruises below both knees. There were no abnormalities of the back of either leg. There was an abrasion on the front of the left ankle. None of the bones of the legs or feet appeared to be fractured or dislocated.

The arms were in normal position. The fingernails were unbroken and appeared normal. There were numerous small abrasions on the knuckles and a 5½-by-2-centimeter area of bruising on the back of the right hand as well as several bruises and abrasions running lengthwise on the back of both fore-arms. Those on the right forearm were most prominent. There were no marks on the upper arms. All arm bones appeared to be intact. No evidence of injury of the thoracic, lumbar, or sacral regions of the spine or back was found, and because the head did not move freely on the neck, McHugh concluded that the neck was not broken.

McHugh noted an incision, presumably made by the AMO, around the skull. The incision had been closed by suture. The right-upper-middle incisor of the teeth was missing, leaving a cavity on the gum.

On the right side of the skull he found a wound about 4½ centimeters by 1 centimeter long near the eye socket, which extended down to the bone. The edges of the wound were sharp. He found bruising of both right eyelids and on the bridge of the nose. McHugh thought the tip of the nose had been pushed slightly to the left.

Along the right side of the head, McHugh found several wounds between ½ and 2 centimeters in length, some extending to the bone, some diagonal and some horizontal in orientation. Several of the wounds had a flap of skin attached to them.

On the left side of the skull, McHugh found two adjacent wounds, one posterior to the other. The first wound was about 1 centimeter long, and the second was almost 2 centimeters in length. The second was in the shape of a triangle with a triangular flap of skin attached. Both wounds extended through "all layers of scalp to the bone of the skull." When McHugh pressed the skull through these wounds, he found the bone structure damaged as well, further indicating a fracture of the skull. McHugh found no blood in the ears, no lacerations of the mouth or tongue, and no fractures of the facial bones.

Following this external examination and based on the order issued by the Maswa magistrate, McHugh prepared the body to be flown to Mwanza for examination by a specialist. The body was placed in a coffin along with Peppy's clothes and shoes. The towel, however, was left in the morgue in error. The cof-fin was then taken to the Maswa airport to be flown to Mwanza.

After taking Peppy's body to the Maswa airstrip, McHugh, accompanied by Father Bob and Inspector Kifunta, went to the Nyalikungu Maryknoll Mission. They found Bill with two priests and a uniformed policeman. It was 3:00 p.m. on March 29. McHugh took Bill into an adjacent room for an examination, where he found Bill to be suffering from gross anxiety, an upper-respiratory infection, acute bronchitis or early pneumonia in the right lower lobe of the lungs, and multiple, superficial injuries of the arms and legs. At this point, it was unclear whether these injuries were a result of the struggle with Peppy or were inflicted by the Africans while restraining Bill.

Because of the reported poor conditions in the Maswa jail, McHugh asked Inspector Kifunta if Kinsey could be remanded, with guard, to the Nyalikungu Maryknoll Mission. Kifunta said no. McHugh then asked if Bill could be transferred to the prison ward of a hospital—either Mwanza or Shinyanga. Kifunta said that it could be done only by court order, and the courts were closed for the day.

Inspector Kifunta said he could transfer Kinsey to nearby Malya Prison, where proper beds would be available. However, Malya was quite some distance away, and there would be no medical care available. Father Bob said he could provide a bed and some medical assistance from a Maryknoll sister-nurse, so it was decided that the Maswa Jail was the best option. McHugh gave Kinsey a shot and left some antibiotics with Father Bob to give to the nurse.[8]

At about 4:00 p.m., the Peace Corps group, including McHugh, Sack, Parekh, and the Peace Corps driver, returned to Mwanza, arriving at the Peace Corps office about 6:00. McPhee told McHugh that Peppy's body had been placed in the morgue of the Mwanza Government Hospital, and he introduced McHugh to Dr. Gerald Dockeray, the pathologist from Nairobi, who had arrived at the Mwanza airport a little earlier.

Dockeray's assistance had been obtained by Dick Richter, the deputy Peace Corps director for Kenya, based in Nairobi. Several months earlier, a Peace Corps volunteer in Kenya had committed suicide, and the Peace Corps needed a pathologist to investigate and to document the death, so after a bit of research Richter had found Dr. Dockeray and had arranged for him to perform a postmortem in that case. When the call came in from Tanzania seeking a pathologist, Richter immediately contacted Dockeray, who fortunately owned and flew his own plane, and he agreed immediately to fly to Mwanza to perform the postmortem on Peppy.[9]

31

Tom McHugh remembers Dockeray as elderly, tall, jocular, and moderately overweight. Dockeray was friendly, professional, and thorough in his approach to the medical examination needed. McHugh, who had little experience with performing an autopsy, was enormously relieved upon meeting Dockeray. McHugh was also cognizant that because of his own limited experience his testimony would be vulnerable to challenge.[10]

After meeting and discussing his prior observations, McHugh accompanied Dockeray to the hospital, where they were met by Dr. Salu, the AMO on the staff of the hospital, and by Nancy Churchill, the Peace Corps volunteer nurse assigned to the hospital. The postmortem began at 7:00 p.m., with Dr. McHugh assisting Dr. Dockeray and Nancy Churchill acting as scribe. They completed their work by 8:30. Dockeray's examination notes are preceded by the following introduction:

On the 29th of March 1966 at Mwanza Hospital, I made a post-mortem [sic] exam of Mrs. Peverley Dennett Kinsey, aged about 24 years. The body was identified to me by Dr. C. T. McHugh, and the examination was attended by Dr. Salu, a medical assistant at the hospital.

In the coffin with the body was a heavily blood-stained white sleeveless blouse [McHugh described it as blue in his autopsy report], a blue denim wrap-around skirt, and gray rough leather shoes.

He recorded the height of the deceased as 5 feet 7 inches. The details of his examination can be broken down into two lists (my summaries, with a few quotations and numbering taken directly from the postmortem report):

External Examination; Bruises and Abrasions

Palms of the hands and the fingers normal; fingernails intact.

A 2-by-¾-inch bruise on the back of the right hand.

A "skid-mark" abrasion over the ulna of the right arm "extending from below the elbow halfway down the forearm."

Small abrasions on the left forefinger, middle finger, and the thumb side of the forefinger.

On the back of the hand an abrasion ½-inch long and ¼-inch wide at the base of the middle finger.

Two bruises on the left forearm, one just below the elbow and one above the elbow, each about ½ inch in diameter.

No bruises on the back of the legs.

A few bruises below the left shoulder blade covering an area of about 2½ by ¾ inches.

Three small abrasions on the back, each about ⅓ inch by ½ inch in diameter; also three other abrasions on the back covering an area of about 3 inches in length with about 1½ inches between each abrasion

"The right upper central incisor tooth had been knocked out."

Bruises at the corner of the mouth; a bruise over the front of the nose; a large bruise around the right eye; and bruises on both cheeks.

Wounds to the Head

1. "This was the most serious injury. It was a vertical penetrating wound 1½ inches long. (Caused by a stab of some object, stick or stone.) This wound penetrated to the orbital plate of the front part of the base of the skull. The base of the skull was broken over an area about the size of a fingertip and from this area fractures radiated in several directions."
2. A 2-inch-long cut inside the hairline that exposed the frontal bone but did not penetrate it.
3. Another cut running parallel to cut number 2 about 1-inch long.
4. Above the right ear and separated from number 2 by a ½-inch-wide piece of skin, a circular jagged cut 1½ inches in diameter and 1½ inches above the ear.
5. Between cut number 4 and the ear, a ¾-by¼ -inch cut.
6. Above and behind the right ear, a 1½-by-½ -inch cut.
7. and 8. Two cuts in the scalp on the top of the skull, ¼ inch by ½ inch running across the skull.
9. and 10. Two jagged cuts to the left of cuts 7 and 8, each about 1½ inches long.
11. A 2-inch cut on the back of the head.
12. A 2½-inch cut behind and above the left ear.[11]

This numbering system for the wounds became the basis for further discussions, testimony, and the judge's decision in the case and so was a significant indicator for how Peppy's death came about.

Except for wound number 1, Dockeray found no fractures of the base of the skull. There was a separation of the suture line (joint) between the frontal and parietal bones of the skull, with a linear fracture running from the suture line for 2½ inches horizontally and through the left parietal bone.

> With the exception of the penetrating wound number 1, which broke the orbital plate of the base of the skull, all the other wounds except number 4 were clean cuts exposing the skull, but not damaging the skull. These cuts might have been caused by fairly hard blows of an object such as a stick or bar, but insufficiently hard to damage the skull. They might have been caused by the head hitting sharp edges of rock in falling, but the head would have to have rolled about to explain the number and situation of the cuts.
>
> Wound number 1 would have to be caused by a narrow object going into the face above and inside the right eye and penetrating in an upward and backward direction to the base of the skull. A stab with a stick or bar or a narrow projection of rock could account for this injury, which may have been the fatal injury, although the other wounds and the fracture of the left parietal bone would have also contributed to the shock and concussion of the brain. Death, in my opinion, was due to these head injuries causing shock and concussion of the brain.[12]

Visit to the Scene

On March 30, Dockeray went to the "scene of the accident" with Superintendent Kifunta and Paul Sack. He was shown the large boulder from which Peppy allegedly fell and a blood-stained rocky area below it. Kifunta showed him where the bar and the stones with blood stains and hair were found, but Dockeray did not see either the rod or the stones at that time. "I have not seen the bar, but a bar might have caused the cuts on the scalp, although it is peculiar that none marked the skull. But this argument could also be used for cuts produced by falling on rocky ledges. The penetrating wound, number one, could not have been caused by a blow other than a penetrating or stab like blow. The jagged cut number 4, which was circular, would be likely to be caused by a stone rather than a bar." The postmortem report ended with the following description of Dockeray's professional status:

G. C. Dockeray, M.D., M.S.C., D.P.H.,
FRCPI, Director Laboratory of Clinical
Medicine, Nairobi
Consulting Pathologist, Nairobi Hospital
and Aga Khan Hospital
Former Government Pathologist, Kenya
Former examiner in Forensic Medicine, National
University of Ireland and University of
East Africa, (Makerere College)[13]

Dockeray believed that his finding that Peppy's skull was undamaged beneath the scalp wounds was very significant because if she had been struck by an iron bar or a large rock or both, he would expect the skull to be fractured or crushed. However, he found head wound number 1 difficult to explain. It would depend on whether the iron bar fit the wound; he later determined that it did not.[14]

Thus, by the third day after Peppy's death, while announcing a position of neutrality, Peace Corps officials had acted quickly to investigate the case and to obtain high-quality, professional medical assistance. These early decisions would turn out to be crucial in Bill's defense. None of the activities appeared to focus on demonstrating that Peppy's death had not been an accident—that is, murder.

5

Peace Corps Officials Visit Scene, Bail Is Sought, Peppy's Body Is Flown to Dar es Salaam

This man will be out of the country in 24 hours if you release him.
—*Tanzania state attorney*

On Wednesday, March 30, 1966, Sack and Dockeray, together with a professional photographer, flew to Maswa in Dr. Dockeray's plane. In Maswa, Inspector Kifunta showed Sack, Dockeray, and the photographer the scene of the "crime." Both the photographer's photos and Dr. Dockeray's testimony, informed by his visit to the scene, would play important roles at the trial. Kifunta reported there were two witnesses, an elderly woman and a man. However, later it was found that there were three witnesses.

The elderly woman, Humbi Sayuda, had come to the scene because she had heard a woman's cries, but she had poor eyesight, and, according to measurements made by Sack, was approximately 105 feet away from Peppy and Bill when she saw them. Kifunta told Sack that Bill had motioned to her, and they discussed how there might have been confusion in Bill's signal to her: Europeans (Americans) and Tanzanians normally gesture in different ways to direct someone to go away and to come near. Sack understood that the woman would not have been able to see something in Bill's hand, but she could testify to a struggle.

The second witness, Maganda Vilindo, was about 90 feet away according to Sack's measurement. This witness, according to Kifunta, claimed to have seen Bill and Peppy standing and pushing each other, that Bill pushed Peppy back with an iron bar, put Peppy on the ground, sat on her, and beat her head up and down on the rock. He also says he saw Bill carry the body over his shoulder to a second location—to hide the body, he assumed.

Kifunta could not show Sack the iron bar because it had been sent to Dar es Salaam, "carefully sealed in wax," for analysis. He did show Sack where the iron bar was found at the scene.

Kifunta pointed to where the bloody rock was found, which was about 8 feet from the second resting place of the body. Kifunta felt that the place where it was found was definitely of the "hiding place" sort, so it could not have been casually flung to that spot, the way the iron bar seemed to have been. Sack thought the location and use of the rock were particularly troubling to Bill's defense. Sack observed that the rock was about the size of a man's head and heavy. If used to strike the head, it would have fractured the skull, but no fractures were found. (When Sack later asked Bill about the rock, Bill said that he had no recollection but that he might have placed it under Peppy's head.) Sack and the photographer went on to take many photos, to make measurements, and to draw diagrams of the scene. The photos and their descriptions would be key exhibits at the trial.[1]

Presumably based on the facts provided by the eyewitnesses, Kifunta seemed to have come to the conclusion that Bill and Peppy never climbed to the higher rock, and so a fall such as Bill described never happened. Kifunta theorized that all the action instead took place below, as seen by the witnesses. Kifunta apparently did not believe Bill's story.

At 10:00 a.m. on March 30, McPhee and McHugh went to the Mwanza High Court to testify on an application for bail for Bill Kinsey. Gurbachan Singh, partner at Singh and Parekh, had been brought into the case to handle the early proceedings. He had studied law in England and was considered one of the leading criminal lawyers in Tanzania. Judge Harold Platt presided, but the application proceeding was postponed until 2:00 p.m. It is not known why, but the delay was not unusual for a busy court.

When the bail hearing resumed at 2:00, Singh argued that bail should be granted on the basis of Bill's illness, as reported by Dr. McHugh. The state attorney countered that bail was unprecedented in such a case and said, "This man will be out of the country in twenty-four hours if you release him." After further argument, the judge granted bail to Bill for 30,000 Tanzania shillings and Bill's passport. The passport could not be found at the time, but McPhee and Mr. Karim, owner of Karim Stores in Mwanza and a friend of McPhee's, posted 15,000 shillings each for bail.[2] Presumably Mr. Karim added a level of credibility to the application because he was well known in Mwanza.[3]

McPhee later reported that he had overheard a conversation around the court between the state attorney and several Africans: "The State Attorney [complained] about the granting of bail on the basis that it was favoritism by a white man for a white man." McPhee and Sack also understood that the state attorney planned to report the matter to the attorney general with a request that Judge Platt be removed from the case. Apparently, nothing came of that plan, however, because Platt would eventually preside at the trial.[4]

Despite Judge Platt's ruling, Bill was never released on bail. Not long after the bail-application hearing, he was placed in Butimba Prison in Mwanza. Butimba was considered quite a good prison, with medical support and appropriate food, and, if not exactly comfortable, it had reasonably good accommodations. The Peace Corps and Bill's attorneys then dropped the bail issue. On March 31, Paul Sack wrote a memo to the Peace Corps file on the case arguing that, in fact, it was important for Bill to be kept in prison. He pointed out that the various doctors had stressed the importance of keeping a person accused of murder under close supervision and observation because of the potential for self-harming or even suicide. Such attention would not be available elsewhere. Sack urged that Bill be placed in Butimba Prison as soon as his immediate health issues were under control.[5]

Although the prosecutor, Peace Corps officials, and the doctors agreed on where Bill should stay, it doesn't appear that Bill was ever consulted on whether he would prefer to spend the next six months in prison or continue to seek bail and possibly go free until after the trial. Such an effort would probably have been fruitless because the option of bail was unavailable with a charge of murder, although Judge Platt was initially willing to grant it.

Another potential problem for Bill's defense arose when it was discovered that he had taken out an insurance policy on Peppy's life, but copies of the policy, which had been on Bill's desk, could not be found. It was later confirmed that the police had confiscated the documents as further proof of Bill's malevolent intent. When McHugh heard that the state attorney had told Singh that the state had an "airtight" case, McHugh assumed the insurance issue might have prompted the prosecutor's confident feeling.[6] The prosecution, however, was unlikely to know that the Peace Corps provided a $10,000 insurance policy on each volunteer's life, so a policy on Peppy's life, with Bill as beneficiary, was not unusual.

At 7:00 p.m. on March 30, Sack returned from Maswa and reported that Bill's passport was in the hands of the CID in Maswa.

That same day McHugh and McPhee were informed that the CID had ordered Peppy's body be taken to Dar es Salaam and placed in the morgue of Muhimbili Hospital. McHugh and a uniformed police officer accompanied the body to Dar es Salaam, leaving the Mwanza airport at 11:00 a.m. Tom McHugh remembers that it was the same plane and pilot as the ones that had taken him to Maswa. The seats were removed to accommodate the casket; McHugh sat in the copilot's seat, and the policeman was in the back with the casket. As the plane neared Dar es Salaam, the plane began coughing and sputtering. The pilot switched fuel tanks and issued a mayday alert to the airport, but they landed safely—McHugh was left to reflect on his second "experience" in two days with the dangers of flying in Tanzania.

When McHugh mentioned the incident to Dr. Dockeray, Dockeray asked him what kind of plane was involved. McHugh told him it was a Piper Aztec, and Dockeray laughed, saying the Piper Aztec was famous for having the glide angle of a brick! McHugh had been calm during the descent because he was under the mistaken impression that a Piper could glide for long distances.[7]

They arrived in Dar es Salaam at about 3:30 p.m. and took the coffin directly to Muhimbili Hospital, where the body was placed in the refrigerated morgue. However, they soon learned that the CID in Dar es Salaam disclaimed any desire for the body (despite Ijumba's supposed order to perform an autopsy). The calvarium (skull cap) and scalp, which Dr. Dockeray had removed as exhibits, were retained in the Peace Corps office under Dr. Morrissey's supervision.

Later that day, PCDC cabled PCDSM expressing concern about Bill's mental state and suggesting that since Peace Corps mental health experts would be in Nigeria in early April, they could be made available for consultation.[8]

A second cable that day contained instructions for Anthony "Tony" Essaye, Peace Corps deputy general counsel, who would soon arrive in Dar es Salaam:

ASSUME ESSAYE WILL PROCEED KIRECTLY [sic] [TO] KIN-SEY. OBVIOUSLY DESIRABLE HE TALK TO HIM, LAWYER, PATHOLOGISTS AND CID OFFICIALS. HE SHOULD OBTAIN FROM LATTER FULL ASSESSMENT EVIDENCE, DETAILS PROBABLE COURSE LEGAL PROCEEDINGS, POSSIBLE CHARGES AND MAXIMUM PENALTIES THEREFORE. IF AT ALL POSSIBLE, HE SHOULD VIEW DEATH SCENE, EXAMINE

QTE [quote] HIDDEN OBJECTS UNQTE [unquote], OBTAIN COPY ANY KINSEY STATEMENTS AND ENSURE ALL EVIDENCE BEING CAREFULLY PRESERVED.

The cable reported that the Kinsey family had inquired about the advisability of their traveling to Tanzania. The Peace Corps suggested they await further developments.[9]

Also on March 30, PCDSM cabled PCDC with the latest developments as provided to them by the CID deputy director C. F. Ijumba. He told the Peace Corps officials that Bill had been formally charged with murder and that under Tanzania law there was no possibility of bail. The law provided for a hearing in about thirty days in the local court in either Shinyanga or Maswa to allow time for completion of police investigations and court scheduling. The preliminary procedures would generally follow the traditional British system.[10]

On Thursday morning, March 31, at 8:00 a.m., Bill's attorney, Mr. Singh, left by charter airplane for Maswa with the bail notice to bring Bill back to Mwanza for medical treatment. At 9:00 a.m., McPhee learned that Bill had already been moved to Butimba Prison in Mwanza. Sack provided information on the visiting times and who could be authorized to see Bill in the prison.[11]

By Thursday, Tony Essaye had arrived in Dar es Salaam, and he and Deputy Director Norm Hummon reported that they had met in Dar es Salaam with the attorney general, the CID deputy director, and the assistant chief education officer. The meetings were satisfactory, and all the officials appeared to be sympathetic. The cable also reported that Bill had been moved to Butimba Prison, where medical facilities were good, so the reason to seek bail had been removed. PCDSM hoped these factors would satisfy the officials who had complained about bail being granted in a capital case. Hummon and Essaye also reported that a lawyer for Bill had been obtained and asked that PCDC ratify this action and that the Peace Corps continue to pay for the lawyer for the "immediate future." They made clear, however, that the lawyer was Bill's, not the Peace Corps.[12]

Tony Essaye was a graduate of Harvard Law School (1961), working in the spring of 1966 as a deputy general counsel for the Peace Corps. He was a tall, slender, craggy-faced man with a gentle but resolute demeanor. As soon as the Peace Corps had heard that Bill had been charged, Peace Corps general counsel William Josephson had called Tony in and told him to go to Tanzania immediately. Essaye had gotten on the next available flight and arrived in Dar es Salaam within a day or two. After conferring with Paul Sack, who had returned from Mwanza, Essaye flew to Mwanza.[13] Essaye's detailed records supply a clear picture of subsequent events and activities of the various participants in the case.

The foresight and ability of Peace Corps officials, in particular Paul Sack and Jack McPhee, to visit the scene, take photos, obtain information from the police, and quickly meet with Bill may have been the crucial factors in the conduct and outcome of the subsequent trial. Although relations between the Tanzania government and Peace Corps officials had been cordial, the bail hearing began to demonstrate developing tension between Africans and Americans. It became important for the Peace Corps to find ways to improve the relationship, which they hoped to do by taking a position of neutrality and by withdrawing the bail request. But the cable from PCDC with instructions for Essaye seemed to suggest that he should play a more partisan role as a representative of the Peace Corps.

6

Life in Prison for Bill

For Bill Kinsey, Butimba Prison in Mwanza, which was rated a "Class A" prison in the Tanzania system, would become his home for the next six months. Although few consider a prison a pleasant place to reside for six months, by all indications Butimba Prison was comparable to high-quality prisons in the United States. Dr. McHugh visited Bill at the prison and talked with the medical staff about the facilities. He wrote that the "conditions are very good. There was bedding, good diet, adequate facilities, some opportunity for exercise and fairly good medical facilities." However, while Bill's mental health and morale had been fair in Maswa, McHugh observed that they had deteriorated over the first few weeks at Butimba and that Bill had become mildly depressed and anxious.

McHugh reported that Bill had devised a program to keep busy, which included exercising in the morning and the evening, teaching math and English to some of the prisoners, and reading books and magazines brought to him by visitors. Bill expressed his wish to be treated as much as possible like other prisoners and had requested reading material and "teaching English" materials that he could share with other inmates. McHugh, however, was looking forward and became worried about medical and physical facilities at the other prisons where Bill might be placed over the next several weeks.[1]

In the middle of April, Bill was moved to the prison in Malya, which was about 40 miles from Mwanza and the same distance from Maswa. Unfortunately, the move was made in a truck with an open bed, where Bill was drenched by a rainstorm. Before he left Butimba, he was handed all his medications. Although the facilities in Malya Prison were good because it, like Butimba, was a Class A prison, Peace Corps officials were disconcerted that they had been informed of this move only when Father Bob came to the Peace Corps office in Mwanza on April 12 to tell them that he had gone to Butimba to visit Bill but was told Bill had been moved to Malya. The apparent reason for the move was to make Bill easily available for hearings in Maswa. The police were concerned about holding hearings in Mwanza because it was in a different administrative district and would be inconvenient for witnesses. In Malya Prison, Bill was given a one-person cell, and the sanitation, water, and food seemed to be adequate. Bill, however, had little to do and was not able to exercise easily. Peace Corps staff were also concerned about their ability to visit him because of the distance from Mwanza.[2]

Bill's attorneys in Mwanza, Parekh and Singh, were also unhappy with the move and planned to request his return to Mwanza because the distance made it impossible for them to work with him in preparation for hearings. Their effort was unsuccessful, and Bill remained in Malya through April 29, 1966. They were able, however, to arrange for the doctor at Butimba Prison to request that Bill be returned there because of concerns about his health. Attorney Parekh thought the doctor's request would be met with more consideration and likely be successful; however, it was not.[3]

While in Malya Prison, Bill had several visitors, who provided insight to his mental state at the time. Dan and Betty Clemmer, American teachers based in Mwanza, visited the prison on Thursday, April 14, and reported to Jack McPhee that they found Bill quite discouraged.[4] In contrast, Dr. McHugh reported that Bill was in "fine spirits" when he talked with him in Malya on April 17.[5]

When Dr. McHugh and Father Bob visited Bill at Malya toward the end of the month, they came away concerned about his mental health because they observed that he seemed depressed and never talked about Peppy's death. McHugh forwarded his observations and requested an analysis from Peace Corps psychiatrists in Washington. He was relieved to hear from the chief psychiatrist that Bill's reaction seemed perfectly normal under the circumstances.[6]

Tony Essaye expressed a concern that Bill had still not written to his father and that he appeared in no hurry to do so. Essaye and others urged him to communicate soon because his father had been complaining about Peace Corps abandonment of Bill. Bill Sr. had received information only from Peace Corps officials, not from Bill directly, so he reasonably might feel that he wasn't getting the true picture and that perhaps Bill had been abandoned.[7]

Although the Mwanza legal team was concerned about Bill remaining in Malya Prison, when Jack McPhee visited, he concluded that Bill was probably better off because of the proximity of Father Bob and the very helpful attitude of the prison officials there. During his visit, McPhee talked with the prison superintendent, who told him he would do everything permitted under the regulations to help Bill. In fact, as reported in a cable to PCDC, Bill was "assigned [a] servant to prepare special 'European' meals, including afternoon tea, sweep room, etc. English speaking prisoner assigned as roommate."[8] Peace Corps volunteers Phil and Ann Ellison also visited Bill in prison and described the situation in relatively positive terms: "We just visited Bill . . . in prison. . . . It's a good place, actually, clean, lots of flowers, not bad food. The only thing is many of the prisoners are sick—TB, and the like. The man in the cell next to him has smallpox."[9]

Finally, after the preliminary hearing in Maswa was completed, Bill was returned to Butimba Prison on May 7, 1966, where he would remain until the trial.[10]

On May 27, Peace Corps country director Paul Sack sent a letter to the volunteers in Tanzania describing conditions at Butimba and Malya Prisons:

> Both prisons are large, sunny enclosures around a central recreation field. The facilities are kept scrupulously clean, and the staffs of both prisons have made it clear that they wish to do everything appropriate to ensure that Bill's confinement will be as physically comfortable as they can make it.
>
> Bill has been quite satisfied with his diet which has been tailored as much as possible to his tastes.
>
> Medical personnel of the prison system have been equally solicitous of his welfare. They have taken excellent care of him and have consulted the Peace Corps physician whenever they felt it necessary.
>
> Bill has received considerable reading material from the Peace Corps and other friends in Mwanza, and the Peace Corps maintains a close contact with him to aid in any other requests he may have.[11]

During the next few months, Peace Corps officials, volunteers, and other friends regularly visited Bill in prison, although visitors were allowed to visit only on weekends. In early June, Paul Sack responded to a PCDC request that it receive reports on visits two times per week, reminding these Washington officials that visitors were permitted only on the weekends. Bill's attorneys had attempted to arrange for Jack McPhee to visit on weekdays, but the prison superintendent was understandably reluctant to allow special treatment of Bill. Sack felt it was a bad idea to push the issue with the prison.[12]

By early June, Bill was settling into a prison routine. The Clemmers and the McPhees had recently visited him and reported that his sense of humor had returned and that he seemed to have made friends among the prisoners. Their report goes on to describe his high level of reading: *Is Paris Burning* by Larry Collins and Dominique Lapierre, *A Thousand Days* by Arthur Schlesinger, a Faulkner novel, the Paris edition of the *New York Herald Tribune*, the *Saturday Review*, and *Africa Reports*. He also requested copies of the *New Statesman* and *Esquire*.[13] This collection of reading material would probably not have been permitted in an American prison.

Bill was placed in a three-person cell, where, fortunately, one of his roommates who was from Uganda spoke English and was interested in literature and reading. In early July, Dan and Betty Clemmer as well as Jack and Sandy McPhee visited Bill. They brought him a bacon-and-tomato sandwich and fruit, much to Bill's delight. He told them he was even starting to gain weight. The Clemmers and McPhees visited again later in the month, bringing more food and magazines. They found Bill in good spirits. He reported that his Swahili was becoming very good. His attorneys continued to visit on a regular basis to prepare for the trial. One interruption to the day-to-day life in Butimba Prison occurred when on July 20 Bill was subpoenaed to appear as a witness in court in Maswa. His former cook at Binza Upper Primary School was involved in a court proceeding, so Bill, as a potential witness, was required to travel to Maswa for the trial. It was arranged for his Mwanza attorney, Mr. Parekh, to accompany him as a precautionary measure.[14]

In mid-July 1966, Paul Sack wrote to Bill's parents with a report on the prison and Bill's situation:

> My first order of business last Monday on arrival in Mwanza was to visit Bill. His morale, general attitude, and adjustment to his situation can only be regarded as remarkable. He was extremely cheerful and relaxed.
>
> Our conversation covered a fairly wide range of subjects. Bill is making active plans for the future and commented, in an interesting and detached way, on the conditions and the general life of the prison. One of the prison authorities has even commented to Bill that he expects that Bill will write a book on his experiences.

Bill mentioned that while there is plenty of food served him, it is a monotonous diet; he gets the same food everyday. He and an Indian man are the only prisoners entitled to the "Class A" diet, and they have struck up something of a friendship. Bill expressed appreciation for the special food items his friends in Mwanza bring in to him on the weekends and commented that he has even begun to gain weight. He actually looks neither thin nor overweight but very fit indeed.[15]

The usual weekend visits continued on up to the beginning of the trial. In early August, Earl Brown, volunteer teacher from a school in Musoma on Lake Victoria, about 150 miles north of Mwanza; Joan McKinney, an American teacher with the Teachers for East Africa Program; and Dr. McHugh visited. Shortly before the trial began, Peace Corps officials cabled PCDC about Bill's situation: "BREWSTER [attorney Carroll Brewster] CONFERRED WITH KINSEY TWICE SUNDAY AND FOUND HIM CHEERFUL AND IN FINE HEALTH. BILL ALSO VISITED BY MCPHEES, ENGLISHES, MCHUGH, PETER REED [Reid], JOHN OLIVER AND OTHERS."[16]

Dan and Betty Clemmer, who had visited Bill every weekend while he was in prison, finished their tour of duty and returned to America in early August. Betty had written Bill's parents every week, and her letters were a great comfort to them. The Clemmers planned to visit the Kinseys in North Carolina later in August.[17]

Bill reported that he kept busy exercising and teaching English and other skills to the prisoners. John Oliver and I had an airmail subscription to the *New York Times* weekly news summary, and Bill was delighted to get a copy. One time John brought along a copy of *Playboy* magazine, which helped satisfy Bill's interest in current fiction.

Although some people were concerned about Bill's calmness and lack of agitation over not only the loss of his wife but also his imprisonment, it seemed that he was doing his best to get through a very bad situation.

Bill's incarceration caused not only health problems, both physical and mental, but also difficulty in communicating with his attorneys, difficulty for Peace Corps officials in knowing where he was at all times, and access issues for friends who wanted to visit him. However, the quantity of cables, letters, and memos he received demonstrated the efforts made to provide him with support from the community. Although some volunteers openly accused the Peace Corps of abandoning him, it was clear that he was not left alone.

7

The Peace Corps and Tanzania

The Peace Corps and Tanzania share 1961 as their birth year, although at the time Tanzania was known as Tanganyika. Shortly before the U.S. election in 1960, John Kennedy had been convinced, primarily by a group of students at the University of Michigan, to endorse the idea of what became the Peace Corps. After the election, President Kennedy lost little time in implementing the idea. On March 1, 1961, he signed Executive Order 10924, which formally established the Peace Corps. At the same time, he named his brother-in-law, Sargent Shriver, to head the new agency.

The Peace Corps leadership was initially uncertain whether any countries would request Peace Corps volunteers. Many critics complained that such a program was a useless endeavor. Richard Nixon predicted it would become a "cult of escapism" and a haven for "draft dodgers." Shriver and the Peace Corps leadership felt it necessary to reach out to countries in Asia and Africa and to encourage them to step forward with requests for volunteers. In April 1961, Shriver left on a three-and-a-half-week tour of nations in Africa and Asia to speak with the leadership of the countries there and to negotiate agreements for the placement of volunteers.[1]

Shriver's first stop was in Accra, Ghana, to meet Prime Minister Kwame Nkrumah. As a stroke of good fortune, Prime Minister Julius Nyerere of Tanganyika was visiting Nkrumah at the time, so Shriver was able to meet and talk with both of them. Through the efforts of Under Secretary of State Chester Bowles, the Peace Corps had already been in touch with Nyerere, who had told Bowles that Tanganyika could use some road engineers. The meeting in Accra solidified Nyerere's position, and Nkrumah also agreed to accept Peace Corps volunteer teachers. The support from these two prominent African leaders substantially improved Shriver's reception as he traveled to Nigeria, India, Thailand, the Philippines, and several other countries.

Nyerere's response may also have been informed by the expansion of the Kennedy administration's support for African issues, in contrast to the weak connections under President Dwight Eisenhower. Soon after Kennedy's election, the State Department improved famine-relief shipments, increased grant assistance from the U.S. Agency for International Development, set up a student-exchange program, and, of course, offered to supply Peace Corps volunteers to Tanganyika.[2]

During the Eisenhower years, not only did the U.S. government show its unfriendliness in general to efforts at independence in Africa, but it also treated Julius Nyerere in particular rather shabbily. When Nyerere came to New York in 1954 to argue for Tanganyikan independence, the State Department responded by "restricting his movements to an eight- block radius of the UN headquarters and limiting his stay in the United States to within twenty-four hours of his appearance before the Trusteeship Council."[3] In addition, the Eisenhower administration often chastised its representatives for having any contact with Nyerere and other Africans, whereas under Kennedy the State Department welcomed such contacts, and Barrington King, the American vice consul, often invited Nyerere to dinner.

In an interview for a State Department oral history project in 1990, King provided an interesting, no-nonsense picture of the time before Tanganyikan independence. He was surprised and amused by the fact that he had been sent for expensive, comprehensive training in French, served briefly in Cairo, then found himself "in a really run-down seaport on the Indian Ocean." Since Tanganyika was not yet independent, the American mission there was a consulate rather than an embassy, with a staff of only six people. King was impressed with the ability of the British to run the country with just a few hundred people. However, the British had done nothing to develop the country: almost no paved roads, a largely missionary-run school system, and little infrastructure. King arrived shortly after President Kennedy was inaugurated, at a time when former Michigan governor G. Mennen Williams came to the State Department as assistant secretary for Africa. With Kennedy's support, Williams embarked on an aggressive program to boost America's interest in Africa, a move much different from the Eisenhower administration's policy.[4]

Women and the Peace Corps

An issue that might be considered in this case is the role of women in the Peace Corps and the view of domestic violence in America at the time. In the early days of the Peace Corps, there were few women in leadership positions, as was the case in most government, corporate, and other public entities at the time. Although the Peace Corps was considered somewhat more advanced in its acceptance of women, it remained in the 1960s essentially led by men, often relatively young men in their twenties and thirties.[5]

The women who did play larger roles in the PCDC administration tended to be young and well connected politically. Sally Bowles, daughter of Under Secretary of State Chester Bowles, was in her early twenties. Jane Gore, daughter of Senator Albert Gore and sister of later vice president Al Gore, was of a similar age. Nan McEvoy was a bit older and had been a reporter with the *San Francisco Chronicle,* the *New York Herald Tribune,* and the *Washington Post.* Her grandfather had founded the *Chronicle* in 1865. When she died in 2014, her family was listed at number 27 on the *Forbes* list of richest families.

One of the most experienced and forceful women in the Peace Corps administration at the time was Elizabeth (Betty) Harris, a thirty-nine-year-old political organizer from Dallas, Texas. When Harris came to PCDC in 1961, she thought she would head the women's division of the Office of Peace Corps Volunteers. "She was disappointed," states Coates Redmon in her book about the Peace Corps; "her appetite had been whetted to deal with women's issues in an agency dominated by men who didn't want to deal with them at all." Harris was instead put in charge of a newsletter for volunteers in the field. Within a few weeks, however, the hard-driving Harris became deputy associate director of the Office of Peace Corps Volunteers.[6]

The Peace Corps was suddenly faced with a "women's issue"—a volunteer became pregnant. When an "emergency" meeting on a Saturday was called, Harris was the only woman invited. She describes the discussion as follows:

> Well, obviously, if you send all these young, healthy women overseas, and for the first time in their life they would be free, and, well, yes, equal—uh, in a sense—then one or two of them, perhaps, out of a thousand, might be expected to succumb to the temptations of the flesh, and, uh, might actually, uh, sleep with a male Volunteer in

some isolated post. You know, out of loneliness and loss of home-town moral compass. And who knew? There was nothing on the Peace Corps application form to screen out a nymphomaniac. Then the thought began to occur to these grown men that possibly the pregnant Volunteer had got herself in the "family way" by means of intimate contact with a national. Oh, God! Well the guys were just falling apart. A Peace Corps woman is pregnant and she's not mar-ried to anybody! And who's the father? And what happens now? Do we bring her home? Do we inform her parents? Do we throw her out of the Peace Corps? One fool present at this meeting actually sug-gested that we "can" women Volunteers altogether. No one ever sug-gested that our male Volunteers might be shacking up with female "nationals," getting them pregnant, or what the implications of that might be in the host country. Oh no, it's the women.

. . . . For the first time I had come to realize fully the discrimina-tory nature of men's attitudes toward women.[7]

Harris supplied Director Shriver with a memo urging the Peace Corps not to adopt a policy that required a pregnant volunteer to return home to have a baby. Despite considerable pressure from the all-male Peace Corps lead-ership, especially the health professionals, Shriver, after going to the Kennedy compound at Hyannis Port for the weekend, adopted Harris's suggestion that a volunteer could have a baby overseas if she desired.[8]

The sense was that these male administrators were not antithetical to women's role in the Peace Corps but that they had little idea of the issues women faced. In fact, the legislation proposed by Senator Hubert Humphrey (D–Minn.) in 1960 aimed at establishing an all-male version of the Peace Corps.[9]

Even whether the Peace Corps would accept married couples was an issue in the early days. After considerable debate, it was decided that married couples were acceptable, and by the end of 1963 four hundred such couples were volunteers.[10]

Although Shriver had spoken out early on about the Peace Corps' need to include women as volunteers and as administrators, by the mid-1960s there were few women in leadership positions.[11] In 1966, there was only one woman in an administrative position among the Peace Corps staff in Tanzania. How-ever, there were many women among the volunteers in Tanzania. For example, in my own group of secondary-school teachers, fifty-two were women and sixty-seven men. In Peppy's group of primary-school teachers, sixty were women, and twenty-eight were men.

Some of the Peace Corps' efforts to combat sexism were laudable, but in at least one area its record is flawed: "If a single female Volunteer became pregnant, she was sent home immediately; the father—often a fellow Volunteer—was allowed to remain in the program. Many women Volunteers deemed this a blind spot in the Peace Corps' otherwise undiscriminating attitude toward the sexes."[12] The policy Harris worked on, mentioned earlier, would have applied only to married couples. An unmarried female volunteer was still sent home to have the baby.

During the mid-1960s in America (and much of the rest of the world), domestic violence was a somewhat invisible, largely ignored phenomenon. Although it certainly existed at all economic levels, few resources were available to the suffering woman—no shelters, no hotlines, no advocates, few cases in court, few woman lawyers, few women judges, and little research on the subject. Even in the late 1960s and early 1970s, little effort was focused on the issue of domestic violence in the federally funded legal-services programs for the poor. Only when women became a significant part of the population of lawyers and judges did the legal community begin to focus on the issue. By 1974, there were only a few shelters for battered women in the United States, but by 1995 there were about two thousand. In 1979, President Jimmy Carter established the Office of Domestic Violence, but it was not until 1994 that the federal Violence against Women Act was passed and signed by President Bill Clinton.[13]

Although there is no evidence to suggest that the Peace Corps in 1966 either intentionally or through ignorance in some way failed to fully accept the possibility that Peppy Kinsey had been murdered, at the same time one must be aware of the social environment of male leadership and a lack of understanding of the issues of domestic violence at the time.

Indeed, it was only recently that the scale of rape, sexual abuse, and other harassment of women began to be fully taken into account in the Peace Corps. Although it was known that in many countries female volunteers faced myriad challenges in dealing with local customs in which women were often at the mercy of men, in recent years many women have come forward to report on their experience of various forms of sexual abuse. The Peace Corps has found that half of all sexual assaults of its volunteers even today are never reported. In 2015, *Time* magazine published an article reporting on a study prepared by the Peace Corps: "Peace Corps Report Says 1 in 5 Volunteers Are [*sic*] Sexually

Assaulted."[14] The Peace Corps has long struggled to find a suitable balance between the autonomy and independence sought by female volunteers with the very real dangers that they, unlike male volunteers, face in many overseas posts.

Early American Involvement in Africa

Until the advent of the Peace Corps, most people of the third world had "seen few Americans who were not missionaries, GIs, businessmen or affluent tourists." Of course, Ernest Hemingway had shared his African adventures in "The Snows of Kilimanjaro" in 1936. American businessmen developed operations in the early 1900s with Firestone Rubber in Liberia, copper and diamond mines in the Congo, and copper mines in Northern Rhodesia (now Zambia). Between 1919 and 1939, most U.S. trade in Africa involved supplying cars and trucks. In 1923, it is estimated that 93 percent of the cars in British East Africa (now Tanzania, Kenya, and Uganda) were American made. American scientists undertook many expeditions in East Africa from the 1890s on. The National Geographic Society sponsored fourteen projects before 1965, and the Field Museum of Chicago sponsored sixteen expeditions during the same time.[15]

Tanganyika's Road to Independence

Late in the spring of 1961, the first groups of Peace Corps volunteers for Tanganyika and Ghana began training. On August 30, 1961, the first volunteers to leave for a foreign country arrived in Ghana. The road engineers for Tanganyika, who had actually begun training before the Ghana group, arrived in Dar es Salaam shortly thereafter.[16] While the Peace Corps was going through its birth pains in the spring and fall of 1961, Tanganyika experienced a similar process beginning in late 1960.

For nearly a century prior to independence, Tanganyika had been administered by European countries. German colonists occupied the area in 1884, and East Africa was placed, through the division of Africa by European powers, under control of the German government in 1891. During World War I, German East Africa was conquered by the Allies, and Britain was given a mandate by the League of Nations to oversee the country that became Tanganyika.

According to the British explorer Richard Burton, when he discovered the great lake between Tanzania and the Congo in East Africa in the 1850s, it was known locally as "Tanganyika," a name that apparently derived from a Swahili word that means "a meeting place of waters." Burton confirmed that name, which Europeans then used for the lake. In contrast to his fellow explorer, John Hanning Speke, who preferred to utilize British names, Burton favored native names. Speke named the other great lake in the area after the reigning British monarch—Lake Victoria.[17]

In 1922, the British Colonial Office spent an enjoyable time seeking a name for the former German East Africa colony. "Eburnia" (Latin for "ivory") was discarded, as was "New Maryland," "Windsorland," and "Victoria." The Colonial Office secretary insisted on "a native name prominently associated with the territory," so during that year the name "Tanganyika Territory" was formally adopted, and the country became part of the British Empire.[18]

Although Tanganyika had been Germany's most valued colony, the British merely desired to deny others access to it, so they did little to develop imperial structures in the country. Rather, private British companies took over whatever German economic developments were available. Fortunately for Tanganyika, the Colonial Office policy was aimed at protecting Africans' interests against European encroachment.[19]

U.S. president Woodrow Wilson played a prominent role at the end of World War I in ensuring that conquered African countries such as Tanganyika were turned over to administering countries, such as Britain, as mandated territories rather than as colonies. In a mandated territory, the administering government had certain restrictions in its operations in the territory; for example, Britain was required to make annual reports to the League of Nations on its operations and the conditions in Tanganyika. From 1919–1920 until it became independent, Tanganyika remained a mandated territory, although its designation was changed to a "trusteeship" when the United Nations succeeded the League of Nations in 1945.[20]

Early Efforts toward Independence

The Sukuma tribe, based around Mwanza and Maswa, was the most populous tribe in Tanganyika when the Sukuma Union was formed in 1945. Although formation of the union gave tribal members a stronger feeling of tribal connectedness, the colonial Tanganyika government worked hard to block the union's activities and to undercut its drive for power. By the mid-1950s, the Sukuma Union had almost disappeared, although it did provide Paul Bomani, its longtime secretary, important training that he would later put to good use both before and after Tanganyika became independent.

In the 1950s, Bomani, the son of a Sukuma Adventist minister, led the effort to set up a cotton cooperative among the Sukuma. His work led to the establishment of the Victoria Federated Cooperative Union, which became one of the most powerful African-owned and managed entities in the country. It was formed because the Sukuma felt they were not receiving fair prices for their cotton from the Asian traders. By 1961, the cooperative had 363 member societies and 150,000 members.[21]

Julius Nyerere was a prime mover on Tanganyika's road to independence. The son of a chief from a small tribe located on the shores of Lake Victoria near Mwanza, Nyerere was a bright, capable student who obtained a place at Tabora Secondary School in the early 1940s. At the time, Tabora was the premier secondary school in Tanganyika, whose graduates would later become leaders in the Tanzania government. Upon graduating from Tabora, Nyerere entered Makerere College in Kampala, Uganda, from which he obtained a diploma in education in 1945. Nyerere taught for several years in Tanganyika and then went to the University of Edinburgh, Scotland, where he obtained an MA in history and economics in 1952. He was the first Tanganyikan to obtain a graduate degree from an overseas university.[22] Upon his return to Tanganyika, he continued teaching and became involved in the movement for independence.

In 1953, Nyerere was elected president of the Tanganyikan African Association, a political group that had begun to explore possible roads to independence some years earlier. Within a few years, the association was replaced by the Tanganyika African National Union (TANU), which began to work much more aggressively for independence. Nyerere led TANU and found much support among the Sukuma tribe along the southern edge of Lake Victoria. Paul Bomani had been establishing cooperatives among Sukuma farmers since 1950, and with his organizing skills and his following among the Sukuma he came to play an important role in TANU as it pressed for independence.[23]

In 1958, an election for the Tanganyika Legislative Council was held, and TANU candidates battled candidates from the United Tanganyika Party (UTP), which was sponsored by the colonial government. At this time, the Legislative Council served as a legislative body for the government. In the election, each province was to elect one member each from three racial groups: Africans, Europeans, and Asians. TANU put forward candidates from each racial group in each of the provinces, and its candidates soundly defeated candidates from the UTP in most provinces. The UTP chairman, Ivor Bayldon, was easily defeated in his province by the European candidate supported by TANU, Lady Marion Chesham, the American-born wife of a British farmer.[24]

Lady Chesham, née Marion Donaghue, was born in Philadelphia in 1903. She married Leonard Brooke-Edwards, an American civil engineer who took her to India, where he worked on various engineering projects. The Brooke-Edwardses had two daughters in Calcutta and a son, Richard, in Philadelphia. (As an adult, Richard "Dick" Brooke-Edwards, who lived in Tanzania, was in Mwanza at the time of the Kinsey trial and became fascinated by it.) Marion divorced Leonard in 1929 and in 1930 married Theobald Carrick, the eighth earl of Carrick. They divorced in 1937, and she married John Chesham, the fourth Baron Chesham. Lord Chesham had established a large farming estate in southern Tanganyika in 1937, and the family lived there until they returned to England at the beginning of World War II. During the war, Lady Chesham held several important positions with the American Red Cross in England, including assistant director in charge of personnel.

After the war, the Cheshams returned to Tanganyika and to their estate, Rungemba. After Lord Chesham died in 1952, Lady Chesham continued to manage the estate. When she became a member of the Legislative Council, she lost her American citizenship but retained her British citizenship (her previous marriage to the earl of Carrick had given her dual citizenship).

Lady Chesham went on to become a strong supporter and close confidante of Julius Nyerere. In 1960, she was a TANU candidate for the Legislative Council and was elected unopposed. Not only were they closely allied, but Nyerere also often stayed at Lady Chesham's home as a respite from the political battles at the time. During one stay, Nyerere was reading the U.S. Constitution and commented that the framers were the same age as he and his colleagues, yet many people said the latter were too young to lead the movement to independence in Tanganyika.[25] In 1961, Lady Chesham traveled to England to lobby the government for support of Tanganyika's independence. While there, she became disillusioned with British intentions toward Tanganyika and so renewed her connections with American officials. In 1962, she journeyed to the United States on a fund-raising trip. As a result of the trip, she established the Community Development Trust Fund in Tanganyika to gather funds from overseas contacts, ultimately funding more than 2,500 projects in villages throughout the country.

Lady Chesham continued to serve in the Tanzania legislature until the 1970s. In 1964, she moved from her estate in southern Tanzania to a home in

Dar es Salaam; part of her farm was given to her farm laborers, and part was used as a National Service and Women's Union Training Center. Lady Chesham died in 1978 at Guildford, England.[26]

In 1957 and 1958, TANU maintained that independence should come by 1969, but in the meantime it was still seeking universal adult suffrage and parity between Africans and all other races in the Legislative Council. In May 1960, the United Nations Visiting Mission to Tanganyika, as part of its trusteeship status, issued a report praising the progress being made toward independence with "the peaceful and harmonious atmosphere of good will." By this time, the process for independence took on the nature of a race. In July 1960, TANU won a sweeping victory in the elections. On September 1, 1960, colonial governor Richard Turnbull asked Julius Nyerere to form a government. This was "responsible" government, but not yet independence. After the election, Nyerere made a radio broadcast to the nation in which he said, "We must learn to forget the arrogance and prejudices of the past. The people of Tanganyika have become fervent nationalists without becoming racialists."[27]

This rapid move to independence caught the British government in Tanganyika by surprise, as U.S. vice consul Barrington King noted. When someone asked the head of the British administration, "What about Independence?" he replied, "Well they'll be ready in about 300 years, but will probably get it in 25."[28] The local British seemed unaware of what the government in London was planning.

In March 1961, a two-day conference was held in Dar es Salaam between the British government, led by Ian MacLeod, the Colonial Office secretary, and the Tanganyika government, led by Nyerere. At the end of the conference, Macleod announced that Tanganyika would have full internal self-government on May 1, 1961, and independence on December 28, 1961. (In late June 1961, it was announced that the duke of Edinburgh would represent the queen at the independence ceremonies, and so for his convenience the date of the ceremonies was changed to December 9, 1961.)[29]

With the rapid move to independence, the government leadership discovered during the spring and summer of 1961 that a major problem became the need to retain many expatriate officials until Tanganyikan Africans could be trained for such positions. At the time and for the next several years, few Africans had adequate training to function effectively in the civil service. Nyerere wrote to senior expatriate civil servants to ask them to remain in office. Nevertheless, by the end of 1963 several hundred British expatriate civil servants had left the country. At that time, roughly one-half of the senior and midlevel posts had been filled by Africans, but many of the rest of the positions were vacant. The remaining expatriates were unsettled, however, when several Europeans were swiftly deported for insulting Tanzanians. With little regard for the niceties of procedural due process, the deportees were unceremoniously removed from the country.[30]

A. J. Hughes, a British journalist in Tanganyika during the time leading up to independence and later, summed up what many observers felt at the time: "Nyerere's qualities—his integrity, his intellect, his organizing talents and his ability to translate his idealism into practical terms—played an important part in this advance [to independence]."[31]

Tanganyika Becomes Independent

Once independence was obtained in December 1961, the new government went about organizing itself to govern and to create a functioning nation. After elections in December, many officials from Tanganyika and from other countries were shocked when Nyerere resigned in January 1962, as he said, to rebuild TANU. Rashide Kawawa, the sitting vice president, took over as president. In December 1962, however, Julius Nyerere was elected again and installed as president, and the country became a republic.[32]

The year 1964 turned out to be a most tumultuous year for Tanganyika, beginning in January with President Nyerere announcing that "Africanization" would be coming to an end and that Tanganyikan citizens of all races would be equally eligible for jobs. Many unions objected to this change. Later that month, members of the army rebelled, led by a small group of noncommissioned officers who wanted to oust the British officers still in charge of the Tanganyikan army. After considerable back-and-forth negotiations, President Nyerere called on Britain to send troops to help him put down the rebellion. Britain did, and the rebellion was soon terminated. However, the fragility of the young Tanganyikan government had been clearly demonstrated.[33]

Union of Tanganyika and Zanzibar

In April 1964, Tanganyika and Zanzibar agreed to unite, and the union was soon ratified by the two countries. A few months later, after a naming contest, it was announced that the name of the new republic would be "United Republic of Tanzania," soon shortened to "Tanzania." As with many such swift actions, unintended consequences followed. Zanzibar had recognized the government of East Germany, which West Germany objected to. When Tanzania, which had maintained cordial relations with West Germany since independence and had received considerable German economic aid, proposed a solution to this conflict, West Germany refused to agree and quickly withdrew all of its aid to Tanzania.

Conflicts between Tanzania and the United States

In November 1964, as the Kinseys were coming to the end of their Peace Corps training in the United States and preparing to leave for Tanzania, Tanzania government ministers produced three diplomatic messages suggesting a plot by the United States to overthrow the government of President Nyerere. Although the documents were later shown to be forgeries, at the time they caused a great deal of anger among the Tanzania people.

Later that month, U.S. Air Force planes carried Belgian troops into the Congo either, as the United States declared, to save hostages or, as Tanzanians believed, to protect the rebel leadership in the Congo, which Tanzania strongly opposed.

A third Tanzania-U. S. conflict arose in January 1965 when cables from U.S. State Department officials obtained by the Tanzania government suggested that the United States was engaged in subversive activities in Tanzania. The two officials accused of leading the conspiracy were expelled from Tanzania within twenty-four hours. It later turned out that the diplomatic documents, written in somewhat opaque bureaucratese, had an innocent explanation, but by the time this was clarified, significant damage had been done to the U.S.-Tanzania relationship.[34]

All of these strains existed and influenced relationships as the Kinseys began working in Binza School in Maswa. However, in June 1965 Nyerere addressed the National Assembly and pointed out the need to recruit skilled workers from overseas to balance the loss of personnel from retirements and expiring contracts.[35] At first, President Nyerere was extremely pleased with Peace Corps volunteers: "They come to Tanzania and if you tell them to go anywhere, they go. They don't complain. If you tell them to go to Kigoma, they go; or to Masailand, they go. . . . The Volunteers have a spirit I would like to see more of in Tanzania's teachers."[36]

During the next several years, new issues generated conflict between Tanzania and the United States and other Western countries. Paramount among them was the Vietnam War, which Nyerere strongly opposed. Tanzania also supported a boycott of South Africa over its racial policies; pushed Britain to give independence with majority rule to Rhodesia; accepted Chinese help, over vehement U.S. objections, to build a railroad to Zambia; and, perhaps most importantly, adopted the principle of African socialism, or *ujamaa,* as it was called in Swahili. Nyerere defined the meaning of *ujamaa* in a speech in 1966:

> I was the first to use the word *ujamaa* in order to explain the kind of life we wish to live in our country. The word *ujamaa* denotes the kind of life lived by a man and his family—father, mother, children and near relatives. Our Africa was a poor country before it was invaded and ruled by foreigners. There were no rich people in Africa. There was no person or group of persons who had exclusive claim to the ownership of the land. Land was the property of all the people, and those who used it did not do so because it was their property. They used it because they needed it, and it was their responsibility to use it carefully and hand it over in good condition for use by future generations. Life was easy. It was possible for a man to live with his wife, his children and other close relatives. Wealth belonged to the family as a whole; and every member of a family had the right to the use of family property. No one used wealth for the purpose of dominating others. This is how we want to live as a nation. We want the whole nation to live as one family. This is the basis of socialism.[37]

As these conflicts accumulated, they soon led to deep distrust and friction between the United States and other Western powers on one side and Tanzania on the other. The Peace Corps became a victim of this conflict, and by 1969 all volunteers had left the country. However, in 1979 Nyerere invited them back. Despite these conflicts with the European and U.S. governments and subsequent economic failures, Julius Nyerere's banishment of tribalism and racialism, his establishment of democracy in Tanzania, as well as his example of personal frugality will perhaps endure as his greatest legacy.[38]

8

Peace Corps Officials Assess the Situation and Plan Future Action

> A metal rod and two rocks covered in blood will be offered in evidence.
> —*Tony Essaye*

By early April, Peace Corps officials were beginning to better understand the parameters of the Kinsey situation and what needed to be done. Peace Corps counsel Tony Essaye had now been in Tanzania for a few days and had spoken to Peace Corps staff, Tanzania officials, and others involved. The disposition of Peppy's body had been determined, and detailed reports on all the actions that had been taken were sent to PCDC. After the frantic, chaotic first days of the affair, people were settling into a balanced rhythm of planning for next steps.

On Friday, April 1, 1966, Essaye cabled PCDC with his thoughts about legal representation for Bill. He emphasized that the case would be difficult and complex and that high-quality legal assistance, possibly even the assistance of expert witnesses, would be required, which would likely be expensive. He felt that Gurbachan Singh, the attorney in Mwanza, seemed quite capable, but even Singh recommended an additional attorney for the actual trial.[1]

PCDC responded to Essaye's recommendation to pay for legal representation in a cable that same day, stating that under section 1031 of the Foreign Service Act of 1946, a lawyer could be retained where it is necessary to protect U.S. interests. Based on this reading, PCDSM was authorized to retain a lawyer if it made the determination required by section 1031. The cable went on to suggest that the representation be limited to the emergency situation while arrangements with Bill's family were negotiated. By April 4, however, PCDC officials reported that they had urged the Kinsey family to hire their own attorney to advise them.[2]

PCDC underscored its great interest in the case and how the affair was proceeding with a detailed request for information on the autopsy, the pathologist's qualifications, blood types, and the items found at the death scene. It also requested copies of any autopsy reports.[3]

The issue of bad press coverage continued to worry PCDC, as evidenced by a cable urging local Peace Corps officials to coordinate on information to be given to the press. The cable pointed out that misleading and inaccurate stories attributed to Peace Corps officials in Tanzania were appearing in the American press.[4]

On April 2, PCDC supplied information that might turn out to be helpful to Bill's defense:

DENNETT FAMILY REPORT PEVERLEY'S "WILD DELIRIUM" TOTALLY CONSISTENT HER PAST BEHAVIOR.

TWO ACCIDENTS: (1) BROKEN ARM (2) THROWN OMTO [sic] SHORE BY LARGE WAVE ILLUSTRATE REACTIONS. BOTH TIMES SHE REPEATEDLY SCREAMED TO THOSE WHO ATTEMPTED TO HELP HER—"DON'T TOUCH ME—STAY AWAY." EACH TIME FAMILY HAD TO CALM HER CONSIDERABLY BEFORE SHE WOULD ACCEPT ASSISTANCE. BOTH INCIDENTS OCCURRED DURING PEVERLEY'S ADOLESCENCE. DENNETT FAMILY WILLING TO TESTIFY TO THESE FACTS.[5]

Although it is unclear who was included in "Dennett family," the cable suggested that there was strong support for Bill and that members of Peppy's family were willing to help in the trial, perhaps a bit hastily because much about the evidence was yet unknown. At this early point, the Dennetts appeared to be in total acceptance of Bill's account of the event. They believed him innocent, and their unswerving support would provide the Peace Corps considerable comfort in their efforts to help Bill.

On April 1, Paul Sack sent a letter to the volunteers then serving in Tanzania, informing them that Peppy had died a violent death on March 27, that the police were holding Bill on a charge of murder, and that he denied the charge. Sack also explained that Peppy had died from a fall. The letter closed with this paragraph: "Peace Corps is taking every step possible to help Bill with assistance in securing legal counsel, providing medical attention and support while under detention, maintaining contact with his family, and—most important—ensuring protection of all his rights."[6]

On April 6, Sack followed up with more detail in a second letter to Tanzania volunteers. In the letter, explaining that Tanzania law is based on English law and so very similar in many respects to U.S. law, he reported that a preliminary inquiry would be held sometime in the next few weeks in Maswa. If the magistrate determined that there was sufficient evidence to require Bill to stand trial, a trial would be held before the Manzwa High Court, presided over by a judge and two assessors. Sack also described Bill's current incarceration in Butimba Prison in Mwanza, where conditions seemed good even by American standards. Because of the seriousness of the charge, Bill would not be allowed out on bail. Sack noted. "It would be unprecedented in Tanzania for him to be so released (and would be practically unprecedented in the United States as well)."[7]

On Saturday, April 2, PCDSM reported that Bill had agreed to the burial of Peppy's body in the United States and that the attorneys and the pathologist felt that no more tests were needed, so attorney Singh would prepare and execute the documents required to ship her body to America.[8]

On the morning of April 2, Peace Corps deputy director Norm Hummon had a telephone conversation with Mark Bomani, Tanzania's attorney general. Hummon told Bomani he was calling because Bill's attorney, Gurbachan Singh, had requested bail in the court in Mwanza on medical grounds, but since Bill had been moved to Butimba Prison, where he could obtain adequate medical attention, the defense was no longer pursuing bail. Bomani pointed out that Bill had been transferred to Butimba before the court hearing and wondered why Hummon was raising the point now. Hummon said the Peace Corps was concerned that it might appear as if it were trying to interfere with court procedure. Bomani said he was pleased to hear that because release on bail would be extraordinary, if not unthinkable, in a capital case. Hummon said that he and other Peace Corps officials cared only about Bill's welfare and that they had confidence that justice would be obtained in a fair trial. Bomani said he certainly understood their concern for Bill's welfare.[9]

Later that day Hummon and Peace Corps staff member Leon Parker met with CID deputy director C. F. Ijumba to tell him about the press release to be issued by the United States Information Service. Mr. Ijumba said they were free to issue whatever statement they liked but that the CID would provide only the barest essentials of the case. He told them that he had just received a telephone report from Mwanza informing him that Bill's attorney had requested bail. He then commented that the case had become too big for the state attorney in Maswa and so had been transferred to the court in Mwanza.

Because Ijumba was under the impression that Peppy had been buried, Hummon explained that the body was actually still at Muhimbili Hospital in Dar es Salaam but that plans for her burial place would be made soon. Ijumba said that the CID had no further need for the remains and that as long as the legal requirements were met, there would be no objection to shipping the remains to the United States.

Ijumba also offered his understanding, from reports received, of what had happened on that Sunday in Maswa. He reported that witnesses said the man had been beating the woman, and after she fell down, he picked up a big rock and struck her on the head. The man and woman appeared to have been drinking, perhaps too much, and this may have led to a quarrel. According to Hummon, "Mr. Ijumba said this looked to him like a case of murder although he said the evidence and the testimony of the witnesses may not stand up in court."[10]

On Sunday, April 3, Tony Essaye, then back in Dar es Salaam, sent PCDC his evaluation of the case and the known evidence at the time. The prosecution's case, he summarized, would include two eyewitnesses who saw the Kinseys struggling, and Bill running from the scene. They might testify that they actually saw him strike Peppy. In addition, a metal rod and two rocks covered in blood would be offered in evidence. The police might have other evidence. The defense case would offer Bill's explanation that while he and Peppy were picnicking near Maswa, they climbed up some high rocks, and Peppy fell; he went to her and tried to restrain her in order to prevent her from causing herself further injury.

Essaye believed that Kinsey's story and lack of motive provided a fairly good chance for Bill to establish "reasonable doubt." In his report to PCDC, Essaye described the criminal procedure, which would commence with a preliminary hearing, where the prosecution would present its evidence, but the defense need not present any evidence. Bill's local attorneys felt it best not to present their evidence at this time because it was likely that the prosecution could establish a prima facie case (one for which there is sufficient evidence), anyway, and so the magistrate would order a trial. Essaye agreed. If a conviction resulted, an appeal could be taken to the East African Court of Appeals, and, if necessary, a plea for clemency could be made to the president of Tanzania.

Essaye thought Bill's local attorney quite capable and discussed the potential cost of representation. He also pointed out that Paul Sack, the Tanzania Peace Corps director, and Tom Quimby, the Africa Region Peace Corps director, felt strongly that it was in the Peace Corps' best interests to pay the entire cost of Bill's defense.[11]

In a cable to PCDC on that same day, April 3, PCDSM stressed the need for a careful response to the press:

> Regret PC/W [PCDC] press release states "Peace Corps officials in Tanzania relayed the following account" without indicating it was Kinsey's account not ours. Fear that wording of release makes it appear that defense position is official PC account. His story has been challenged by police on basis of considerable evidence. PC position must be one of giving Kinsey full moral and medical support and of assisting him to secure best possible defense and full protection his rights. But believe it great mistake to endorse defense contentions that injuries result from fall. Court must decide, and PC must avoid any implication of taking position on facts of case or being on trial itself. If any further release to be made by PC/W request it include complete clarification this point.[12]

Meanwhile, Bill's father, the North Carolina press, and the state's congressional delegation let the Peace Corps know, once the Peace Corps had informed the Kinseys that it could not pay for Bill's defense, that they felt Bill was being abandoned. At the same time, the Kinsey family asked for help in finding an East African attorney.[13]

In an effort to demonstrate that Bill had not been abandoned, over the next several days PCDSM sent PCDC a lengthy description of all that had been done (my summary):

1. Paul Sack immediately went to Mwanza after arranging for a highly qualified attorney to meet his plane.
2. Sack had arranged for Dr. Dockeray, a leading pathologist, to fly to Mwanza to perform a postmortem examination.

3. In Maswa, attorneys obtained orders allowing Dr. Dockeray and Dr. McHugh to perform the postmortem.

4. On March 30, Sack, Singh, and Dr. Dockeray flew to Maswa on a chartered plane, met with Bill, and reviewed the scene with the police inspector. Valuable evidence was obtained, and the scene photographed by a professional photographer.

5. On March 31, Tony Essaye met with police officials, the attorney general of Tanzania, and Ministry of Education officials in Dar es Salaam.

6. Extensive staff work had been provided in supporting Bill in prison, attending to his medical needs, arranging for Peppy's remains, and attending to the couple's personal effects.[14]

Although the Peace Corps' relationship with Tanzania officials in Dar es Salaam was amicable at the time, the situation in Maswa and Mwanza had become quite testy. At the bail hearing, the state attorney had objected strenuously to granting bail and stated his feeling that Bill was getting special treatment; meanwhile, reports from Maswa indicated great hostility to Bill's story within the community. On April 12, Father Bob told Jack McPhee: "The stories in the Maswa community about the Kinsey tragedy are unbelievable."[15] Apparently, people in Maswa were convinced that Peppy had been murdered.

Generally, when an American dies in a foreign country, the Consular Section of the U.S. embassy in that country is contacted for assistance in handling the remains. The assigned consular officer ordinarily contacts the next of kin and asks him or her what he or she wishes to happen. In this case, the next of kin was Bill Kinsey, who was under arrest and charged with the murder of the person who died. The Consular Section is also contacted when an American is charged with a crime in a foreign country. It then might supply a list of attorneys, visit the American in jail or prison to see that conditions are acceptable, and generally offer any other assistance necessary.[16]

Because the Kinseys were Peace Corps volunteers, Peace Corps staff stepped forward to provide these services. Despite substantial questions about the Peace Corps' ability to provide defense counsel for Bill, its staff were able to see that Peppy's body was properly taken care of and returned to the United States for burial at a location her mother chose. Similarly, the Peace Corps was able to help in finding counsel for Bill, and Peace Corps staff visited him in the various jails and prisons to ensure that the conditions were acceptable.

At the outset, Peppy's mother thought that it was up to Bill to decide about the disposition of Peppy's body, but by Thursday, March 31, 1966, she had changed her mind and expressed a desire for Peppy to be buried in a family plot in Middletown, Delaware. She reasoned that both families would then be able to visit the grave, and, given Bill's youth, he would likely remarry, so it would be better for the Dennett family to have the ongoing responsibility for the grave. It was unclear whether further tests might be needed, and so the body could not be released. At this point, the Peace Corps still considered the final decision regarding Peppy's burial to be Bill's.[17]

In Tanzania, the issue of what to do with a person's remains was not a simple one. Under Tanzania law, it was illegal to bury, cremate, or otherwise dispose of a body without a certificate issued by the local health officials. Such a certificate would be issued when either a certificate of death signed by the attending physician or a certificate of "no objection" by the local police is presented. There was no prescribed time for burial, but because of the hot, humid conditions, as a practical matter it was ordinarily necessary to move rather quickly. Muhimbili Hospital in Dar es Salaam, where Peppy's body had been taken, did have a refrigerated facility where a body could be kept for up to one week. There were no professional undertakers or embalming facilities in Tanzania at the time, so families or churches generally handled burials. The only crematorium in Dar es Salaam was operated by the Hindu *mander* (temple), but a non-Hindu could be cremated there if permission were obtained. In order for a body to be sent out of the country, a special casket was required, and a certificate executed by the American consular officer needed to be obtained. The estimated cost of shipping a body to New York at the time was $1,000.[18]

According to a cable from PCDC sent on April 3, 1966, Mrs. Dennett sought assurance that Peppy's remains would be treated in full accord with the teachings of the Anglican (or Episcopal) Church. The cable also sought a letter from the archdeacon in Dar es Salaam providing assurances that the proper procedures were followed.[19]

In the end, all of the requirements were met, and on Tuesday, April 5, 1966, Peppy's remains were placed on a plane leaving Dar es Salaam for New York. Prior to the departure, a moving memorial service was conducted by the Anglican archdeacon of Dar es Salaam, Venerable Taylor. The service was held at St. Albans Anglican Church and attended by approximately forty people, including the U.S. ambassador. Archdeacon Taylor escorted the remains to the Dar es

Salaam airport and said that he would write to Mrs. Dennett with the requested assurances.[20]

The Dennetts also held a memorial service at St. Paul's Episcopal Church in Riverside, Connecticut, on April 4, 1966. Paul Sack cabled the following message to Mrs. Dennett, care of the minister of St. Paul's, Jack Hawkins: "On behalf all Peace Corps Staff and Volunteers in Tanzania wish to express deepest regret and keen sense of loss. Peverley was outstanding Volunteer, an inspiration to her fellow teachers and students and a joy to her fellow teachers and students and a joy to her fellow Volunteers. The sympathies of all of us in Tanzania are with you at this sad time."[21] Father Bob, the Maryknoll priest stationed at Sayusayu Mission near Maswa, also celebrated a memorial mass for Peppy and had written to Bill's parents at Bill's request.[22]

A number of documents were prepared to accompany the body:

1. The official death certificate
2. An affidavit signed by the Peace Corps physician in Dar es Salaam, James D. Morrissey, describing how the remains had been prepared for transit
3. A permit from the Tanzania government permitting the remains to be transferred to the United States, signed by C. F. Ijumba, assistant commissioner of police in the CID.[23]

Early in April, Peace Corps officials in Tanzania were able to forward to PCDC a list of suitable attorneys to represent Bill. The Kinsey family had requested help in finding the "best-qualified" East African attorneys, and PCDC suggested contacting James Read, acting dean of the Law Faculty at University College, Dar es Salaam:

Following lawyers recommended as top lawyers EAST AFRICA by all persons contacted including SINGH and JIM READ. All are NAIROBI lawyers but have been assured this no drawback re case in TANZANIA. Also, NAIROBI closer to MWANZA than is DAR.

1. ACHROO RAM KAPILA, LINCOLN'S INN 1947, admitted KENYA BAR 1947, outstanding criminal lawyer who has represented JOMO KENYATTA and presently representing OBOTE before commission of inquiry into UGANDA GOVERNMENT

2. BYRON GEORGIADIS, Master of Arts OXFORD, INNER TEM-
   PLE 1951, admitted KENYA BAR, 1953. Primarily Civil lawyer, but
   DOCKERARY[sic] has worked with him in criminal cases and rec-
   ommends above all others;
3. BRYAN O'DONOVAN, MIDDLE TEMPLE 1945, admitted KENYA
   BAR 1953, named QUEEN'S COUNSEL in KENYA, 1958.[24]

The cable also provided additional information about Gurbachan Singh. He was born in India but educated in Mwanza, where his father was chief of police. He became a barrister at Lincoln's Inn, London, in 1958 and practiced in England for a year. He knew the Mwanza area and local officials and was thought to be the most skilled criminal lawyer in Tanzania.[25] At the time, officials in Tanzania estimated the cost of defense at about $10,000 (approximately $70,000 in today's dollars). Byron Georgiadis would eventually be hired as the lead trial attorney.

On April 5, 1966 (although apparently not received in Dar es Salaam until April 7), William "Bill" Josephson, Peace Corps general counsel, cabled Tony Essaye in Tanzania, expressing great concern that Dr. McHugh had retained Peppy's scalp and skull cap. Josephson warned that Tanzania officials might object and that Bill and Peppy's families might be most unhappy.[26]

Essaye replied that the scalp and skull cap were being kept at the behest of Dr. Dockeray, the pathologist, not to be introduced as evidence but for viewing by the judge privately and to be used to support the conclusions from Dockeray's autopsy. Dockeray said such a procedure was common practice in East Africa. Essaye did go on to express his shared concern about the Kinsey and Dennett families' possible reaction but thought a final decision should wait until the defense team was in place. Interestingly, he also thought Bill should have the final decision despite his being charged with murder, further demonstrating the complicated legal, ethical, and social issues involved in the case at this point.[27]

With Bill still in prison, his attorneys worked diligently to move the case forward rapidly. The next procedure would be a preliminary inquiry, where Bill would submit his plea, the prosecution would present its case, and the magistrate would decide if Bill would be tried. By the middle of April, the inquiry had not been scheduled, and Bill's attorneys were frustrated. To set the date for the inquiry, a "mention hearing," a hearing in court to set a date for the preliminary inquiry, must first take place. But each time such a hearing was scheduled, the prosecutor claimed he was not ready, so nothing happened. On April 8, Singh traveled to Maswa for the mention hearing, but again nothing happened. At that point, Singh pressured State Attorney Ededen Effiwat to agree to set the preliminary inquiry within one month.[28] The inquiry was eventually set for May 5. It is not surprising that the prosecution kept delaying because under Tanzania law they must present their entire case at the preliminary hearing, a daunting task even for a well-equipped prosecutor's office, which the office of the state attorney in Mwanza certainly was not.

By April 6, the Kinsey family had hired American attorney Carroll Brewster to represent Bill's interests. Brewster was a graduate of Philips Exeter Academy, Yale University, and Yale Law School. Between college and law school, he had also studied history at King's College, Cambridge. In 1962, he had been clerking for a U.S. District Court judge in New Haven, Connecticut, when he accepted a unique opportunity for a job with the government of Sudan. The job came about through the Fellows for Africa Program based at the Massachusetts Institute of Technology. Brewster stayed in Sudan until December 1964; while there, he compiled and published several volumes of Sudanese legal cases that had never been published. Brewster became the official reporter of cases for the Sudanese judiciary. Through his work in the Sudanese legal system, he became familiar with the interrelationship of British common law, Islamic law, and tribal law, which is so much a part of the legal system in many African countries, including Tanzania.

According to Peppy's sister, Charlotte, Brewster was brought into the case through their mother's connections at Yale Law School. However, according to a cable from PCDC to PCDSM on April 6, 1966, Brewster had been recommended to the Kinseys by Professor Robert Stevens of Yale Law School, a British lawyer with extensive Tanzania experience. Stevens became a barrister as a member of Grays Inn in 1956. In 1958, he was awarded an LLM from Yale University, and by 1965 he was a professor at Yale Law School.[29]

At the time Brewster became involved in the case, he was practicing law with the New Haven law firm of Gumbart, Corbin, Tyler & Cooper. Interestingly, the March 5, 1966, issue of the *New Yorker* included a long article by John McPhee (unrelated to the Peace Corps regional director Jack McPhee) on the MIT program that featured a profile of Brewster's work in the Sudan. McPhee described in detail Brewster's activities in the Sudan, including swimming in the supposedly polluted Nile River, drinking camel milk, eating a raw camel liver with sheiks, and making himself very much a part of the indigenous

Sudanese society. McPhee was obviously impressed with the prodigious body of work Brewster had completed, including several volumes of Sudanese reports of judicial decisions.[30] Brewster fell in love with the Sudan, the Sudanese people, and the Sudanese judiciary. He continued to give back to the friends he made there by obtaining scholarships for more than a dozen Sudanese judges to study law in the United States.

Given Brewster's fame in the American press at the time, it is not surprising that, with his knowledge of Africa and African law, he would be a perfect candidate to assist Bill Kinsey in his trial. On April 7, 1966, Bill Josephson wrote a memo to Peace Corps director Jack Vaughn informing him that the Kinsey family had hired Brewster and that they did not seem to have a problem with the cost, which was estimated at the time to be $10,222.[31] Coincidently, Gurbachan Singh had been trained in the same London chambers as Brewster and by the same well-known prosecuting attorney, and they had at times used the same desk, although not in the same years.[32]

When I contacted Carroll Brewster in 2008 seeking an interview about the case, he declined to discuss the case with me because of attorney–client privilege, despite my assurance that I did not seek any privileged information but sought general impressions and a feeling of the atmosphere in Mwanza.

9

Syracuse University Training
and Marriage

[We will] provide you with a sound introduction to the
environment in which you will live and work.
—*Dean Clifford Winters to Peace Corps trainees*

Bill Kinsey and Peverley (Peppy) Dennett met in Peace Corps training at Syracuse University in the fall of 1964. They were part of a group of volunteers to
be trained as schoolteachers to work in Tanzania and Malawi. In the beginning, Bill was assigned to the group destined for Malawi, while Peppy was
assigned to the Tanzania education group. A third group also in training at
Syracuse at the time was scheduled to assist in the management of cooperatives in Malawi.

The welcoming letter from the dean at Syracuse in June 1964 described
the goals of the training program as follows:

(1) to provide you with a sound introduction to the environment in
which you will live and work during your assignment; (2) to provide
you with the technical skills you will need to perform effectively in
your assignments; (3) to produce informed and knowledgeable students of African and American affairs, the machinery of international relations, and the significance of the international Communist
movement; (4) to enable you to achieve fluency in the languages of
Malawi and Tanganyika [Tanzania]; (5) to develop an awareness of

71

health and medical problems in the host countries; and (6) to provide you with an understanding of the purposes and objectives of the Peace Corps.[1]

To accomplish these goals, the Syracuse administration and the Peace Corps had developed a rigorous training program. Syracuse University at the time had a well-known program in African studies, with many experts on staff as well as African students from throughout the continent, who could be called upon to provide language instruction, cultural insights, and political perspective. The training materials gave the following description of Tanzania (Tanganyika at the time):

> Situated between the great lakes of Central Africa and the Indian Ocean, and lying just south of the equator, Tanganyika has a coastline of some 500 miles. The two extremes of topographical relief of the whole continent of Africa lie within its boundaries; Kilimanjaro, with a permanent ice-cap rising to 19,340 feet above sea level, and the deep trough-like depression filled by Lake Tanganyika (the world's second deepest lake). Along the coast lies a plain, 10 to 40 miles wide; behind this the country rises to the great central plateau of some 4,000 feet, which is sharply defined along its eastern and western margins by steep and eroded escarpments but falls, on the west, to the level of the lakes (Tanganyika 2,534 feet; Nyasa 1,568 feet) which lie in the Great Rift Valley. Along the eastern and western escarpment ridges the plateau forms narrow belts of high country; in the east this is cut by the Great Ruaha River, and, in the west, by the valley of the Malagarasi River. About half of the two great lakes, Victoria and Tanganyika, lie within the borders; lakes Natron, Manyara, Eyasi and Rukwa account for most of the remainder of the 20,000 sq. miles of inland water. The main rivers are the Pangani or Ruvu, the Wami, the Ruvu (Kingoni), the Rufiji, the Great Ruaha, the Matandu, the Mbwemkuru, the Lukuledi, and the Ruvuma—which drain the central plateau and flow into the Indian Ocean; and the Mori, Mara and Kagera, the Malagarasi, the Songwe and Ruhuhu—which feed the great lakes.[2]

The basic schedule for the four months of training followed a fairly rigid format, as shown in table 9.1.

Table 9.1 Syracuse Peace Corps Training Schedule

Hours	Monday	Tuesday	Wednesday	Thursday	Friday	Saturday
8:00–10:00 a.m.	Technical Studies					
10:00 a.m.–12:00 p.m.	Technical Studies					
12:00–1:30 p.m.	Lunch					
2:00–3:45 p.m.	Language Studies					
4:00–6:00 p.m.	Cross-Cultural Studies					
6:00–7:30 p.m.	Dinner					
7:30–9:30 p.m.	Language Laboratory or Classroom Instruction					Supervised Study
9:30–10:30 p.m.	Supervised Study					

In Tanzania, the volunteers would be assigned to upper primary schools (Standards VII and VIII), roughly equivalent to junior high school in America. The volunteer teachers would teach English and mathematics, and they might also teach one or more classes in history, geography, home economics, music, art, physical education, or sewing.[3]

In the early years of the Peace Corps, Sargent Shriver and his fellow administrators debated long and hard on whether education programs were suitable for the Peace Corps. Many staff members felt teaching situations were too comfortable and didn't reflect the "real" Peace Corps concept of digging latrines and living in difficult situations. When President Kennedy issued the Executive Order establishing the Peace Corps in March 1961, he underscored the idea of sacrifice expected of the volunteers: "Life in the Peace Corps will not be easy. There will be no salary and allowances will be at a level sufficient only to maintain health and basic needs. Men and women will be expected to work alongside the nationals of the country in which they are stationed—doing the same work, eating the same food, talking the same language."[4] However, "the Peace Corps stayed in education because African governments requested it and because Sargent Shriver himself strongly supported the Peace Corps role in education."[5] Although America had a long history of overseas education programs, they never were as pervasive as ones established by colonial powers, especially the British. From the early 1900s until the 1960s, American education programs were created primarily by religious missionaries. One exception took place in the Philippines, which had come under U.S. rule at the end of the nineteenth century. In 1901 and for many years afterward, thousands of American teachers were sent to the Philippines and to other new territories to teach in "U.S.-sponsored public schools." In addition, during the twentieth century between 150,000 and 200,000 American missionaries taught in primary and secondary religious schools in Asia, Africa, and Latin American. For much of the century, American leaders viewed their efforts in establishing education programs in other countries as bringing "civilization" and the face of "American exceptionalism" to the third world. After World War II, however, educators began questioning these concepts, culminating in the Peace Corps' thrust to provide education within the host country's cultural context.[6]

While Peace Corps volunteers continued to debate whether they were in a country to mold their students into Americans or simply to provide a professional education, Peace Corps leaders worried that teaching assignments were too "cushy" and did not meet the Peace Corps image. However, assignments to African primary schools came much closer to the Peace Corps ideal than those to secondary schools.[7] For example, the Kinseys' house had no electricity, no running water, and an outdoor toilet with a hole in the floor. Because of the remoteness of their school, the Kinseys had few English speakers as neighbors, and so they quickly became fluent in Swahili.

Shortly after Bill and Peppy met at the Syracuse training, they began dating and spending increasing time together. Before long, they began considering the idea of marriage. One substantial obstacle stood in the way of their getting married and working in Africa as volunteers: Bill was assigned to Malawi, whereas Peppy was scheduled to work in Tanzania. For bright, creative Peace Corps volunteers, such an obstacle was not a major problem. John Coyne, just back from Ethiopia and working in the Division of Volunteer Support at the Peace Corps at the time, has written his account of how he helped resolve the issue: "Peppy and Bill, hearing that 'someone from Washington' was on site, sought me out and asked if Bill might be reassigned to Tanzania. In those early years of the Peace Corps rules were stretched and bent and I helped with some paperwork and Bill was transferred out of the Malawi project and into Peppy's Tanzania one." Coyne went on to describe Peppy and Bill in glowing terms: "Bill and Peverley were two young good looking kids just out of college. Bill, as I recall, had a bright smile, blond hair cut into a crewcut, an[d] All-American good looks. Peppy was sweet and shy and very pretty. They were the picture of what Peace Corps Volunteers were all about: bright and articulate and good looking kids going off to the developing world to do good."[8]

Over the past thirty or more years, John Coyne has been known as the prime resource for Peace Corps authors, of which there have been many. He has regularly published information on books about the Peace Corps, encouraged writers, and published their books. Coyne has also published several accounts of the Kinsey affair in various online postings.[9]

Several years ago, John submitted a Freedom of Information Act (FOIA) request to the Peace Corps about the Kinsey case. In response, he received a large box of documents. When I caught up with him in 2011, he had passed the documents on to Dick and Joan Richter. Dick had been deputy director of the Peace Corps in Kenya at the time of Peppy's death and helped provide resources for the Kinsey trial, including arranging for Dr. Dockeray to perform an autopsy. Joan Richter is an author and was interested in writing a book about the case. In 2011, the Richters had retired and moved to Washington State near my home. I contacted them, and Joan confirmed that indeed she had the files but had abandoned her plans to write a book and that I was welcome to make copies of the documents. I soon visited them, enjoyed a lengthy discussion about the case and the Peace Corps in the 1960s, and made copies. The documents were an enormous resource for me. I had submitted an FOIA request to the Peace Corps in 2010 and received quite a few documents, but many documents had disappeared between the time of John Coyne's request and my own. The stack of materials I received from my FOIA request consisted mainly of newspaper articles about the case, whereas the Coyne files included letters, memoranda, research reports, cables, and much more.

Once the issue of Bill's transfer to the Tanzania group was resolved, plans for marriage accelerated. In early November, Peppy called her mother to announce that she and Bill planned to marry before leaving for Africa. Peppy's mother was appalled and told her she couldn't.

Despite this objection, three days before they were to leave for Africa, the Dennett and Kinsey families were present for a wedding at Peppy's home in Connecticut. Peppy's mother had given in and within three weeks had made all the arrangements for the wedding, including a posting in the *New York Times*. Peppy's father had died several years earlier, so Peppy's uncle escorted her down the aisle. When the priest asked, "Who giveth this woman to be married to this man?" Peppy's mother stood up and said, "I do." Peppy's sister remembers that there seemed little time for anyone to get to know Bill and his family. Two days later Peppy and Bill flew to Tanzania.[10]

When Vicki Ferenbach and her friends heard that Peppy was going into the Peace Corps, they were surprised. The life and work of a Peace Corps volunteer didn't seem to fit what they knew of Peppy, although her father, who had separated from her mother when Peppy was a teenager, had been involved in international work.

Peppy's college friends were even more surprised when they heard she was getting married. They had no sense that she was looking to get married so soon after graduation. Bill Kinsey remained an enigma for the group of friends as well as for Peppy's sister, Charlotte. The wedding took place immediately after the Peace Corps training at Syracuse, and Peppy's friends met Bill at that time and saw him for only a day or so. Immediately after the wedding, Bill and Peppy left for Tanzania. Other than receipt of a few letters, the next thing Vicki heard was that Peppy was dead. At that time, Vicki was about to be married. At the wedding on April 16, 1966, only weeks after Peppy's death, Peppy's mother gave Victoria a silver coffee service that Peppy had received as a wedding present from her aunt, Justine Woodall.[11]

10

Peace Corps Training in Tanzania, Binza Upper Primary School

Her husband wouldn't talk to her.
—*Delores Ledbetter*

When the members of Bill and Peppy's Peace Corps group arrived in Tanzania, they were sent to a small town named Mbeya in the southern highlands of the country, where they lived for several weeks at Iyunga Secondary School, about four miles south of town, to receive further training, assignment to schools, and preparation for travel to their assignment. In Mbeya, they would learn more about the country and about the Peace Corps organization in Tanzania and hear from local teachers and administrators about the actual teaching format in their schools.

Mbeya is in the southwest corner of Tanzania, about 550 miles from Dar es Salaam—about only 40 or 50 miles from the northern borders of Zambia and Malawi. The town is located in the "southern highlands," an area of gentle mountains and lush vegetation. Mbeya is nearly a mile high, so the climate is generally comfortable year-round: cool evenings and mornings, warm days, but without the humidity of coastal Dar es Salaam. During colonial times, the area provided fertile soil and a beneficial climate and so had attracted a large contingent of British farmers. There were very few mosquitoes and other bothersome insects—though you might encounter the occasional cobra. Mbeya, with a population of about 11,000 in the 1960s, was the regional capital of Southwest Tanzania. A market square in the center of town was the focus of commercial and social life.

Prior to independence, Iyunga Secondary School had been a primary boarding school for children of expatriate (mostly British) families, tea planters, and government officials from throughout Tanzania. By 1965, it was in its second year as a government school attended by Tanzanians, so there were only two forms (grades) at the time. Because it had been a school for expatriate children, it was inordinately well equipped for a Tanzanian school: it had a gym, science labs, an auditorium and stage, and even a swimming pool, although the pool was not currently functioning.[1]

Peppy Kinsey's sister, Charlotte, remembers Peppy telling her that marriage had at least one tangible benefit: married couples were flown to Mbeya from Dar es Salaam, whereas single volunteers had to endure a twenty-four-hour, hot, dusty bus ride.[2] The volunteers remained in Mbeya over Christmas and New Year's Day. Because the school was closed between terms, space was available for the volunteers in the student dormitories and in teacher housing. Patricia Ann Royce (now Trish Daniels) was part of the Peace Corps group with the Kinseys in Mbeya. She remembers in particular a very detailed lecture by Tom Law, a Peace Corps doctor, as part of the training. Using an assistant with flip charts, Law covered health issues, eating, drinking, auto accidents, travel in the country, features of various tribes, and more.[3]

Delores Ledbetter grew up in Seattle, Washington, and graduated from Seattle University. In August 1963, she began Peace Corps training at Syracuse University and left for Tanzania at the end of the year. In Tanzania, her Peace Corps group spent some weeks in Mbeya for in-country training before she moved on to Tosamaganga Girls Upper Primary School near Iringa in central Tanzania in January 1964.

After completing her first year of teaching in December 1964, Delores and her roommate used their Christmas break to travel to Rhodesia to see Victoria Falls, and she stopped in Mbeya on the way back to school, around Christmas. She spent about a week in Mbeya with the new group of volunteers, which included Bill and Peppy Kinsey. Delores and her roommate stayed in the girls' dormitory, while the Kinseys were in married couples' housing.

Many of the women in the new group sought out Delores to learn about her experience in the first year of her assignment. One of the women who joined in these discussions was Peppy Kinsey. She was very interested in knowing what life was like in the school, what the teachers and students were like, how Delores got along with Africans, and many other things. One time when they were alone, Peppy talked to Delores about how unhappy she was. She said that she had met her husband in training and that after the few months at Syracuse they were married. Now they were in Tanzania, and her husband wouldn't talk to her and hadn't talked to her in several days. She didn't know what to do. Delores commiserated with her and said she had met a man in Peace Corps training who wanted to marry her, but she couldn't imagine getting married at that time and facing all the needed adjustments of being newly married, moving to Africa, and starting teaching. Peppy and Delores discussed the situation, but Delores, not being married, felt she was in no position to offer much advice. She thought that Peppy seemed overwhelmed by getting married, going to Africa, and preparing to teach.[4]

From Mbeya, the Kinseys traveled to their assignment at Binza Upper Primary School in the northwestern Tanzania town of Maswa. This Tanzania upper primary school included two grade levels, Standard VII and Standard VIII, roughly equivalent to junior high school in the United States. At the school, they taught English and mathematics as well as some geography or history and possibly music and some home economics. Teachers also had responsibility for after-class activities, such as games, sports, the monitoring of dormitories, and so on. The Kinseys remained at the school until Peppy's death in March 1966.

At the time the Kinseys began teaching in Maswa, Peace Corps volunteers were warmly welcomed in local areas despite developing conflicts between the United States and Tanzania. An anecdote from C. Payne Lucas, one of the earliest Peace Corps staffers and former regional director for Africa, offers a view of the complex relationships between the volunteers and the local people: "When a Tanzanian village chief was instructed in 1965 to make an anti-American speech to his people, he complained that he could not understand the order. 'The only Americans I know are the missionaries in our village and the two Peace Corps teachers,' he said, 'and they are nice people. I guess it is the South Americans I am to attack.'"[5]

In March 1965, Peppy wrote to her family that one of the big problems at the school was pregnancy among the girls. Once pregnant, the girl was expelled from the school and lost the opportunity to continue her education. Generally nothing happened to the father, even if he could be found.[6]

In June 1965, Peppy wrote to her family describing corporal punishment at the school, which involved beating the transgressing student with a large stick. Women teachers were expected to punish the girls, so Peppy was strug-gling with her own feelings about whether she could beat someone for any reason. Later in the year she reported that a girl had been hit on the head so many times that she was admitted to a hospital with damaged eardrums, which affected her balance.

By October that year, the Kinseys decided to seek a transfer to another school because they had too many problems with the headmaster at the Binza School. The Peace Corps was generally reluctant to permit such transfers unless absolutely necessary. Because most of the staff shared the Kinseys' antipathy to the headmaster, however, he was finally removed by the Ministry of Education, and a new headmaster was appointed. The Kinseys were happy with the change and decided to stay at the school.

Peppy's mother, Charlotte, and Peppy's aunt, Justine Woodall, traveled to Tanzania to visit the couple in December 1965. While they were in Tanzania, the four of them took the opportunity to travel extensively around East Africa. After the two sisters returned to America, Peppy wrote to her mother about "what a great vacation we both had."[7]

The following January Peppy wrote home that she and Bill were very happy with the new headmaster and other new staff and so hoped to remain at Binza School. In the same letter, she reported that a new Peace Corps couple had been placed at the Sayusayu Mission School, which was only an hour away by bicycle. They were about to go there to meet the couple, the Ellisons.[8]

Phil and Ann Ellison graduated from the University of California at Los Angeles in 1965, joined the Peace Corps the following fall, and began training at Syracuse University in a program very similar to the one that the Kinseys had gone through. Both Ann and Phil were natives of the Los Angeles area and had remained there to attend college.

In January 1966, the Ellisons arrived in Tanzania, and after a brief in-country training session in Dar es Salaam they traveled by train and bus to their assignment at Sayusayu Upper Primary School near Maswa. Shortly after the Ellisons' arrival, the Kinseys went to Sayusayu to meet them, and over the next several months the two couples became good friends. In March, they planned a joint trip to Uganda during the school holidays.[9]

In the early days after their arrival, the Ellisons wrote home often, giving their families a sense of life at the school. The Maryknoll fathers at Sayusayu were very jolly and rarely wore priestly garb, except for at mass. The Ellisons were the only American or European teachers at the school, although many of the priests, brothers, and nuns were from America. The Ellisons were surprised to discover that they knew the regional Peace Corps director, Jack McPhee, and his wife, Sandy, both of whom had been at UCLA with the Ellisons; Phil Ellison had known Sandy McPhee for more than five years.

The Maswa countryside was beautiful and green at this time because it was the middle of the rainy season. In a letter home, the Ellisons painted a picture of their life at Sayusayu:

> Now let me tell you about our house. It really reminds me of camp. Of course no running water, electricity and an outdoor latrine—this is standard. But our house is very large—2 bedrooms, den, living room, dining room, kitchen. All the windows are screened and we have a screen door. We have a kerosene stove, refrigerator, and lanterns. We have very little furniture—the beds were stolen while the house was unoccupied last month—but I guess we'll accumulate gradually. Water is the main problem; we have 2 types: fairly clean from the mission well which we must filter however, and not so clean which we can only use for washing. We must wash everything very carefully. We have vegetables delivered once a week, meat twice. For other things we go into the nearest small town, Maswa. I'm writing this by grace of kerosene. Our cots and mosquito nets are awaiting us. Tomorrow is Mass and our "scheme of work" for the *year's* classes and lesson plans for next week.[10]

Their classes ran from 8:30 to 3:30 and included geography, English, physical education, and art. Phil coached basketball, boxing, and track, while Ann supervised the drama program. Not everything was idyllic, however: "Our past couple of days have been rather tense. As I said we had bats in the rafter. Well, the fathers had someone stop all our roof holes with cement to get rid of them, so for two nights we had them squealing and scrabbling about in panic. Phil massacred three of them and one escaped. But now the living room will be a bit cleaner. Also the carpenter bees that were eating their way into our bedroom have been poisoned and are slowly disappearing."[11]

On March 29, the Ellisons wrote to their parents about Peppy Kinsey's death. They had planned to spend the weekend with the Kinseys at Sayusayu, but late in the week the Kinseys notified them they were not coming. Once they heard about Peppy's death, they were confused by the different stories about what had happened. Bill said she had fallen from the rocks, but the witnesses said they saw him beating her: "It is all so terrible, like a nightmare. I never felt so bad about anyone dying. She was so happy and so nice. Everyone liked her. She will really be missed. . . . During the break (almost a month) we have a P. C. conference to go to, and then Phil and I will go on some sort of vacation, but not the same one we were planning with the Kinseys. We just can't believe it of Bill—they seemed to have no troubles. He was very mild-mannered."[12]

A few days later they followed up with a more detailed description of the events surrounding Peppy's death:

> As you've probably already heard from the Franklins we've had quite a shock here. Last Sunday Peverley Kinsey was killed here in Maswa. It really is a terrible loss, she was a wonderful girl and we had become fast friends. The Kinseys, Bill & Pep, lived 3 miles away and taught at the UPS [upper primary school] in the town of Maswa. They had been here over a year. The previous weekend we had spent Sat. and Sun. at their house and had planned a trip together for next week, Apr. 8 to Uganda etc. They were an ideal couple.
>
> There is some mystery about the death; Bill is being held by local authorities on a possible murder charge, as there may be evidence that may implicate him—we can't believe it and assume it was a fall from the rocks—there will be an inquest soon I believe.[13]

Shortly after Peppy's death, the Ellisons went on their planned trip, which included a Peace Corps Conference in Dodoma in the central part of Tanzania. From the conference, they proceeded to Arusha, Tanzania, and toured the nearby game parks, including the Serengeti. They arrived back at Sayusayu on April 26, and Phil once again took up the matter of Peppy's death and Bill's jailing in a letter to his and Ann's parents the same day:

> About the Kinsey case—there was an inquiry and the trial will be within two weeks. There seems to be quite a bit of evidence against Bill but it is still hard to believe. The Peace Corps has supplied a lawyer from Washington and also two of the best East African lawyers—. He's in prison near here and getting excellent treatment. His father is coming out and I'm sure he'll get a very just trial. There

have been no repercussions here at all. Ann and I cleaned out their house along with Father Bob; and the students, teachers and headmaster all asked for more Peace Corps teachers. The Kinseys were very popular. People here often do take law into their own hands if they suspect evil and that's probably the reason they attacked Bill. Of course misunderstandings could hurt an innocent victim.[14]

The Ellisons would later change their view of the case and attempt to intervene in the trial.

11

Friends of Peppy

Probably the most tragic thing that has ever happened to someone
we know happened last weekend.
—*Dan Clemmer*

The Clemmers

Dan and Betty Clemmer, an American couple, lived in Mwanza next to my
house at Bwiru Boys Secondary School. Both had been teachers in the United
States and had applied to the Peace Corps, but Dan was rejected because of
asthma. He then applied for the Teachers for East Africa (TEA) program and
was accepted. Another member of their TEA group had also been rejected by
the Peace Corps on medical grounds, a prior history of tuberculosis. TEA not
only did not have the various medical limitations that the Peace Corps did but
like the Peace Corps permitted couples to join the program, although only one
of the spouses could be an actual TEA teacher. And many TEA couples had
children. Betty Clemmer remembers that on the plane to East Africa, there
were "loads of kids on the flight, including a newborn, as well as at least one
pregnant woman, maybe more."[1]

TEA, one of the first international initiatives of the new Kennedy administration in 1961, was launched with a grant from the State Department's Agency
for International Development and administered by Teachers College, Columbia University. The TEA program recruited experienced teachers to be placed in
secondary schools in Kenya, Uganda, and Tanzania and paid them salaries comparable to the salaries of Tanzania nationals. Paying at this level was important

because when the TEA teacher left, he or she could be replaced by an African teacher paid at the same level. In contrast, Peace Corps volunteers received only a subsistence-level stipend, equivalent to about $125 per month.

Betty, although not a TEA teacher, was included in all the training programs provided at Teachers College. By the end of the training, the Clemmers had met the TEA requirements, and Dan was assigned to Bwiru Boys Secondary School in Mwanza, Tanzania. Betty was told that although she would not be a TEA teacher, she would have little trouble finding a teaching job in Tanzania. Such was the case, and she taught first at Bwiru Girls Secondary School and later at another girls' school in the Mwanza area.[2]

When the Peace Corps began operations in March 1961, Sargent Shriver wanted the TEA program brought under the Peace Corps' administration. According to R. Freeman Butts, the program's director at Columbia University, the East African governments refused to agree to this proposal because they liked the fact that the TEA teachers had teaching experience; in contrast, the Peace Corps did not require its volunteers to have any prior teaching experience. By 1964, however, TEA teachers had largely been replaced by Peace Corps volunteers. My own group of secondary-school teachers were trained at Columbia Teachers College in 1964, and many of our instructors had taught in East Africa under the TEA program. Once the Peace Corps began supplying teachers for East Africa, Teachers College developed a new program called Teachers Education for East Africa, which focused on training East Africans to teach in elementary schools.[3]

Dan Clemmer was a graduate of Davidson University, and Betty had graduated from Mount Holyoke. He was a tall, slender man with a plethora of freckles on his very fair skin, and he wore a pair of large eyeglasses. He was from the South and maintained a courtly southern demeanor. Betty was a short blonde with an infectious laugh and an easy manner with new people. She had been a senior at Mount Holyoke when Peppy Kinsey was a freshman, and they had lived in the same dormitory.

One day in the spring of 1965, Dan and Betty were walking along the street in downtown Mwanza when Betty heard someone call out, "Betty Lou Campbell!" It was Peppy, and she used Betty's maiden name, as she had known her at Mount Holyoke. Betty, of course, responded, "Peppy Dennett." They chatted for some time, filling each other in on the particulars of their lives since they had last talked, including where they were living and working. The Clemmers invited the Kinseys to visit them the next time they came into

Mwanza. Betty remembered Peppy at Mount Holyoke as a very friendly, outgoing person, so, although a senior back then, she had known Peppy better than she had known most other freshmen. Over the next year or so, the Clemmers and the Kinseys saw each other several times, usually at the Clemmers house at Bwiru. As our next-door neighbors, the Clemmers invited John Oliver and me to dinner to meet the Kinseys.

On the weekend of March 18, 1966, the weekend before Peppy died, the Clemmers had driven out to Maswa to visit the Kinseys and to stay overnight with them. Although Peace Corps volunteers were not allowed to own a car, TEA teachers could, and the Clemmers owned a used Peugeot sedan. Betty Clemmer remembers that she saw no signs of problems or strains between the Kinseys during the weekend. The only unpleasant moment came when Peppy dropped and broke the bottle of wine the Clemmers had brought and became distraught. Betty had never observed any tension or conflicts between Peppy and Bill during any of their many previous meetings, either.[4]

After the March 18 visit, Dan Clemmer included his observations on the visit in a letter home to his parents. He was particularly impressed that the Kinseys were doing well under rather primitive conditions. "They have no electricity and their water is piped into a small shed about thirty feet from their house. They have an outside toilet with a hole in the floor." Dan mentioned that the Kinseys were the only white people in town, other than two priests. The Kinseys seemed to be doing well, although they would have preferred being in a large town, such as Mwanza. At the same time, they felt they knew the "real Africa" and were becoming fluent in Swahili because they had to use it all the time.[5] Their visits to the Clemmers and to John Oliver and me very likely exacerbated their feelings of being "stuck in the bush" because both our house and the Clemmers' had three bedrooms, electricity, indoor plumbing, running water, and complete furnishings. As will be seen later in some of Peppy's letters to friends in America, the contrast was frustrating and depressing for her and Bill.

A few days later, on April 3, 1966, Dan again wrote to his parents. The letter reminded them of his previous letter in which he described their visit to the Kinseys but was largely about Peppy's death and its aftermath.

> Probably the most tragic thing that has ever happened to someone we knew happened last weekend. In my last letter I described a visit to our Peace Corps friends, the Kinseys, near Mwanza. Last Sunday they were on a picnic near Maswa and she, Peppy, fell off some rocks

and was killed, and Bill, her husband, is being held in prison charged with murder. Nobody, except those immediately involved, knows exactly what happened, but it appears as though he might have been temporarily insane and pushed her and then beat her with rocks and an iron bar. According to rumor the only marks on her body were on the head and these could not have been made by a simple fall. There are supposedly some eyewitnesses, but no one knows anything for sure.[6]

The letter goes on to say that many rumors were circulating and that the Peace Corps had originally asked Dan to fly to Dar es Salaam to accompany Bill and Peppy's body but was later told Bill would not be going to Dar es Salaam due to his arrest.

At the time of Peppy's death, Betty Clemmer was teaching at Rosary Girls School in Mwanza. Some of her students asked her if she knew the person who killed his wife. They also told her that they had heard that some of the villagers had moved objects around at the site.

The Clemmers were never aware of any strains in the Kinsey marriage, and, in fact, they made regular visits to Bill in prison and wrote weekly to his parents with news of his condition.[7]

The Dowers

Aileen and Hal Dower trained with the Kinseys at Syracuse University. Aileen had graduated from the State University of New York in Albany, Hal from the University of Minnesota. They had worked and taught for several years in America before joining the Peace Corps. At first, they had been assigned to the Peace Corps in Somalia; however, the Somalia program was closed down after a year, so they returned to the United States and joined the same group as the Kinseys at Syracuse in September 1964, training for teaching positions in Tanzania. Aileen had previously lived in Syracuse and had taught in the schools there, which, as mentioned previously, was helpful experience but not a requirement for becoming a Peace Corps volunteer.

In Tanzania, the Dowers were assigned to Ibadakuli Upper Primary School, a boarding school near Shinyanga, about 100 miles south of Mwanza and enrolling students in standards (grades) 4, 5, 6, 7, and 8. The school had open-air windows and neither running water nor electricity. The Dowers taught English, math, and geography to grades 7 and 8, which they taught in English. Hal also provided physical-education training, and Aileen taught cooking. There were about forty-five students in a class. Although the school was a boarding school, a few students from nearby villages attended on a daily basis. Each child had a set of schoolbooks but no exercise books, so they did math on slate boards. There was a small library but no laboratory. Each child had two sets of school uniforms: on Saturday one set would be washed, and the student would put on the other set for the coming week. The students were also responsible for sweeping the school grounds. The school provided two meals per day; in the morning *uji,* a hot cereal usually made from millet, corn flour, and water, and in the evening *ugali,* made from maize flour and water and worked to a porridge consistency. The *ugali* usually contained a few vegetables, and the students received meat once each week. The faculty lived on the campus. The Dowers' first headmaster had a severe drinking problem, was known to have slept with one of the girl students, and was eventually removed from the school.[8]

Although Aileen and Peppy were not close during training, they became good friends in Tanzania and met frequently when they both were in Mwanza. The meetings were generally at a local restaurant called the Citizens' Delight, which was very popular with Peace Corps volunteers in the area. It was so popular, in fact, that a couple of volunteer jokers had convinced the owner to rename the restaurant the "Greasy Spoon" because, they told him, this was a name used for fine restaurants in America.

When Aileen and Peppy met at the restaurant, Bill and Hal and other volunteers were often present, but Aileen and Peppy usually moved to the side and had private conversations. Aileen had become pregnant in the summer of 1965, and Peppy was especially interested in talking with Aileen about the pregnancy and family life. Peppy told Aileen about the problems she was having with Bill. She told her he would become angry and lock her out of the house at times, and he would not talk to her for long periods, sometimes days at a time. Peppy never mentioned any physical abuse, but, according to Aileen, she did tell Aileen about considerable psychological abuse. She questioned Aileen as to whether this was a common occurrence in marriage. Aileen assured her it was not.

After Aileen delivered her baby on March 19, 1966, she was confined for several weeks to Kola Ndoto Hospital, operated by Canadian missionaries a few miles from Ibadakuli School. While she was in the hospital, Peppy sent her three watercolors she had painted based on scenes from Winnie the Pooh. At the time of Peppy's death, Aileen was still in the hospital and did not learn about it until several weeks later. She was never contacted by any of the attorneys in the case, and she played no role in the trial. She and Hal completed their assignment in Tanzania and returned to the United States in December 1966.

12

The Peace Corps and Criminal Defense

Sargent Shriver firmly believed that the volunteers should live and work as the people in their assigned country did. This principle included the fact that volunteers would be subject to all of the laws of the host country and could be tried for infractions of the law under the host country's judicial system. Although volunteers may have been told in training and in written documents that they were on their own, few if any of them paid attention to these notices. Either they were too excited by the coming adventure, or the information was never actually emphasized. Also, since they had no intention of violating the host countries' laws, they largely ignored this "small" point. Volunteers served without diplomatic immunity, nor were they covered by extraterritorial agreements that might permit them to be tried by U.S. courts.[1] However, when Bill Kinsey was accused of murder and jailed, the situation became much more troublesome for the Peace Corps: Could the organization obtain and pay for highly competent counsel to represent Bill?

Under the Poor Prisoners Defence Ordinance, a judge in Tanzania could have assigned an attorney to represent Bill, and the attorney would be paid out of public funds. Apparently, Bill nor his parents nor the Peace Corps nor his attorneys gave any thought to requesting such an appointment.[2]

The Peace Corps' initial belief that it could not provide an attorney and pay for the cost of Bill's defense was met with displeasure by Bill's father, Bill H. Kinsey Sr., and by others in North Carolina, who felt the Peace Corps was abandoning Bill. Peace Corps officials went to great lengths to inform the Kinseys about all they were doing to support Bill as well as why, under U.S. law, they could not pay for his defense. The Peace Corps urged Bill's father to retain an appropriate American lawyer to advise him how to proceed. Peace Corps officials believed that Bill's father was in a financial position to pay for the representation, so they did not feel they needed to go further in making such arrangements. At this time, Gurbachan Singh had estimated the cost of representation to be 2,700 English pounds (about $20,000 in today's value). That figure, however, did not include the cost of expert witnesses, transportation, and other things that might be required.[3]

After Tony Essaye returned to Washington, he wrote Paul Sack a letter on April 20 describing his impression of the situation with Bill's father:

> Mr. Kinsey has not kept his thoughts to himself, but apparently has spread them throughout the town of Washington, North Carolina, to the extent that we have had a whole host of Congressional inquiries expressing concern about what is happening, and what we are doing on Bill's behalf. I should throw into all of this the fact that Washington, North Carolina, has been an area under considerable pressure in the last few years due to the Civil Rights movement. There is probably no question that racial feelings are not far below the surface there and affect the way both the Kinsey family and their neighbors are viewing this situation.[4]

In response to the determination that the Peace Corps could not pay for Bill's defense, Paul Sack and Tom Quimby, the associate director of Peace Corps Africa, aggressively argued that the organization should do so and asked that Peace Corps director Jack Vaughn reverse the decision. They pointed out that the Peace Corps, as an independent program, should not be bound by such long-standing government policy established for different circumstances. Volunteers were not salaried and were prohibited from receiving financial support from their families; they also had no diplomatic immunity and were asked to submit to all local customs and practices. Finally, Sack and Quimby argued that there would not be a conflict because the government does not assume responsibility even when providing the legal defense for an indigent defendant in the United States, although a malpractice case might be brought against a poor-performing attorney.[5]

Tony Essaye had cabled PCDC on April 5, 1966, with his views on representation and Peace Corps involvement in the case. He believed Sack and Quimby's position to be "well considered," but he remained of the opinion that Peace Corps could not provide such representation. He was also concerned that a high level of involvement by local Peace Corps officials might begin to irritate the Tanzania government. He recommended that local Peace Corps officials shift into the background and that he return to the United States to further remove direct official Peace Corps involvement. At the same time, he pointed out that, given the emergency situation, it had been essential for the Peace Corps to supply a high level of support in the beginning.[6]

Bill Josephson, the Peace Corps general counsel at the time, had been a key player in setting up the Peace Corps. He and Warren Wiggins had drafted the original memorandum to Sargent Shriver describing the structure of the new agency. Josephson, a graduate of the University of Chicago and Columbia Law School, was at that time a twenty-six-year-old lawyer at the International Cooperation Administration, which would soon be renamed the Agency for International Development. Shortly after the Kinsey trial, he joined the New York law firm Fried, Frank, Harris, & Jacobsen, later Sargent Shriver's firm also and now known as Fried, Frank, where Josephson had a distinguished career until he retired in 1999.[7]

On April 7, 1966, Josephson sent Jack Vaughn several memos concerning representation of Bill Kinsey. The first memo defined the issues as follows:

1. Only one authority immediately available to the Peace Corps specifically authorizes the procurement of legal services. That authority is section 1031 of the Foreign Service Act of 1946, as amended. Attached is a memorandum to you recording our opinion that that section does not authorize the procurement of legal services to defend Tanzania Volunteer Bill Haywood Kinsey, Jr., against the murder charge currently pending against him.

2. Two extraordinary Peace Corps Act authorities, section 15 (a) and section 15 (b)(7), may or may not provide the necessary authority. We are now turning to this question.

3. If none of the legal authorities available to the Peace Corps authorize the procurement of legal services in the instant case, and if the Peace Corps should decide as a matter of general principle that it should have such authority, we could of course, seek it from the

Congress. But I am not sure that it could be applied retroactively to the instant case.[8]

As Josephson soon discovered, there did not appear to be legal authority for the Peace Corps to provide and pay for counsel to represent Kinsey in the murder trial. One of the general counsel's memos reviews at some length the Peace Corps Act, the Foreign Service Act, the Foreign Service Manual, other relevant legislation, intercountry agreements, legislative history, and administrative decisions. It begins by pointing out that generally "all persons, citizens and aliens, are responsible for their criminal conduct to the Government of the place in which the acts complained of occurred." It goes on to mention some limited exceptions, for foreign diplomatic personnel and, by Status of Forces agreement, military personnel.[9]

In an early fundamental decision, the Peace Corps chose to claim for Peace Corps volunteers only the equitable treatment to which all Americans residing abroad are entitled under international law. The decision sought to separate volunteers from the U.S. government. The privileges and immunities accorded to diplomatic personnel of American embassies overseas by custom and to nondiplomatic U.S. government agency personnel by agreement were not to be sought for Peace Corps volunteers. The friction these agreements and the Status of Forces agreements have caused is well known and perhaps can best be understood if one reverses the situation and contemplates the U.S. Senate's likely reaction to a proposal that the United States, by international agreement, accord diplomatic privileges and immunities to nondiplomatic personnel of foreign countries living in the United States.

One of Josephson's memos sets out the relevant section of the Peace Corps handbook, which was allegedly given to all volunteers and reiterated the basic policy:

24. LEGAL STATUS: This is a section we hope you never have to worry about: it concerns offenses committed by Volunteers. As Volunteers are not officers or employees of the U. S. Government, and do not have diplomatic immunity, their legal liability usually does not change as a result of their enrollment as Trainees or Volunteers.

Thus, they generally are subject to State and Federal laws in the United States and to host country laws overseas. An agreement between the Peace Corps and the host country usually provides that

Volunteers shall receive the same treatment as is accorded private
U. S. citizens residing there.[10]

This provision did notify volunteers of their status, although in somewhat con-
fusing language, but it made no mention of criminal defense and who would
pay. The volunteers may have been cognizant of this fact, but it is likely that
few, if any, thought seriously about it when they signed up. As to the issue of
legal expenses, the question seems never to have arisen until the Kinsey case.

Similarly, the Peace Corps program agreement with Tanzania did not
provide for any different resolution of the question of the status of a volunteer.
"The Government of Tanganyika will accord equitable treatment to Peace
Corps Volunteers . . . and fully inform and consult and cooperate with representatives of the Government of the United States of America with respect to
all matters concerning them."[11] This particular memo continues at some length
to review other potential sources of authority but in the end concludes that the
Peace Corps was without authority to procure such legal representation.

This same memo then examines what level of assistance an American, if
arrested in a foreign country, might expect from the U.S. government:

> To what United States Government assistance, then, are American
> nationals entitled if they are arrested abroad? This is outlined in 7 F. A.
> M. 350. In general, the United States Government will undertake to
> insure [sic] that its nationals may at all times communicate with an
> American Foreign Service officer and, unless lawfully detained, visit
> him in his office. If arrested, there should be probable cause for the
> arrest and trial, the American national should be informed of the
> charge against him, the national should have an opportunity to defend
> himself, and the national should not be mistreated while in prison:
>
> > In substance, the officer of the Foreign Service must determine
> > whether the American national's treatment was similar to that
> > accorded nationals of the foreign country faced with a similar
> > charge. 7 F. A. M. 352.4–6
>
> The only authority for further action we have found is Revised
> Statutes §2001 (1875), 22 U.S.C. §1732 (1964). That provides that
> whenever the President learns that any citizen of the United States

"has been unjustly deprived of his liberty by or under the authority of any foreign government, it shall be the duty of the President forthwith to demand of that government the reasons of such imprisonment." That section further provides that if the imprisonment "appears to be wrongful and in violation of the rights of American citizenship, the President shall forthwith demand the release of such citizen." Finally, the section provides that if the release is unreasonably delayed or refused, "the President shall use such means, not amounting to acts of war, as he may think necessary and proper to obtain or effectuate the release." *We have no evidence that Tanzania's action in arresting Volunteer Kinsey is wrongful or in violation of the rights of an American citizen.*[12]

The complexity and importance of the provision of counsel were underscored when Josephson's office produced on April 14, 1966, a second lengthy, detailed analysis of the Peace Corps Act and why it did not support providing counsel for Bill Kinsey. Josephson then concluded that the better course would be to ask Congress to change the legislation to make clear that the Peace Corps could pay for attorneys in these circumstances.[13]

The general counsel's memos on the subject indicate that Peace Corps officials took a rather conservative view of the law. A more vigorous and bold analysis could probably conclude that the Peace Corps might have leeway to cover the costs of legal representation. However, given the vagaries of Washington politics and the fact that the Peace Corps was still a relatively new agency, with not a few severe critics, it made sense to proceed cautiously. Even a decision to seek a change from Congress was not without complexity.

In the middle of May 1966, Josephson was quoted in the press as saying that the Peace Corps did not have authority to provide representation to Bill Kinsey: "'We don't have the authority, under the Peace Corps Act, to pay for a lawyer for a volunteer who is charged with a crime in a foreign country,' Mr. Josephson said. 'Up until now, we have never needed to have the authority because we haven't had any such incidents.'" Josephson added that the Peace Corps planned to seek legislation authorizing it to provide such representation.[14] Although the decision that the Peace Corps could not hire a lawyer to defend Bill substantially weakened the organization's ability to oversee the case, it had the benefit of further supporting the organization's position of neutrality, which it thought important vis-à-vis the Tanzania government.

As the general counsel's office began work on a proposed amendment, a number of questions were raised about what should be covered:

1. Should this authority apply to volunteer representation in *all civil* (contract, tort) and *criminal* cases or should it be limited to the latter
2. Should the authority be limited to the defense of volunteers . . . or should it extend also to volunteer *plaintiffs* . . .
3. . . . should it include petty crimes . . .
10 . . . Would Peace Corps retention or financing of counsel, particularly to defend criminal cases (espionage, smuggling, black market transactions), unduly complicate relationships with the host country? . . .
   Picking lawyers and making sure they do a good job is never an easy thing. Does the Peace Corps want to take on that burden?[15]

In the end, it was decided that a fairly short and general amendment should be made to the Peace Corps Act. The language finally adopted was:

(a) Section 5 of the Peace Corps Act, as amended,[72] which relates to Peace Corps volunteers, is amended to add immediately after the end thereof a new subsection as follows:

> "(1) Notwithstanding any other provision of law, counsel may be employed and counsel fees, court costs, bail, and other expenses incident to the defense of volunteers may be paid in foreign judicial or administrative proceedings to which volunteers have been made parties."

(b) The authority contained in subsection (a) shall extend to counsel fees, costs, and other expenses of the types specified therein that were incurred prior to the date of enactment of the Act.[16]

The congressional delegation from North Carolina, Bill's home state, had pressed the Peace Corps, beginning shortly after Bill was arrested, to take over the cost of representation. North Carolina senator Everett Jordan was particularly aggressive in this effort, most particularly that the coverage must be retroactive to ensure that all of the costs of Bill's representation were taken care of. The proposal to seek legislative change received considerable attention in American and East African newspapers, which also included reports that some volunteers felt abandoned by the Peace Corps and did not realize that they needed to "go it alone" in defending themselves overseas.[17]

Although the bill was introduced shortly after the Peace Corps determined it lacked the authority to pay for Bill's representation, it did not pass Congress until August 31, 1966—near the end of the trial, and it would not become effective until later, after the president signed it. By the end of August, critics in Congress were satisfied that the bill provided for retroactivity and so supported paying for Bill's defense.

Even as the Peace Corps general counsel's office began its analysis of the authority to supply legal counsel to Bill Kinsey, it became known that Bill's family had moved forward and retained Carroll Brewster. Because Brewster would not be able to practice law in Tanzania, he planned to go to East Africa and arrange for local legal counsel. He would be responsible for the selection of a trial attorney in East Africa and for making whatever financial arrangements were necessary.[18]

In late April, Bill's initial attorney Gurbachan Singh proposed that he travel to Nairobi to interview prospective trial counsel. He planned to go during the week of May 2. At this point, Singh was considering three potential counsel; Byron Georgiadis, Bryan O'Donovan, and a Mr. Wilkenson (first name not known). Paul Sack suggested to Singh that Carroll Brewster might want to participate in selection of trial counsel, but Singh responded that he was much more familiar with the attorneys, had watched them in court, and knew their reputations. He also asked for approval of his authority to retain counsel and for a determination of who was responsible for the fees.[19]

13

The Preliminary Inquiry

A crowd of solemn-faced African villagers sat on the stone
benches around the whitewashed walls of the court, squatted on
the concrete floor and stood four deep outside.
— *"Peace Corps Man Faces Trial," Boston Globe, May 8, 1966*

In late April, Father Bob wrote to Bill's father that the preliminary inquiry (PI)
was to be held on April 21. Mr. Kinsey became very upset because Carroll
Brewster, the Kinseys' American lawyer, could not be there at that time. PCDC
requested clarification, and PCDSM responded that the hearing date information was incorrect; the date had not yet been set.[1]

Carroll Brewster arrived in Nairobi on May 1 to interview Dr. Dockeray
and Byron Georgiadis. Brewster was impressed with Georgiadis but did not
hire him at this point, in part because he felt that Gurbachan Singh could more
than adequately handle the PI.[2] About the same time, Singh wrote Georgiadis
that the hearing was now set for May 5 and that it would likely last one day,
with no chance for an adjournment, which would make it difficult to bring in
additional counsel. At the same time, Paul Sack talked to Georgiadis about
possibly attending, but Georgiadis said he was in trial in Nairobi, couldn't
attend, and had not actually been hired yet for the Kinsey case.[3]

The *Boston Globe* described the scene for the PI:

On 5 May, the PI began early in the morning in Maswa. The hearing
took place in a small courthouse where the Magistrate laboriously
recorded every word of testimony in longhand. Bats fluttered among
the rafters of the courthouse and insects hummed through the open

98

side of the building. All testimony from African witnesses was given in the Sukuma dialect of this district and laboriously translated into Swahili and then English.

A crowd of solemn-faced African villagers sat on the stone benches around the whitewashed walls of the court, squatted on the concrete floor and stood four deep outside.

The magistrate occasionally ordered police to silence a crying child or move the crowd back.[4]

Magistrate Vinno Mhaisker had left his home in Shinyanga at 4:30 a.m. to arrive in time to begin the hearing. The government's case was presented by Assistant Superintendent of Police Peter Kateti, not by one of the state attorneys. Bill Kinsey was present and represented by Gurbachan Singh, with Carroll Brewster assisting because he was permitted to participate despite not being admitted to practice in Tanzania.[5] The PI was less formal than a trial; consequently, the prosecutor was a policeman rather than a state attorney. The informality extended to Bill as well: he was not manacled and ate his meals at the Maryknoll Mission with the prosecutor, Carroll Brewster, Gurbachan Singh, and Jack McPhee.[6]

PCDC continued to express concern that the Peace Corps' "neutral" position be made clear to the Tanzania government. Tony Essaye cabled Peace Corps Tanzania to be sure that the number of Peace Corps officials at the PI be kept to a minimum and that the local office should make clear that Carroll Brewster was not connected with the Peace Corps.[7]

Prosecution witness number 1, Assistant Superintendent of Police Martin Kifunta, testified that on March 27 he had been called to a hill outside Maswa, where he found Bill Kinsey being held by a group of villagers: "Effendi" (a title of respect in many Middle Eastern and African countries), he was told, "two Europeans are fighting, and it is believed one is dead, and you are wanted urgently." He testified that Kinsey's clothes were bloodstained and that Kinsey told him that his wife had fallen from the rock and his clothes became covered in blood when he tried to move her. Bill's shirt and pants were identified as exhibits 1 and 2 for the PI.[8]

Kifunta went on to testify that he found Peppy Kinsey's body a short way away, her face covered by a towel and her head resting against the side of a rock. He moved the body to his Land Rover and then began his investigation. At the spot where Bill said she had fallen, he found a pool of blood, pieces of a broken beer bottle, and two white buttons. He subsequently found nearby a short length of iron pipe covered with blood and what looked like hair sticking to it.

It was getting dark (this area of Tanzania is very near the equator, so the days consist of twelve hours of night and twelve hours of day, with the sun setting at 6:00 p.m.), so Kifunta drove Bill home and had him change his clothes. He then took the clothes Bill had been wearing, secured them at his office, and later brought them to court, where they were marked as exhibits. Kifunta took Bill from his house to the police station, where he administered the usual caution and took a statement but did not arrest or charge him. When he offered Bill's statement to the court, Singh objected. After some argument, Assistant Superintendent of Police Kateti agreed with Singh's argument and withdrew the statement.

Kifunta then continued his testimony, reporting that he allowed Bill to go to the Sayusayu Mission to spend the night with Father Bob. When they returned the next morning, Kifunta charged and arrested Bill prior to bringing him before the district magistrate. Over the ensuing days, District Magistrate D. J. Gumbo held several hearings concerning the charges, whether to grant bail, and where the PI should be held.

On March 28, Kifunta took Bill and several police officers to the site of the incident and continued the investigation. While there, Corporal Silashi found a rock covered in blood and what appeared to be hair. Kifunta took the stone into his custody.

Kifunta produced a sketch map of the area where Peppy died. He identified points on the map, such as the top of the hill, which was some 20 feet above the place where Bill said Peppy had landed; the place where Bill said he fell down while carrying Peppy, which was 41 feet from where she landed; the place where Kifunta found the body; the place where the iron pipe was found; and the place where the rock with blood on it was found. He also pointed out on the sketch where the witnesses told him they stood, provided measurements from those places to various points on the hill, and described whether the view was obstructed or not.

Kinsey was taken back to his house, and the house searched, testified Kifunta. During the search, a handwritten diary, apparently Bill's, was found, which was confiscated because of certain entries. "It was seized because of entries on page 12, written March 26, the day before the wife's death," said Kifunta. Kifunta then gave an account of the various steps he had taken to proceed with the case: (1) sent Bill to the doctor; (2) signed the order for the postmortem; (3) sent Bill to the area secretary to give a statement; (4) sent Bill to Malya Prison.[9]

On March 29, Kifunta continued, he arranged for a blood sample to be taken from Bill and sent several of the exhibits (a piece of metal pipe, clothes, specimen of Peppy's blood and hair, the stone, and a specimen of Bill's blood) to the government chemist in Dar es Salaam. On April 4, Kifunta received the chemist's report along with those items sent to Dar es Salaam, which he produced as exhibits.

Kifunta then called the court's attention to page 12 of the diary, at which point Magistrate Mhaisker read portions of the entries from the diary:

> What frigging bore it is to get to know people. Don't you think they are nicer before you know them? That's what's good about the good old days. The other fellow got the girl . . .
>
> When she asked her if anything unusual had happened Etoile had been obliged to say that it might have but she would not really know until about the 27th of the month.[10]

Kifunta was then excused.

The area secretary for Maswa, Mr. A. S. Swai, submitted and read a written statement given to him by Bill Kinsey two days after Peppy's death. Swai testified that he made the police officer accompanying Bill leave the room, so Swai and Bill were alone. He told Bill the statement could be used against him and asked him if he was making the statement on a truly voluntary basis. Bill replied that he was. Swai asked him if anyone had threatened him. He replied no, that everyone had been very helpful to him. Swai then began writing Bill's statement, which was given in English.

In his statement, Bill recounted how he and Peppy had gone to the hill for a picnic after grading exams. They climbed to a higher rock to look around, and Bill heard the sound of breaking glass. He rushed to the edge of the rock to look down. He saw Peppy below, so he went down to her. He tried to assist her and keep her quiet, but she struggled to get up. He moved to carry her down to get to a doctor, but he fell with her in his arms. So he left her there and went to get his bike to ride for help, but he was restrained by local villagers.[11]

In response to Swai's testimony, the defense submitted a lengthy written argument and gave an oral presentation at the hearing that Bill's statement should not be submitted into evidence. The magistrate withdrew for a full hour to write an opinion on the issue. Citing sections of the Indian Evidence Act concerning what evidence can be introduced in a case, which had been adopted in Tanzania, Mhaisker admitted the statement into evidence. The defense expected that result but wished to preserve its right to object at the trial. Brewster later said he was impressed by the magistrate's legal opinion.[12] Mhaisker, however, bemoaned the inadequacy of his law library on the issue of admitting the statement.[13]

It is interesting that the effort to keep Bill's statement from being admitted was one of the few arguments the defense made at the PI. Its admission would eventually turn out to be very helpful to Bill's defense because later the trial court was favorably impressed that Bill's account of the events was so consistent every time he gave it.

Philip Mganga, the AMO for the Maswa area, testified next that he had examined Peppy's body in Maswa. After setting forth his qualifications as a medical officer (completing courses at Muhimbili Hospital and Sewa Haji Hospital, completing the AMO course in 1961, concentrating on pathology and medical jurisprudence, and performing medicolegal work since 1961), he described the circumstances leading to the postmortem.

Once these preliminary matters were out of the way, Mganga reviewed his findings and described each of the various injuries he found on the deceased. His testimony was based on the notes he took at the time of the postmortem, and the notes were admitted into evidence. The injuries included, among others, (1) a 3-by-½-inch wound on the right parietal region of the scalp; (2) a 2-by-½-inch scalp wound on the top of the head; (3) a 3-by-½-inch wound on the occipital region of the scalp; (4) a lacerated wound on the left temporal region about 2 inches by 1 inch; (5) a fissured fracture of the left temporal bone about 4 inches long; (6) a depressed fracture of the right temporal bone about 2 inches in diameter; (7) a fissured fracture of the right frontal bones about 4 inches long and slanting upward; (8) a 3-by-½-inch wound on the right eyebrow running from the socket of the eyeball upward.

Based on the injuries and on his assessment of Peppy's build, Mganga came to several conclusions: (1) she would have passed out very quickly: (2) if she fell down, she would not have been able to stand up; (3) she would soon have become unconscious, although her subconscious might allow her to call out names; (4) the injuries could have been caused by a club, an iron bar, a stone, a stick, or any blunt object, but not by anything pointed.

Mganga believed that Peppy had died as a result of hemorrhage from a fractured skull. In his opinion, a fair amount of force had caused the injuries, and the injuries happened at different times. "These injuries are not consistent with having been caused by a fall. They are so scattered they could not have been caused by a fall," Mganga testified.[14]

Several other witnesses also testified: (1) Corporal Silashi testified that he found the stone at 2:00 p.m. on March 28. The stone was approximately 8 inches by 5 inches by 3 inches. The blood and hair on the stone were identified as Peppy Kinsey's. (2) Detective Constable Thomas testified that he found the iron bar on March 27 in the evening and that Bill stated it was part of a camera stand. The blood and hair on the bar were identified as Peppy's. (3) Constable Mohammed testified that he accompanied Peppy's body and the physical evidence to Dar es Salaam. (4) Father Charles Liberatore testified that he identified the body. (5) Stanley Mhardo, a teacher at the Kinseys' school, testified that Bill had access to the school workshop, where iron bars could be found. (6) Humbi Sayuda testified she heard wailing that she thought came from her daughter and that her cries summoned Mr. Maganda Vilindo.

Each of the witnesses was identified as either a Christian or a pagan or a follower of some other religion, so they could be sworn in on a Bible, the Quran, or some other document. Humbi was identified as "pagan" and so "affirmed" her testimony.[15]

Late on Friday, May 6, 1966, a local Sukuma villager, Maganda Vilindo, took the stand dressed in a white robe. As a pagan, he also affirmed his testimony. "Vilindo testified that he ran toward the hill when he heard a cry. There he came upon an old woman, who pointed to a white man and woman who were fighting. Vilindo said the man was hitting the woman on the head with something. He went around the hill to get a better look and saw the man sitting on the woman." The court clerk lay on the floor in front of the witness to demonstrate how Vilindo described the scene. "We were afraid of the man because he was fierce," he said. "We saw him get up and we saw blood on his clothes."[16]

Padre Masunzu testified that he came to the scene when he heard a woman cry out. There he met Vilindo, who told him to look at the hill, where Padre saw a man lying on top of a woman. Padre then bicycled to the police station to alert the police.[17]

On that same Friday, Magistrate Mhaisker ruled that there was sufficient evidence to warrant a High Court trial of Bill Kinsey on a charge of murder. He ordered Bill remanded to custody until the trial.[18]

Under Tanzania law, the prosecution was required to present its full case before the magistrate in order to obtain a ruling that Bill should be charged with murder.[19] The defense was not required to and did not present its defense to the charge at the preliminary hearing. Thus, the defense knew everything about the prosecution case and could plan accordingly, whereas the prosecution knew nothing of the defense case. The defense could then develop information to impugn prosecution witnesses' testimony. As the trial shows, the defense efforts were largely successful because the judge discounted much eyewitness testimony. Similarly, the defense medical experts were able to review AMO Mganga's testimony in depth and to develop a detailed rebuttal. Because a written transcript of the PI proceedings was prepared and made available, the defense could also easily spend time examining every nuance of the prosecution case. Given this situation, one can readily understand how the prosecution could be taken by surprise by many aspects of the defense case. This requirement that the prosecution present its full case at the PI offered an enormous benefit to the defense.

In addition, the prosecution case was presented not by an attorney but by a police inspector, which likely meant a lower level of advocacy and preparation than an attorney could offer. Although the use of a policeman was not required by Tanzania procedure, it was probably compelled by the lack of resources available to the state attorney. By not participating in the PI, the prosecuting attorneys were also denied the opportunity to see their witnesses in action and to be able to prepare countermeasures against defense efforts to impugn witness testimony at trial.

It is surprising that Tanzania legal practice required the prosecution to present its entire case at the PI. It is instructive to compare PI practice in England and America at the time of the Kinsey trial. By the early 1960s, a PI in England and the United States generally followed the same model, although in the United States each state defines its own procedure, and the federal courts have their own distinctive rules.

Generally, in England and America in the 1960s, a PI consisted of an effort by the prosecution to show only enough of its case to meet the prima facie case standard or probable cause. These terms are used somewhat interchangeably to mean that the prosecution must present facts or evidence such that a reasonable person would believe that the suspect committed a crime. The usual prosecution strategy is to present only enough evidence to meet that test, thereby denying the defense the opportunity to find out much more of the evidence. The usual defense strategy is to force the prosecution to present the maximum amount of evidence, leading to the highest level of trial preparation by the defense.

Historically, there has been conflict over how much the prosecution needs to present because guilty defendants might profit by their knowledge of the evidence and so defeat appropriate prosecutions. For the defense, the right to avoid self-incrimination means that the prosecution is unable to obtain much, if any, information about the defense case. In recent years, many jurisdictions have relaxed these rules to allow more opportunities for both sides to discover evidence at the PI and later.[20]

However, as we have seen, at the time of the Kinsey trial the defense was able to avail itself of a powerful tool to find out about the prosecution case and to prepare for trial.

The prosecution case at the PI was presented entirely by a police officer, Peter Kateti. No one from the state attorney's office appeared. Carroll Brewster was very impressed by the competence and fairness of Magistrate Mhaisker and by the performance of Gurbachan Singh for the defense. Singh's performance was excellent, showing great technical competence, and his knowledge of local practice and participants was most helpful.[21] However, considering that the defense presented no evidence and did not question witnesses at the PI, Brewster's praise of Singh seems a bit excessive.

The PI received extensive newspaper coverage in the United States. Many newspapers in Bill's home state, North Carolina, published reports, but articles also appeared in newspapers throughout the country, including in Waterbury, Connecticut; Boston; Salem, Oregon; San Antonio, Texas; Boise, Idaho; Pottstown, Pennsylvania; Richmond, Virginia; Wichita, Kansas, and Montgomery, Alabama.[22]

After the PI, Brewster and Singh traveled to Nairobi, where, based on several recommendations and personal interviews, they engaged Byron Georgiadis to handle the trial.[23]

In early May 1966, Carroll Brewster had met with Georgiadis for several hours in Nairobi. Brewster then reported to the Kinseys that he was very impressed with Georgiadis and that they got along "splendidly." Georgiadis was energetic and interested in getting involved immediately. Whereas many senior attorneys would normally sit back and wait to get to work a few days before a trial, Georgiadis would soon go to Mwanza and get to work. He was flown in a Cessna 210 to interview Bill in jail. He found Bill "an intelligent young man [who] gave a consistent account of the incident in more detail than he had given to the police or magistrate." After the interview, he flew back to Nairobi and began many conferences with doctors and other experts. In a lecture given in London in 2007, Georgiadis complained that Carroll Brewster used to tease him because American newspapers had referred to him as the "East African Perry Mason. Having seen several T. V. depictions of the lawyer, I was not exactly flattered."[24]

Byron Georgiadis, although from a Greek family, had been born in Tanzania and raised in Uganda and Kenya. His family immigrated to Kenya from Greece in 1922 after the Greek war with Turkey. In East Africa, Georgiadis's father was the owner of the Uganda Tobacco Company. Georgiadis attended one of the best-known and most prestigious schools in Kenya, the Prince of Wales School, which catered primarily to Europeans living in East Africa. At that school in 1945, Georgiadis was very active, serving as head of Hawke House, head of school, and captain of the hockey team. The Old Cambrian Society was made up of alumni of the Prince of Wales School in Nairobi. At the time of his death, Georgiadis was fondly remembered in the society's newsletter: "With an international reputation and able to command high fees, Byron never forgot his background and his roots, and several penniless Old Cambrians on serious charges had cause to feel grateful to him for defending them free of charge, invariably successfully, out of the goodness of his heart."[25] He attended Oxford University to study law and was called to the bar in England before returning to Kenya to practice. At the time of the Kinsey trial, he was thirty-eight years old and had by then developed a reputation as a brilliant trial lawyer.

Georgiadis went on to become one of the most famous and expensive trial lawyers in East Africa. Before he retired in 1998, he handled several high-profile cases in Kenya, including the Julie Ward murder case, involving an American woman found dead in Masai Mara Reserve; the initial case against former Kenyan Treasury permanent secretary Wilfred Karuga Koinange; and the case against Member of Parliament Stanley Githunguri on charges of violating the Foreign Exchange Regulations.[26]

Sometime after the Kinsey case, Georgiadis joined the prominent Kenyan law firm Kaplan and Stratton, where he remained until shortly before his death. Despite all the famous cases Georgiadis handled during his career, when he died in 2010 at the age of eighty-three, it was the Kinsey case that led his obituary in the *Nairobi Daily Nation*. The obituary went on to quote Justice Minister Mutula Kilongo on Georgiadis: "Other than the late S. M. (Silvano Melea) Otuno, the country has not produced such a charismatic criminal lawyer."[27]

By this point in the Kinsey case, the defense had assembled a powerful legal team, including the lawyers Singh, Brewster, and Georgiadis: Singh, the experienced local trial lawyer from Mwanza; Brewster, the respected trial lawyer from the United States; and Georgiadis, perhaps the most prominent defense attorney in East Africa. Tony Essaye publicly followed the Peace Corps' position of remaining neutral; however, he would also supply help to the defense. In terms of medical expertise, the defense would use Dr. Dockeray to great purpose, and Dr. McHugh would supply detailed medical analyses for the defense, not only based on his familiarity with the Kinseys but also based on research he performed at Georgiadis and Brewster's request. In addition, the defense would eventually engage a head-and-neck injury specialist from Nairobi, who would supply valuable support for certain aspects of the medical testimony.

14

Peace Corps Faces Challenges

> The prosecution case by itself is so damning that to distribute it
> might appear as an endorsement of the charges.
> —*Paul Sack to Tom Quimby, May 14, 1966*

Once the PI was concluded, Peace Corps officials struggled with how to inform volunteers and others on the status of the case. Not only were the facts coming out of the PI extremely damaging to Bill's case, but the Peace Corps also continued to be battered by complaints from volunteers and others that Bill had been abandoned. On May 14, 1966, Paul Sack wrote to Tom Quimby, Africa Region director for the Peace Corps, describing his efforts to update Tanzania volunteers; it was difficult to decide what to say. Because the prosecution had presented its case at the PI, but the defense had not, the only public details available were the damning ones presented by the prosecution. "We considered giving to the Volunteers more of the facts of the prosecution case to familiarize them with the seriousness of the charges. We decided not to do so, however, because we are not yet able to give out any of the details of the defense. The prosecution case by itself is so damning that to distribute it might almost appear as an endorsement of the charges against Bill by the Peace Corps."[1]

In a similar letter to Will Lotter, the Peace Corps director in Malawi, Sack underscored the seriousness of the charges:

> The prosecution has produced three eye-witnesses to the struggle described by Bill. One of these witnesses testifies to having seen Bill beating his wife over the head. The prosecution has further intro-

duced into evidence an iron bar about 12 inches long and a rock about 8 inches long, which the police claim to be weapons with which Bill beat his wife. Both these items are covered with blood and hair identified to be of the same type as Peverley's. Although there were a large number of serious head wounds, there were virtually no marks anywhere else on Peverley's body. Obviously, the prosecution has a serious case which would result in an indictment in any state in the United States.[2]

Newspapers at the time reported that other Peace Corps volunteers in East Africa expressed the view that Kinsey had been abandoned by the Peace Corps. In one newspaper article, a volunteer was quoted:

Volunteer Mr. Seeba, a 22-year-old engineer from Dothan, Alabama, apparently is one of the minority. "When we joined the Peace Corps we didn't realize that if we got into trouble we were on our own. We thought the American Government would do something for us," he said. "Kinsey's case has brought this home to us. I think there must be some change in our status as a result." Mr. Seeba said in an interview he had discussed the position with several of his colleagues, and they felt there should be some agreement between governments by which an accused volunteer could stand trial in the United States rather than in the country to which he is assigned and where the legal procedure is likely to be strange to him.[3]

Peace Corps volunteers and members of Congress were not the only ones complaining that Bill had been abandoned. Peppy's uncle was heard on several occasions demanding that U.S. marines be sent in to Tanzania to rescue Bill and bring him home. He apparently even called Peace Corps director Jack Vaughn pressing him to see that it was done.[4] Although many newspapers in the United States carried stories about the case, no groundswell of popular demand for extreme action ever took place.

Jack Vaughn received a letter dated May 16, 1966, from Vance Barron, pastor of the Presbyterian Church of Chapel Hill, North Carolina. Pastor Barron was closely interested in the case because his son was a Peace Corps volunteer and a near neighbor of Bill and Peppy in Tanzania.

Specifically, I think that there is considerable justification for the growing opinion among my friends here that the Peace Corps has failed to support Kinsey and his family in this matter. The explanation offered in the press today, i.e., that the Peace Corps is not legally authorized to finance legal counsel, does not carry much weight with me, or with others who are acquainted with some of the operations of the Peace Corps. It stands to reason that you do have funds which can be used for emergency situations, such as this one, if you so choose.

It seems to me that it *is* the responsibility of the Peace Corps to provide adequate legal counsel in this instance. I have discussed this with a number of persons here in Chapel Hill who have various connections with the Peace Corps, and each one has agreed with my own judgment. If the impression is created that the Peace Corps is *not* going to stand behind the volunteers in such cases, then I think that all parents of prospective volunteers would have serious reservations about sending their children on such assignments. The fact that Kinsey may well be guilty of the charge, as the evidence seems to indicate at this point, does not change my conviction at all. What he did, if he did it, can hardly be considered the act of a normal person. The presumption is that he broke under the stress of the situation in which he found himself.[5]

As Reverend Barron pointed out, even if Bill were guilty, as seemed to be the case, he still needed the best representation possible, and the Peace Corps' position created a substantial obstacle to achieving that goal.

Director Vaughn answered the letter on May 25, 1966, with a detailed recapitulation of all the steps taken to support Bill: Peace Corps officials rushing to the scene, the deputy general counsel Tony Essaye flying to Tanzania the day after notice was received, Paul Sack locating local counsel, visits to Bill in prison, discussion with the Tanzania attorney general, retention of attorney Carroll Brewster, and the hiring of Byron Georgiadis. Vaughn concluded his letter with a lengthy discussion of the legal issues involved in the Peace Corps paying to defend Bill. He reported that on May 23, 1966, the Peace Corps asked Congress to provide authority for the agency to cover the costs of such representation.[6] In a subsequent letter to Pastor Barron, Vaughn pointed out, however, that the legislation might not pass or might not apply retroactively to Bill's situation, so in the end it might be necessary to undertake private fund-raising to defray the costs of his defense.[7]

Later in May, Sack wrote to Quimby again with his concerns that Bill might in fact be guilty. He stressed the importance of ensuring that volunteers recognize the possibility that Bill might be convicted and urged Quimby to alert various people in the United States, such as the North Carolina congressional delegation, that "Bill may have done the things of which he is accused."[8]

While the concern about Bill's guilt continued and in the face of some volunteers' feeling that he had been abandoned, the Peace Corps maintained its public position of neutrality. However, it continued to make efforts on Bill's behalf and to pay expenses incurred by the case—for example, on May 18, Leon Parker, Peace Corps associate director in Dar es Salaam, authorized payment to Dr. Dockeray for his travel from Nairobi to Mwanza.[9] At the same time, the Peace Corps undertook no efforts to develop evidence that might show Peppy was in fact murdered. It left such work entirely in the hands of the prosecution.

One may wonder why few, if any, voices were heard urging significant steps be taken by American authorities to show that Peppy's death might not have been an accident. Paul Sack seemed deeply troubled by the evidence, but his primary actions were aimed at supporting Bill's case. As mentioned earlier, some volunteers had information from Peppy that the relationship was not as successful as generally portrayed.

In contrast, much of the complaining came in support of Bill—he had been abandoned; he should be forcibly removed from Tanzania and returned to the United States; and so on. Peppy's family seemed to believe in Bill's innocence and failed to pursue any alternative narrative, so the Peace Corps was left with nothing to encourage its officials to look deeper into the situation on Peppy's behalf and possibly to supply the prosecution with resources and suggestions.

15

Tanzanian Criminal Law

If a person is convicted of murder, the death penalty is obligatory.
—*J. S. R. Cole and W. N. Denison, Tanganyika*

By the time of Bill Kinsey's trial in August 1966, Tanzania laws and legal system had passed through many changes. Shortly after Tanganyika became a League of Nations–mandated territory under British control, the British government passed a law setting forth the laws to be applied there. That law, dated July 22, 1920, established a High Court that was to act in accordance with certain Indian Codes and locally enacted ordinances and in conformity with the common law of England, the doctrines of equity, and the statutes of general application that were in force on that date in England.[1] The described laws, however, would generally apply to Europeans, whereas Africans would be governed by customary laws that had developed over the centuries among the tribes, and Islamic Law would apply to Muslims.[2]

The Indian Codes—that is, the Penal Code, the Evidence Code, and certain civil codes—had been developed by legal scholars in England starting in the mid-1820s. The authors took the unwritten common law of England and produced coherent, consistent codes to be used in the British colony of India. In India, much of the law was applied to Indians by administrators untrained in the law. The Colonial Office and legal scholars felt that such administrators, not being lawyers, could not apply the unwritten common law in a consistent, logical fashion, so codification was necessary. These codes became the basis for the legal systems in many of the countries ruled by Britain during the early years of the twentieth century. The Indian Codes were adopted in East Africa, including in Tanganyika, in the early 1920s.[3]

112

At least with respect to criminal law, starting in the 1930s the Tanganyika High Court began to bring African defendants within the parameters of the general law rather than letting it remain solely within the customary law. From this time until the 1950s, there were vigorous battles between Tanganyikan administrators (i.e., British colonial officials), Tanganyikan judges, and other legal officials over what legal system should govern Africans. The administrators pushed for a simplified, African-based law, whereas the judges and others argued that only pure English law could function properly in Tanganyika.[4]

The tenor of the debate can be seen in a report from 1932 by a district officer in Mwanza:

> I consider that the present system of professional magistrates and judges should be abandoned. The conception that, because a man has passed Bar examinations and has eaten a number of dinners in one of the Inns of Court, he is fit to be a magistrate is, in my opinion, fallacious. It is a relic of the old English guild system, the modern relic of which in more humble occupations is the trade union. . . . A knowledge of the language, customs and psychology of the people is necessary and this can never be acquired by sitting in court. . . . I submit that the class of official most qualified to exercise judicial functions is the administrative official and I would base a reorganization of the judiciary on this fact. Provincial commissioners would be presidents of provincial courts, administrative officers would hold courts and the native courts would be part of the system. All jurisdiction over cases, civil and criminal, in which both parties were natives would be removed from the High Court. Provincial commissioners' courts would have no jurisdiction over non-natives. A diminutive High Court would be necessary to deal with non-natives—one judge would suffice. Where I have attacked the legal profession it is because I feel it has a stranglehold on the country which should be loosened; the territory is rapidly becoming a lawyer's udder to the enrichment of the advocate and the impoverishment of the people.[5]

Under traditional or customary African law, what we might consider "crimes" were generally treated as civil matters because the usual penalty was for the transgressor to pay compensation to the aggrieved party rather than be sentenced to prison or executed. Once the British took control of Tanganyika, homicide was brought under the principles of criminal law and was no longer a "civil" matter.[6]

From the 1930s to the early 1950s, as a general rule—at least in rural areas, which made up almost all of Tanganyika—the residents were governed by native authorities established under the Native Authority Ordinance. These "native authorities" were mainly the hereditary rulers or chiefs and were appointed by the governor of Tanganyika. "Native authorities" would generally apply customary law to native Tanganyikans.[7]

In the 1930s, Tanganyika adopted a model Criminal Code and Criminal Procedure Code, which had been drafted by the British Colonial Office with modifications by the attorney general of Kenya. The codes included various provisions of the Indian Criminal Procedure Code.[8] Although these codes clearly covered "Europeans," as mentioned earlier, the High Court began to treat natives under the Criminal Code starting in the 1930s.

At independence in 1961, Tanganyika adopted the Independence Constitution, which was followed by the Republic Constitution, in force from 1962 to 1965. In 1965, another interim constitution was adopted when the country moved from a multiparty state to a one-party state. It was anticipated that a permanent constitution would be adopted shortly, but the new constitution was not adopted until 1977.[9]

At the time of Peppy's death and the Kinsey trial, the Interim Constitution was in effect, and so the Penal Code, the Criminal Procedure Code, and the Evidence Code, which had been adopted in the early 1960s along with the various constitutions, were the law of the land. The codes in large measure followed the law as it had been established under British rule, based on the English common law, doctrines of equity, certain English statutory laws, and various Indian Code provisions. In 1963 under the Magistrates Court Act, Tanzania had fully integrated the court system and removed the distinction between courts that applied the general law and those that applied customary law.[10]

The most significant variation from English criminal law provides that the judge try a case with two assessors rather than with a jury. Assessors are not considered jurors. They are not sworn in, and there is no mechanism to challenge them, although as a practical matter the judges try to make sure the assessors are acceptable to the parties. They give their individual opinions, not a collective opinion, which does not amount to a verdict. The judge must ascertain and consider their views "but has complete freedom to decide contrary to them." "The concept of appointing assessors to sit with a judge and advise him in questions of fact and custom, was taken from the Law of India."[11] The exact role of assessors has long been a vexed one. Are they to be considered experts on customary laws, or should they be viewed as "expert witnesses" who may give an opinion, but the meaning of customary law must still be proven. Most commentators and the courts, at least in written opinions and documents, suggest that the assessors should not be considered experts in customary law.[12]

The procedure to assign assessors to a case and their role is relatively straightforward; the law provides that the registrar of the High Court direct the appropriate magistrate to summon the number of persons that the registrar considers necessary for the current court sessions. From this pool, the judge then selects the assessors for his case. At the end of the case, the judge sums up the evidence and requires each assessor to give his opinion orally on the case generally and on "any specific question of fact addressed to him."[13]

At the time of the Kinsey trial, under section 196 of the Tanzania Penal Code, "murder is defined as causing the death of another person of [sic] malice aforethought, by an unlawful act or omission."

> "Malice aforethought" is defined, in section 200, as (i) an intention (a) to cause the death of, or to do grievous harm to, any person, whether that person is the person actually killed or not; or (b) to commit a felony ; or (c) by the act or omission to facilitate the flight or escape from custody of any person who has committed or attempted to commit a felony; or (ii) knowledge that the act or omission causing death will probably cause the death of or grievous harm to some person, whether that person is the person actually killed or not, although such knowledge is accompanied by indifference whether death or grievous bodily harm is caused or not or by a wish that it may not be caused.[14]

"If a person is convicted of murder, the death penalty is obligatory."[15] In 1963, the latest figures available, which were from 1961, indicated that 652 offenders had been charged with a crime in the High Court of Tanzania. Of the 652 cases, 444 involved murder or manslaughter. In 46 of these cases, the death penalty was imposed, but only 21 of those convicted with the death penalty were executed. Cases were likely resolved in favor of lesser charges, or the president of the country pardoned such persons given the death penalty. It is unlikely the numbers would vary significantly by the time of the Kinsey trial.[16]

To most observers, Tanzania had a well-run, competent judicial system based largely on the laws of England. As Peace Corps officials would often say to newspaper reporters, legislators, and Bill's friends and relatives, they had every confidence that he would receive a fair and just trial.

16

McHugh and Singh Re-create the Scene of Peppy's Death

On Monday, May 30, 1966, Dr. Tom McHugh and Gurbachan Singh traveled to Maswa and nearby Impala Hill so McHugh could see the site where Peppy died, examine the exhibits, and review the facts and the conclusions presented by the prosecution at the PI. McHugh planned to see if he could construct a scenario that would not only support Bill's account of an accident but also be consistent with the prosecution's evidence. They went first to the Magistrates Court to look at the exhibits: the iron bar, the rock, and the blood-stained man's clothing.[1]

McHugh and Singh then drove to Impala Hill and attempted to re-create the scene as described by Bill and the prosecution. (The prosecution would contend that there had been no climb up the hill and thus no fall.) At the top of the hill, they placed themselves in the positions described by Bill to examine the likelihood that his statement that "he did not hear or see Peppy fall" could be true. Bill and Peppy had apparently climbed the hill to look for the steeple at Sayusayu Mission.

McHugh first noted the "omnipresent" wind in the area, which he had experienced on previous visits to Maswa. He thought the wind's noise level might be high enough to keep Bill from hearing Peppy's fall. With Singh standing in Peppy's place, behind Bill and to the right (according to Byron Georgiadis, there was insufficient room on the rock to stand side by side[2]) and McHugh in the place where Bill stood, as described by Bill, McHugh assessed whether Bill would see Peppy fall. McHugh knew that Bill was quite nearsighted and wore thick-lensed glasses, which would distort his peripheral vision, and McHugh felt that the combination of the thick lenses and the distortion would make it most unlikely that Bill would have seen Peppy fall.

McHugh thought that Peppy could have passed out, fallen forward, slid down the rock face first, and landed on the rock below with little or no sound that Bill might hear. It seemed likely that such a fall could lead to sufficient impact to cause the separation of the "fronto-parietal suture." This suture is where the bones of the skull join, and this injury was the one that Dr. Dockeray thought led to Peppy's death. The surface of the rock onto which Peppy would have fallen was not smooth but rather broken "in an exfoliative or scaling fashion," which could easily have led to the lacerations Dockeray found.

Bill stated that Peppy was holding a beer bottle, and he heard it break. McHugh conjectured that Peppy retained it in her hand as she fell, and it broke as she landed below. In McHugh's experience, bottles tend to break so that the mouth and neck are left intact but with jagged edges on the shoulder. It seemed to him that the jagged edges of the bottle could have caused some of Peppy's injuries, particularly the wound around her right eye. In addition, no other object likely to cause such an injury had been found in the area. The broken shards of glass could also have caused some of the cuts found on Peppy's head.

AMO Mganga had stated that a person with head wounds like Peppy's would immediately lose consciousness. McHugh's experience and his extensive research on this type of head injury informed him otherwise. A person with these injuries might be very active for a time, flailing, getting up and down, and so on—all of which could have led to additional injuries. Bill had described his efforts to carry Peppy to get help. They had fallen at least twice. McHugh postulated that further injuries might have occurred as she was moved, and blood and hair could then have ended up on the iron bar and rock as well.

McHugh believed that although he had not necessarily proved exactly what had happened, he was able to demonstrate a logical scenario that combined Bill's statement and the prosecution's evidence, leading to the conclusion that Peppy died by accident. He and Singh had determined that Bill's account could very well be true.

McHugh found no reason to question Bill's account of an accident. He knew both Peppy and Bill, had cared for their medical needs, and would later testify that they seemed perfectly compatible as a couple. Had McHugh known of Peppy's complaints to other volunteers, however, he might very well have viewed the events on Impala Hill with a more critical eye.

17

Trial Preparation after the Preliminary Inquiry

There is no question in my mind that the Kinsey trial contains a great deal of potential dynamite for the Peace Corps in the United States.

—*Jack Vaughn to Paul Sack, August 1966*

Once the magistrate at the preliminary inquiry ordered Bill to stand trial in the High Court, the defense could begin preparing for and securing a date for the trial. Meanwhile, the Peace Corps spent considerable time worrying about press coverage, attempting to pass attorney-fee legislation, dealing with complaints from Congress and from North Carolina, and monitoring Bill's prison situation.

The defense team focused much of their preparation and planning on the medical evidence, believing it could be the key to a favorable verdict. Although the defense already had the postmortems from Dr. Dockeray, Dr. McHugh, and AMO Philip Mganga, only the AMO's report was readily available to the prosecution because the defense had presented no evidence at the PI. McHugh became the key player in this effort because of his personal knowledge of the Kinseys, his participation in the external exam in Maswa and the postmortem, and his ability and willingness to research the medical issues. In Byron Georgiadis's mind, the medical issues were so important that he later told Paul Sack that without Dr. Dockeray's postmortem and testimony, he would have been in big trouble.[1] In a letter to Carroll Brewster in June 1966, McHugh described how the defense was relying on his work: "I visited with Mr. Georgiadis on May

23, and at that time we had a very useful discussion. He has given me enough homework to do justice to a semesters course."[2]

At Peace Corps headquarters in the United States, Tony Essaye began gathering potentially useful documents, such as Bill's medical records, including mental health reports. As part of the final decision whether a Peace Corps enrollee would be sent overseas or be "deselected" from the program, he or she received a comprehensive mental assessment by Peace Corps psychologists and psychiatrists: "Volunteers underwent repeated psychological testing, which for many constituted the most stressful aspect of training. In the Peace Corps, psychiatry was king. Psychological testing had gradually come into its own over the twentieth century, but it became more accepted after its use by the military during World War II."[3]

The psychiatric profile became the primary basis for determining whether a person would be sent overseas. The decision was usually not made until near the end of the three-month training program, by which time the enrollee had invested a great deal of time and effort in the Peace Corps. If the enrollee were deselected at this stage, not only would this investment be lost, but the enrollee would also return home with an embarrassing mark on his or her record.

Obviously, Bill and Peppy had "passed" the mental-profile test and succeeded in their quest for a foreign assignment. In his letter to Gurbachan Singh, Essaye reported that Bill's medical records showed no evidence of "psychopathology." Essaye wrote that Carroll Brewster would bring the originals to Tanzania and that Bill's family was obtaining all his school and local medical records, and they would be forwarded as well. In the same letter, Essaye informed Singh that the Peace Corps was not authorized to pay Bill's attorney's fees but that Bill's father had agreed to cover the fees, so there was no cause for concern. In the meantime, the Peace Corps was seeking legislative changes to allow it to pay the fees.[4]

As Dr. McHugh continued to research various medical aspects of the case, he found a paucity of medical texts available to him in Africa, so he requested and received a number of books from Essaye and Brewster. For example, Brewster wrote to McHugh in late May and in early June that he was sending copies of *Goodman and Gilman's The Pharmacological Basis of Therapeutics,* the bible of drug reference books; *Merritt's Neurology,* a classic on the brain; and a book on forensic medicine.[5]

In contrast, I found nothing in the record describing efforts by the prosecution team to enhance their understanding of the medical evidence.

One nonmedical note of warning McHugh passed on to Essaye concerned Bill's insurance. He reported that Bill had taken out insurance on Peppy's life, and several letters concerning the insurance, which were on the desk at the Kinseys' house, could not be located. He wondered if they had been found and taken by the police to be used as further evidence of a motive.[6]

McHugh eventually produced a multipart analysis of the evidence in the case that would deeply inform the defense methodology (see chapter 18.) By August, McHugh was focusing on very specific aspects of the case. For example, he asked Byron Georgiadis to find out the alcohol content of the Pilsner beer Bill and Peppy had been drinking and the total alcohol content of a large bottle.[7] The search continued to determine how best to demonstrate that Peppy had passed out and fallen down from the rock. This issue remained a crucial part of the defense case.

In June, Carroll Brewster contacted a prominent neurological surgeon, Robert Selker, at the Yale University Medical School about the medical evidence. After reviewing the postmortems, Selker raised several issues. He thought the amount of blood (2 cubic centimeters [ccs]) reported by the AMO seemed very small, so he wondered if this amount did not include the blood from the massive hemorrhage indicated elsewhere. (McHugh also thought the amount noted a mistake and suggested 200 ccs to be more likely.) Selker asked if there were signs of an epidural hemorrhage, which sometimes allows for lucid intervals, such as Bill had described, and he raised the possibility that Peppy might have suffered an aneurysm brought on by taking the oral birth-control medication Enovid. A number of recent cases had appeared in the United States where Enovid had been implicated in causing such aneurysms. However, after an exchange of letters between Brewster, McHugh, and Georgiadis, it seemed that no conclusion could be reached as to whether Peppy suffered an aneurysm.[8] On July 8, Dr. Selker followed up with a letter to Carroll Brewster in which he gave more detail on the current research into the connection between use of Enovid and cases of vertigo or loss of balance. Selker found it reasonable to believe that the Enovid might well have caused Peppy to black out or lose her balance or both.[9]

Bill's parents continued to express their discomfort at the situation and pressed for more detail on Bill's status in prison. His mother contacted Carroll Brewster after Father Bob urged them to come to Mwanza for the trial. The defense lawyers and Peace Corps officials thought it a bad idea for them to come. They were worried that the Kinseys might become the focus of press efforts to generate news, and their responses to press questions could upset the Tanzania government and the courts. None of these worries seemed to include whether Bill might feel the need to have his parents nearby for support. In the end, Bill wrote a letter asking them to follow the advice of counsel and not come to Mwanza.[10]

As the Peace Corps' legislative package moved through the U.S. Congress, Senator Everett Jordan from North Carolina played an active role. In early June, he wrote the comptroller general of the United States inquiring whether the amendment as currently written would permit the Peace Corps to pay Bill's legal expenses. Frank Weitzel, assistant comptroller general, wrote back that if the legislative history made it clear that the statute was intended to be retroactive, his office would construe it to do so. However, he urged that the following language be added to the amendment to make clear its intent: "(b) the authority contained in subsection (a) shall extend to counsel fees, costs, and other expenses of the type specified therein that were incurred prior to the date of enactment of the act." Senator Jordan then wrote Senator J. William Fulbright, chair of the Committee on Foreign Relations, urging him to follow the comptroller's recommendation and add the proposed language or at minimum add strong language to the committee report to describe the intent. The Senate committee included both the amendment and the language requested by the Peace Corps in its report on the bill.[11]

The Peace Corps continued its effort to remain publicly neutral and not to be seen asking for special treatment for Bill. One might think that the need for neutrality also necessitated efforts to ensure that justice was done on behalf of Peppy. If her husband had killed her, it was important that justice be obtained with a guilty verdict. However, it seems the Peace Corps did nothing to obtain evidence that would support such a conclusion. It did not assist the prosecution to find potential witnesses or provide it with expert analyses of relevant aspects of the evidence.

Paul Sack summed up the Peace Corps position in a letter to Tony Essaye in early July. He was responding to Essaye's plans to come to Tanzania for "public relations" purposes. Sack urged him not to come because they were trying to keep a low profile and not bring in a number of officials from PCDC. "As you know, all our efforts since your visit have been directed toward demonstration to the Government of Tanzania that the Government of the United States is not interfering in the judicial process here. The results of these efforts have been just what we had hoped. Both the judicial and prosecuting departments of the Government here in Tanzania have made it clear that they have decided to treat this case as a 'routine' one and to leave the entire matter in the hands of the local officials in Mwanza."[12]

The issue would arise again at the time of trial, when PCDC wondered whether lawyers, witnesses, and Peace Corps officials should stay with local Peace Corps officials or at a hotel in Mwanza. Mwanza had one small European-style hotel. To ensure that the appearance of neutrality remained in place, Sack wrote back with a carefully delineated list of who should stay where. For example, Brewster should "not be quartered in official Peace Corps housing." Mrs. Dennett could stay with the regional Peace Corps director, Jack McPhee, because "refusal to do so could be interpreted in such a way to imply abandonment to Dennett, Kinsey families."[13]

It is ironic that shortly before Sack wrote about keeping a "low profile," Senator Robert Kennedy and his wife, Ethel, visited Tanzania, where they were warmly welcomed at the airport "by several hundred jubilant people, who included traditional dancers and members of the American community in Dar es Salaam." They were to spend four days in Tanzania, which would culminate in an address to "a large crowd at the Diamond Jubilee Hall in Dar es Salaam," where Kennedy proclaimed that the "world must do much more for Africa" and praised Julius Nyerere as one of the great leaders on the continent.[14] I found no mention in any of the newspaper coverage of the Kennedys' visit that an American Peace Corps volunteer was facing a murder charge in the country or any discussion in Peace Corps or embassy correspondence raising any potential problems over the connection.

Near the end of July, Paul Sack was able to alleviate concerns, at least Peace Corps officials' concerns, about Bill's supposed abandonment. Sack reported in a letter to Tony Essaye that when he visited Bill recently, the first subject Bill raised was a desire to disassociate himself from complaints from Peace Corps volunteers that he had been abandoned. He said he felt "the Peace Corps had done well and all it possibly could for him."[15]

However, PCDC, especially the press office, remained worried about the reporting being done on the case and the trial. In late May, Thomas Page, the Peace Corps director of public information, sent Paul Sack a collection of clippings of stories about the case in the American press. In response, Sack reported that coverage in Tanzania had been very restrained and that the CID had not released Bill's name in connection with the case. He added that the CID wanted to ensure the case was tried in court, not in the press. Sack went on, however, to observe that the Kenyan papers in Nairobi seemed to feel no such restraint.[16]

In response to inquiries from PCDC in July, Sack responded with information about press coverage at the trial: photography would not be allowed in the courtroom, but photos taken outside the courtroom were permitted. Also, reporters were not allowed to give opinions but must stick to a description of the proceedings.[17]

Peace Corps officials, particularly in Washington, D.C., were very sensitive to the potential for bad press in America arising from this case. Ironically, their concern might have been fed by efforts in the early years of the Peace Corps to seek positive reports and to advertise widely in America in order to obtain volunteers. The National Advertising Council enlisted well-known advertising agencies, such as Young and Rubicam, to provide free service to the Peace Corps.[18] Because the Peace Corps had received so much positive attention in the press, officials worried that bad news about it would also receive extensive coverage throughout the country.

In a memo to Director Jack Vaughn in late July, Information Director Page described several potential danger areas. He was concerned about (1) the indigenous press, especially reporters for "*The Nationalist* [*sic, The Nation*?]"; (2) Asian and expatriate freelance photographers, and (3) expatriate reporters who might seek to sensationalize the trial, especially for the British press, which could set off a competitive battle among the reporters.[19]

The Peace Corps was also worried about what volunteers might say to reporters. In response to requests from PCDC, PCDSM sent out notices to all Peace Corps offices in Africa and to all volunteers in Tanzania, alerting them to the coming trial and urging them to be vigilant and cautious when talking to reporters. The notices requested Peace Corps officials in other African countries to be particularly careful to alert volunteers who might be traveling in East Africa during this time.[20]

Peace Corps director Jack Vaughn expressed his own feelings about the sensitivity of the situation in a letter to Paul Sack in early August: "There is no question in my mind that the Kinsey trial contains a great deal of potential dynamite for the Peace Corps in the United States." Vaughn went on to suggest that if the press coverage got out of hand, Sack should discuss the potential issues with the American ambassador to Tanzania, John H. Burns, and perhaps they could alert the Tanzania government of what might be ahead. There was a fear that Tanzania was not ready for a massive influx of reporters seeking to observe and report on the trial. In closing, Vaughn expressed the ongoing fear that Bill would be found guilty, and so he was sending Tony Essaye to Tanzania for the trial; if Bill were found guilty, Essaye would be able to come back to America and explain what happened.[21] The American ambassador eventually discussed the case and press coverage with the Tanzanian ambassador to the United States, Chief M. M. J. S. Lukumbuzya, and the principal secretary of the Ministry of Foreign Affairs, D. Mulokozi. Mulokozi was well informed about the situation and assured the American ambassador that they would make every effort to prevent any misunderstanding caused by irresponsible journalism.[22]

Tony Essaye wrote to Gurbachan Singh in early August with a report on the American press's great interest in the case: "As I had more or less suggested, there has been a substantial amount of publicity about the case over here in the United States. The publicity has been, of course, the greatest in North Carolina since this is where Bill's family resides, but almost every sizeable newspaper in the United States appears to have carried a story."[23]

One final concern about publicity and confidentiality came when Paul Sack wrote in frustration to Jack Vaughn that much confidential information seemed to have been leaked by Peace Corps or State Department personnel. Carroll Brewster told Sack that he heard a discussion of details about the case at a dinner at the U.S. ambassador's house in Ethiopia. The details should not have been made public, and Sack pointed out that apparently his cables were easily and widely read by any Peace Corps staff member who wanted to.[24] By this time, however, there was not much that could be done about the many leaks.

In the weeks leading up to the trial, the defense team needed not only to develop its case but also to manage a number of procedural issues with the court. Since Bill remained in prison, the defense pressed for an early trial date, but the government, especially the prosecution, was in no hurry. The defense normally prefers to delay things as long as possible, but not when the client is in jail. Gurbachan Singh began recommending suitable assessors and preparing witnesses and other evidence. Despite his aggressive efforts, by July 20 he had been unsuccessful in securing a trial date. At this point, he called the Tanzania attorney general Mark Bomani, but still no date was set. He was able to find out that although a Nigerian judge, a Mr. Erokwu (first name not known), had been scheduled to hear the case, the government was apparently considering assigning another judge, which was causing the trial-setting delay. The issue of which judge would preside at the trial had been in question for some time. At the end of May, Mwanza attorney Mr. Parekh, Singh's partner, reported that Mwanza authorities had requested that Tanzania chief justice Telford

Georges, a native of Trinidad, handle the trial. Georges turned down the request on the basis that it would be poor judicial policy to give special treatment to the case. Parekh believed that the defense would prefer a local judge.[25] When Singh pressed the state attorney in Mwanza to schedule the trial for August 22, Ededen Effiwatt refused because he had a case in Bukoba at that time. Singh's observation that there were three assistant state attorneys, any one of whom could appear in Bukoba, received no consideration, so Singh threatened to appeal to the Tanzania chief justice. Finally, Byron Georgiadis entered the fray with a letter to the chief justice saying that he and the courts in Nairobi were being put in an untenable position because of the delay. The Nairobi courts were unable to schedule hearings involving Georgiadis while they waited for Tanzania to decide on a date for the Kinsey trial.[26]

On August 6, 1966, a trial-date-setting "mention hearing" was scheduled in the High Court in Mwanza; however, the hearing was continued to the following Monday without setting a date. Finally, on August 8 the trial was set to begin on Friday, August 26. However, the identity of the trial judge still remained in question at the end the mention hearing. Dr. McHugh, who attended the mention hearing on August 8, reported that Judge Erokwu was expected to preside.[27]

On August 9, 1966, Sack wrote to Tanzania volunteers with an update. He reported that the trial would begin on August 26. The letter described the high quality of Bill's defense team—Georgiadis, Singh, and Brewster. Sack also took the opportunity to explain that the Peace Corps Act did not authorize the Peace Corps to pay Bill's legal fees but that the U.S. Congress was considering an amendment that would permit such payments. In closing, Sack warned the volunteers to be careful in talking with the press.

> There are likely to be a considerable number of local and foreign journalists covering the case. In order to protect Bill Kinsey's position, all these Journalists—both domestic and foreign, including American—are bound by the above rules. [i.e., no photography in courtroom, no opinions, etc.]
>
> It is not unlikely that some of you will be approached by reporters seeking your views. In order to insure [sic] that Bill Kinsey's case is not prejudiced, we ask that you use careful judgment if approached by reporters and refrain from commenting on the case as far as possible, keeping in mind the rules of the court.[28]

Even though the trial was now only weeks away, questions about the assessors remained. Singh had urged the court to appoint American assessors but not missionaries, medical personnel, or Peace Corps volunteers. Paul Sack attempted to clarify the procedure for choosing assessors in a note to Peace Corps officials in Washington, D.C. Sack said that, contrary to earlier reports, nothing in Tanzania law required that the assessors be of the same race as the accused. As mentioned earlier, even their tribal connection was not a clear requirement. At this point, there seemed nothing to do but wait for the court's announcement.[29]

Many loose ends still needed to be tied up prior to trial. Georgiadis asked Peace Corps officials in Tanzania to supply a stenographer for the court to take verbatim notes. The reply stated that there was no one in Tanzania with such skills. Brewster arrived in Nairobi and spent six hours in conference with Georgiadis, which resulted in, among other things, a request to PCDC for six copies of the book *Ceremony in Lone Tree* (1960) by Wright Morris. Once Brewster got to Mwanza, he and Singh set out for Maswa to try to track down certain government witnesses whose statements had been taken but who remained unidentified. They thought Father Charles in Maswa could help them, but they for some reason seemed to have a negative view of him— Brewster described him as a "villain." At the same time, they were looking for another hammer handle to experiment with the reconstruction of "Bill's curious bi-pod."[30]

Brewster had already described to Bill their plans to bring Peppy's mother to Mwanza to testify and how much he, Brewster, thought of her: "In short, as you know, she is a woman of the greatest courage, and although the substance of her testimony will not be very significant, I cannot imagine that this tremendous demonstration of loyalty will not produce some marked effect for the good. I really admire that lady more than I can say."[31] Her appearance was to be a surprise, especially for the prosecution, which would have no time to prepare for her testimony. A middle-aged lady, the mother of the deceased, appearing essentially as "a character witness" for Bill, would require considerable preparation if the prosecution were to develop a line of questioning to undercut her testimony that wouldn't backfire. The luxury of such time to prepare was, of course, unavailable because the prosecution knew nothing of this plan. Peace Corps officials in Nairobi arranged for Mrs. Dennett and her sister, Justine Woodall, to remain in secret at the Westwood Park Country Club in Nairobi for a week or so before the appearance at trial.[32] In America, in contrast, the names of defense witnesses would ordinarily be supplied to the prosecution ahead of a trial.

Georgiadis wasted little time in preparing the case once he was hired as trial attorney. One of his first steps was to fly to Mwanza to interview Bill in prison. There he vigorously cross-examined him on elements of his story, such as why the bar had been brought along to the picnic. Georgiadis also succinctly set forth the primary issues in the case:

Did she [Peppy] fall, or was she pushed?
Were all her injuries as a result of the fall?
Were the accused's actions after the fall aimed at stopping her from
    injuring herself further or not?
Why did she fall?[33]

Given the uncertainty of the outcome of the trial, Bill and his supporters may have been somewhat cheered by an article published in the *Washington Post* on August 25, the day before the trial was to start. The article reported that President Nyerere commuted 75 percent of all death sentences to life in prison.[34]

However, according to Byron Georgiadis in an assessment of the case made many years later, Nyerere had said, "If [Bill Kinsey is] convicted, the law will take its course and the Republic will hang him," and "the Peace Corps will be expelled from Tanzania." Georgiadis went on to claim that other African countries, especially in West Africa, said they did not like the Peace Corps either and would expel its volunteers. "The presence of the Peace Corps in Africa hung in the balance."[35]

I have never found such a statement in any of the documents and newspaper articles I have reviewed. When I asked Tony Essaye, Paul Sack, and Tom McHugh if they had heard it, they said no. Paul Sack told me that he "went to see President Nyerere to be sure that the issue did not become whether Tanzania had a sovereign right to try and hang an American. I think this was after Jesse Helms had urged that the U.S. military go in and snatch Bill out of prison. President Nyerere assured me that demonstrating the right to hang an American would not become an issue." When I asked Sack whether Nyerere had said what he would do if Bill were convicted, Sack responded, "Nyerere said nothing about interfering if Bill were convicted and sentenced to hang, but I think that Nyerere might well have intervened. But that is only my personal opinion."[36]

It is surprising that Georgiadis would make up such a specific quote for the lecture he gave about the case in 2007. It could have appeared in the Swahili press, and the Americans might not have seen it. Or, as mentioned previously, it may have been given in the Russian press, which had attacked the Peace Corps, reporting that Bill's situation was the last straw and that the Peace Corps should be sent home. Despite early favorable comments on the Peace Corps by Nyerere, he may have been becoming disenchanted with it by the end of 1966, and the Kinsey trial might have been one of the factors leading to his decision to terminate the Peace Corps presence in Tanzania a few years later, in 1969. The quote from Peace Corps director Jack Vaughn at the beginning of this chapter underscores the Peace Corps' perilous status both domestically and internationally.

18

Medical Analysis by Dr. Tom McHugh

By mid-August 1966, as the trial date approached, Dr. McHugh had prepared a lengthy set of documents to assist the defense. Although the Peace Corps had publicly maintained a position of neutrality, McHugh played a powerful role for the defense because he was the Kinseys' physician, performed the external exam shortly after Peppy's death, and could supply medical analysis. He served as the Peace Corps doctor but was actually employed by the Public Health Service, a uniformed branch of the U.S. government. It is unclear whether his "non–Peace Corps" status made a more partisan role possible. McHugh explained later that he saw himself "as their [the Kinseys'] physician and having an advocacy responsibility to Bill, much as a lawyer, while keeping in mind that [this] advocacy required objectivity."[1] Among the documents he prepared for the defense were:

1. "Qualification of Charles T. McHugh"
2. "Statement of Personality Assessment of Bill Haywood Kinsey"
3. "Statement of Personal Relationship with Mr. & Mrs. Kinsey"
4. "Evaluation of Drugs—Relation to Unconscious Episode"
5. "Site of Accident—Relation to Injuries"
6. "Fractures—Cause and Effect—Intra-cranial Bleeding"
7. "Injuries"[2]

In his "Statement of Personal Relationship," McHugh described several meetings with the Kinseys in Maswa and Mwanza. The meetings included physical exams, inoculations and drug prescriptions, as well as long discussions on a wide variety of medical and nonmedical subjects. McHugh stated that from these interactions he could "find no evidence whatsoever to support any contention of marital discord or unhappiness. They were two vital people totally absorbed with each other and with the job they were doing."[3] McHugh's other reports were quite lengthy, detailed, and replete with medical terminology, so I summarize them here in nontechnical language.

Evaluation of Medications

The defense had developed the theory that Peppy, while on the tall rock, might have fainted, fallen down, and slid onto the rock below. To test this proposition, McHugh first evaluated the likelihood that Peppy had fainted and that certain medications she had been taking might have contributed to a loss of consciousness. He thought that the exertion of simply climbing the rock might have led to a fainting episode because excessive exertion under certain circumstances can be a contributing factor. In the months immediately before her death, the Kinseys' house had been infested with caterpillars, which caused severe reactions. Both Bill and Peppy were taking Benadryl to alleviate the itching, so McHugh examined the potential impact of the Benadryl. Peppy had apparently had a prior episode of fainting in their house in January 1966, which suggested to McHugh that she might be particularly sensitive to Benadryl. His evaluation of this medication included several studies indicating that dizziness, fatigue, lassitude, double vision, and hypotension were frequent side effects. In addition, Peppy had consumed a large bottle of Pilsner beer, with an alcohol content significantly higher than American beer. McHugh posited that the alcohol might increase the side effects of drugs, in particular Benadryl, increasing the likelihood that she may have experienced a sudden loss of consciousness.

After reviewing the timing of eating, drinking, and so on prior to the incident, McHugh concluded: "If it is assumed that the accident took place between 4 PM and 5 PM we have the situation of a potent drug (for Mrs. Kinsey) being potentiated by alcohol at the time when the drug would normally be exerting maximum effect, anyway, and at a time when that amount of alcohol can be found to be exerting a maximum influence."

Peppy had also been taking Aralen for malaria prevention and Gantrisin for an infection. McHugh concluded that neither drug would likely have played a role in Peppy's fainting, but that the Orthonovum (called Enovid by retail sellers) she was taking might have contributed to a loss of consciousness. McHugh reviewed recent studies showing that use of oral contraceptives, such as Orthonovum, had led to dizziness, unconsciousness, paralysis, visual abnormalities, and balance problems. He concluded, however, that the research was inconclusive and that the autopsies did not reveal evidence of any problems with the blood vessels of the brain.[4]

Wounds

McHugh made a detailed, precise analysis of Peppy's wounds. He first discussed them as they might support the prosecution's case and then why they did not. He followed Dr. Dockeray's designation of the wounds.

"There were a few superficial injuries of the body and the extremities. There were multiple gross injuries of the head." Dr. Mganga found eight head wounds, whereas Dr. Dockeray found twelve, along with some additional superficial abrasions. McHugh assumed the differences derived from the difficulty of locating the wounds "in the tangle of hair." Because the wounds were widely scattered, McHugh concluded that it would be unusual for them to have occurred in a single incident. This fact supported the prosecution contention that they had resulted from a struggle. All the wounds except one were deep cuts of the scalp penetrating to the skull. The exception was a large abraded area above the right ear. McHugh mentioned a third type of injury—a crush injury—that is likely to occur in a fall but was not present here. Such absence would also support the prosecution's case. He suggested that the iron bar could have caused incised wounds and that the large stone might have caused the abraded injury in the area of the skull and even caused a fracture. The two buttons missing from Bill's shirt supports the argument that a struggle had taken place.

One contention made by the prosecution and its medical witness that McHugh seemed to ignore is that if such a fall occurred, there should have been many more cuts and bruises to other parts of the body. The judge would later state that his own view aligned more with the prosecution's contention.

McHugh then proposed reasons why the injuries were unlikely to have been caused as the prosecution alleged. He started with a finding that all the wounds, except number 4 (see the numbering of the wounds in chapter 4), "were incised, well demarcated, scattered and surrounded by intact, normal

tissue," but they had not damaged the skull. Dr. Dockeray discovered four separate fractures and no other damage to the skull. The similarity of the wounds
suggested to McHugh that the force causing them was likely uniform, which
led him to conclude that they were unlikely the result of a fight and a man hitting Peppy. In a struggle, the wounds would likely vary in depth and placement
and be more uniform in alignment and closer together. In his experience, the
placement of wounds on a scalp gives a "good clue" to an assailant's position
relative to the assaulted person's position. Further analysis of the wounds
found that all the wounds were predominantly in the front and middle of the
scalp on the right side of Peppy's head. It would be extremely difficult for a
right-handed man, such as Bill, to cause such injuries if the victim were facing
him, as would be expected. (Although McHugh discounts an attack from
behind, such an event seems possible, but the injuries extended to the front of
the face, which would be difficult to accomplish from behind, so perhaps
McHugh is correct.)

In analyzing the role the alleged weapons may have played in the injuries,
Dr. McHugh started with the pipe, which had a "lip" at each end. Because no
wound contained an impression compatible with the expected injury that
would be caused by the pipe end, he felt there was little or no possibility that it
could have caused the injuries. The rock suspected of being used against Peppy
weighed almost eight pounds and measured 8 by 4¾ by 3⅝ by 2 inches.
McHugh felt that it was unlikely to fit comfortably in a man's hand, and the
resulting weak grasp would make it difficult to inflict repeated blows. It might
be used with two hands for a single blow, but that would cause wounds different than those found.

McHugh spent considerable time examining wound number 1, the par-
tial damage of the eye socket and the fracture of the base of Peppy's skull. He
observed that characteristics of the wound and fracture indicated that they
must have been caused by a fairly narrow, pointed object, so neither the pipe
nor the rock could have been the cause, and no other object had been identified that might have caused such a wound. He ended the memo with a review
of other factors that suggested an assault did not take place. In a struggle, a
woman will usually scratch the assailant as she tries to ward off blows with her
arms. No material was found under Peppy's nails, nor were characteristic skin
and soft-tissue injuries found on her arms, only a few small abrasions on the
palms and knuckles. Wounds to the scalp usually lead to profuse bleeding, and
McHugh would expect spotting on Bill and his clothes. There were large

splotches of blood rather than spots on his clothes, but these splotches would likely have been caused by direct contact with a bloody surface. "In summary, I think that a superficial examination of all the wounds of Mrs. Kinsey's body presents real grounds for the prosecution that an assault took place. However, *careful consideration of the evidence and inquiry into the necessary mechanics leads* [sic] *one to doubt that these injuries are compatable* [sic]*with the contention that they were inflicted by a man.*"[5] Although the wounds described in this section received McHugh's primary attention, he did examine and analyze each of the twelve wounds listed in chapter 4.

Skull Fractures

McHugh's final memo provided a medical-textbook analysis of the fractures of the skull found in Peppy's autopsies. He began with a review of the various recognized fractures, their likely causes, and their common resulting problems—for example, simple linear fracture, depressed fracture, open fracture, and the forces needed to cause them. He also reviewed fracture locations and the probability that they might cause internal bleeding and other complications.

He then examined four separate fractures of Peppy's skull. Number 1 was located in the roof of the right orbit (bony cavity around the eye), essentially on the right base of the skull. Number 2 was an 8-to-10-inch fracture running from the right sphenoid bone (behind the right eye) to where the suture (joint) of the right frontal and right parietal bone begins and from there along the suture over the top of the head and entering the left parietal bone, to the left side of the skull. Fractures number 3 and 4 were each about 2 inches long and found in the squamous plate above the temporal bone, which is behind the right ear. (The squamous is the thin upper portion of the temporal bone.) Once McHugh had described various forms of fracture and the placement of the four fractures to Peppy's skull, he proceeded to analyze each, what might have caused it, and the likelihood of its causing death.

Regarding fracture number 1, McHugh observed that it was starlike, radiating out from a central point. Only a sharp object would likely cause such a fracture. Although this wound did little damage to the skull, it lacerated several arteries, which might have caused severe hemorrhage. The injury could have slowly led to death, but because no vital functions were involved, it would not have been immediately life threatening. McHugh concluded that none of the objects claimed by the prosecution to have been used as weapons could have caused this injury. "There is no sharp or nearly sharp point [on these objects]. And there is no projection, which could have stuck out far enough to cause the extensive local damage without involving other facial structures as well."[6]

Fracture number 2 was an 8-to-10-inch-long nondepressed but clearly displaced complex fracture, including the separation of the suture between the frontal and the parietal bones. McHugh opined that the fracture was caused by substantial force on the right side of the head and that "the area of impact must have been great." He felt that the injury was unlikely to have been created while Peppy was either standing or lying down because her head would have moved in such a way to cause a different kind of injury. Similarly, he felt neither the pipe nor the rock would have caused this fracture because each also would have led to different kinds of wounds had it been applied with sufficient force. McHugh concluded that the wounds and fracture number 2 were most likely caused by Peppy falling head first down the rock and her skull striking the rocky surface below. Because this fracture crossed several arteries and the central venous sinus (large vein), it also could have resulted in severe hemorrhaging. The two fractures found behind the right ear both crossed the middle meningeal artery, which is quite close to the bone and so is easily torn when the bone is fractured at this location. Tearing of that artery could lead to catastrophic hemorrhaging in the cranium that may be rapidly but not immediately fatal. (The meninges are membranes covering the brain.)

McHugh concluded that fracture number 1 would not likely lead to immediate death, but the other three fractures, the result of severe blows and located in crucial places in the skull, could cause sufficient damage primarily to the skull and secondarily to the brain to lead to death.[7]

One medical issue that doesn't seem to have been discussed in any of the medical analyses is what is known in forensic medicine as a "coup" or "contra coup." In a coup injury, the head is stationary, and a blow would deform the head on the side of the blow. In the case of a contracoup, the injury results from the head striking a surface, and the damage appears on the opposite side of the head as a result of the brain slamming into the opposite side of the skull.[8] Such an analysis might have led to a definite conclusion as to whether Peppy's injuries were caused by a blow to the head or by a fall, with the head striking a rock.

On August 15, 1966, McHugh prepared his "Statement of Personality Assessment," in which he asserted that he knew of no mental illness or personality defect in Bill Kinsey, and from a review of all Peace Corps medical records he found no indication of any mental or personality issues for Bill. McHugh stated in this memo that he "would testify that before and at the time of Mrs. Kinsey's death Mr. Kinsey was in a normal and healthy mental state."[9]

Byron Georgiadis revealed many years later that he was worried at the time about a possible reaction to the use of Benadryl, which Dr. McHugh did not discuss. According to Georgiadis, there are indications that excessive use over a period of time may lead to personality changes. Could Bill Kinsey have been a victim of such a reaction? In the end, the issue was never raised at trial. In his speech in 2007, Georgiadis also took a swipe at what he thought was the oversupplying of drugs to the volunteers: "Peace Corps sends its members to darkest Africa with a cubic yard each [of] a number of possible medicines and pills plus instructions, 'just in case.'"[10]

Kinsey-Dennett *Nuptials*

MRS. BILL HAYWOOD KINSEY, JR.

—Photo By Juliet Newman

Peppy Kinsey, wedding photo (*Old Greenwich Village Gazette* [Conn.], December 17, 1964)

Except where noted, photos are from the author's collection.

Maswa street scene (Phil Ellison Collection)

Scene of Peppy's death, Impala Hill, Maswa (Peace Corps files)

Kopje near Maswa (Phil Ellison Collection)

Mwanza Hotel, Mwanza

Mwanza market, Mwanza

Dar es Salaam Harbor

New Africa Hotel, Dar es Salaam

Maswa Court, Maswa (Getty Images)

Peter Kateti (left), assistant superintendent of police and prosecutor at the preliminary inquiry, and Martin Kifunta, inspector, CID (Getty Images)

Mwanza Harbor and High Court, Mwanza

Byron Georgiadis, defense attorney (photo by Duncan Whitfield)

Peace Corps Book Locker, with Peace Corps director Sargent Shriver at center (courtesy John F. Kennedy Presidential Library and Museum, Boston)

19

The Trial Begins in Mwanza

The Judge entered the court wearing a red robe and with a white wig on his head.

—*Tony Essaye, trial notes*

On Friday, August 26, 1966, the trial of Bill Kinsey for the murder of his wife, Peverley (Peppy) Kinsey, began in a courtroom of the Tanzania High Court in Mwanza. The court was a relatively new one-story building about 100 yards from the shore of Lake Victoria. It was located near the main Mwanza harbor, with the police, customs, and other government buildings nearby. The courtroom for the trial seated about forty persons, and for most days of the trial it was full. Since the courthouse was built by the British while they ruled the country, the courtroom generally followed a British arrangement. The judge sat in front, with the two assessors next to him. There was a witness box next to the judge and a table for the prosecution and one for the defense between the judge and the public gallery. Because the trial was a murder case, at least one policeman was in the room. The court clerk and reporter sat in the front between the judge and counsel tables. Once Bill Kinsey was brought in, he sat with defense counsel at their table.

Mwanza seemed to be filled with reporters, lawyers, and Peace Corps officials. Tony Essaye was in the courtroom gallery every day taking notes for the Peace Corps. His notes became an important record of the proceedings during the trial. Dr. Tom McHugh attended once the judge approved his attendance. I visited the trial on several days, and when I could not attend, Dick Brooke-Edwards gave me a report at the end of the day. He had become friends with

John Oliver and me at a café in Mwanza and wound up living with us for several weeks. Brooke-Edwards was born in America but lived in England until age sixteen. He came to Tanganyika with his mother, Lady Marion Chesham, and her husband, Lord Chesham (see chapter 6). While living with me in Mwanza, he became obsessed with the Kinsey trial and spent every day in court. He planned to write about the trial but apparently never produced a publishable manuscript. In 1968, he authored an eloquent defense of the Masai tribe's way of life in the African magazine *Transition*. His brief biography accompanying the article stated that he "is working on a book based on the Peace Corps murder in Tanzania."[1] In 2015, I undertook a search for Dick Brooke-Edwards. After much digging, the search took me to a member of the family of the earl of Carrick, who reported that his uncle Dick had died in the early 1980s. At the same time, I located Professor Alistair Ross of London Metropolitan University, who informed me that he had contacted Brooke-Edwards at the end of 1973 after obtaining his current address from his half-brother, the earl of Carrick. Ross was seeking Lady Chesham's papers, which Brooke-Edwards had inherited. Ross told me that Brooke-Edwards wrote back to him on January 1, 1974, with a report "that he had just completed a novel based on the murder trial (he describes it as a novel written in semi-fictional style!). He wrote that he attended all eighteen days of the trial in Mwanza, and visited Bill Kinesy [*sic*] 'many times' in prison." Brooke-Edwards, then living in Ibiza, asked Ross "to pay his fare from Ibiza and put him up in London" while he looked for a publisher. Although Ross did not help him with book publishing, he did arrange for the Chesham papers to be donated to the University of York, which paid Brooke-Edwards one hundred pounds.[2]

The defense team was made up of Byron Georgiadis of Nairobi and Gurbachan Singh of Mwanza. During the trial, Georgiadis would fly to Mwanza every Sunday afternoon and fly back to Nairobi every Friday night. Carroll Brewster, American lawyer and Yale Law School lecturer, was involved but unable to sit at the defense table because he was not admitted to practice in Tanzania. Before the trial began, Bill's attorneys had worked diligently to obtain permission from the judge to allow Dr. McHugh to attend the trial before testifying so he could evaluate the medical testimony. Generally, witnesses are not allowed to be present in the court before they testify.[3]

The prosecution was led by Senior State Attorney Ededen Effiwat and State Attorney George Leuridi. Ededen Effiwat was a Nigerian attorney under contract with the Tanzania government to serve as a senior prosecutor. Although he had limited experience trying cases, because of the shortage of Tanzania attorneys he filled a fairly senior position. The prosecution and defense attorneys were dressed in black robes and white wigs. Georgiadis seemed unhappy with the wig-and-robe requirement in hot, humid Mwanza; that custom was no longer required in Kenya.[4] My research has provided no additional information on the two state attorneys. At the beginning of the trial, the prosecution had reason to be quite confident of winning their case. They had not only the classic factors of a successful prosecution—means, motive, and opportunity—but also several eyewitnesses to the events and medical support for a finding of guilty. In their minds, convincing evidence was clearly available.

Judge Harold Platt, a forty-one-year-old British national, although born in Bangalore, India, entered the court in a red robe and with a white wig on his head. Court observers had expected that Judge Erokwu, a Nigerian, would preside over the case. No explanation for the change was given. Paul Sack thought that Platt was chosen because of his superior legal knowledge, long experience, and the governments' desire to ensure the trial was conducted in the most professional manner to avoid potential political issues. Platt had apparently approached Attorney General Mark Bomani several times requesting that he not be assigned the case, but his pleas were obviously ignored.[5]

Judge Platt was educated in India at Breeks Memorial School in Ootacamund (one of the famous "hill towns" of the British Raj), served in the Royal Air Force from 1942 to 1947 in India and Rhodesia, and received a jurisprudence degree from St. Peter's College, Oxford University, in 1950. At St. Peter's, he was president of the Athletics Club and competed at the university level. In 1952, he was called to the bar and practiced law until 1954, when he moved to Tanganyika, where he served in the colonial legal service from 1954 to 1962. He sat as a provincial High Court judge in Tanzania from 1962 to 1972. Judge Platt's father had been a clergyman in India, and his mother was an American living in the United States at the time of the Kinsey trial.[6]

Judge Platt was followed in by the two "assessors": Missourian Gail Bagley, a forty-six-year-old American soil-conservation expert, and Fred Mugobi, a twenty-seven-year-old native of Mwanza who had recently returned to Tanzania after studying in the United States, where he had obtained a degree in economics from the University of Wisconsin. Bill's attorney, Gurbachan Singh, had pressed the court early on for the assessors to be Americans but not missionaries, medical personnel, or Peace Corps volunteers. When the assessors were announced, it was clear that the court had largely met Singh's request.

Some confusion had developed on the appointment of assessors for the case. Newspaper reports indicated that the assessors needed to be from the same race or tribe as the accused and that a number of "white" people in the Mwanza area had been contacted. They also suggested that the defendant had to approve of the assessors before they could be confirmed. Paul Sack cabled PCDC to say that these statements were untrue. He reported that the procedure required the administrative secretary in the Office of the Regional Commission to submit names to the judge, who would make the final decision. It appears that government officials and the court had worked hard to make sure the assessors were acceptable to both the prosecution and the defense, who approved them.[7]

Gail Bagley had graduated from Colorado A&M University and worked for the U.S. Department of Agriculture in Missouri and Iowa. In 1965, he read a notice from the Near East Foundation, which was looking for agriculture experts to work in East Africa. With his wife's encouragement, he responded to the notice, was selected, and sent to Tanzania. He had never previously worked overseas. In Tanzania, he was employed by the Tanzania government under a grant from the Near East Foundation. The Tanzania Ministry of Agriculture assigned him to a research station about ten miles south of Mwanza, the Ukiriguru Agricultural Institute. When Bagley had been in Tanzania for three or four months, his boss, the regional agricultural officer, an Irishman, came to him and said he was to be an assessor in a court case in Mwanza. The officer told him the date and where to go in Mwanza. After the case was over, the officer told Bagley he didn't think the case would last so long, or he wouldn't have asked him to serve. At the time of the trial, Bagley was living alone; however, after about six months his family joined him. He stayed in Tanzania for two years but has never gone back.[8]

As mentioned previously, Fred Mugobi had recently returned from the United States.[9] By the end of the 1950s, with impetus from the conflict between Russia and America in the Cold War, efforts were made to bring East African college students to America to study; however, in the early 1960s it was still unusual for a Tanzanian to study in the United States.

A key institution in this effort was the African American Student Foundation (AASF), which was established through the efforts of American industrialist William Scheinman and Kenyan labor official Tom Mboya. Because Russia and China were luring Africans with scholarships, some Americans thought it vital for the United States to do the same. The U.S. government had helped a small number of Africans to come to America to study, but in 1959 the AASF planned to bring a planeload of more than eighty students from East Africa, mainly from Kenya. One of the students who came that year to the University of Hawaii was Barack Obama Sr., President Obama's father.[10] From 1959 to 1963, the AASF brought more than eight hundred East African students to America, including Wangari Maathai, who would become the first African woman to receive the Nobel Peace Prize.[11] Fred Mugobi was also supported by the foundation.

Funding to expand the number of African students brought to America became an issue in the American presidential election of 1960. The AASF had sought funding from the State Department for several years but had been denied. Tom Mboya, a Kenya labor official, was in the United States for a conference and flew to Hyannisport, Massachusetts, to meet with Jack Kennedy. After the meeting, Kennedy arranged for the Kennedy Foundation to fund the airlift from Africa. At about the same time, an official from the Nixon campaign convinced the State Department to fund the program; however, the AASF had already accepted funding from the Kennedy Foundation before the State Department acted. The Nixon campaign and Republican senator Hugh Scott accused Kennedy of sneakily taking the project away from the U.S. government. Eventually, in 1963, the program was brought under State Department administration.[12]

Fred Mugobi's time in the United States demonstrates that even with a scholarship and transportation supplied, students still faced financial difficulties. In April 1961, while he was working for the Victoria Federation of Cooperative Unions in Mwanza, he wrote to the president of the AASF with a plea for help: "The problem now confronting me is to get money to cover all necessary expenses which is [sic] required by the school. As I do not have finance nor have I a reliable supporter while I am out for studies, I have found it unavoidable to appeal to you."[13]

Gail Bagley and Fred Mugobi were charged with the heavy responsibility of giving Judge Platt their opinion of whether the prosecution had made its case that Bill Kinsey was guilty of murdering his wife.

20

Trial Day One

Friday, August 26, 1966

Not guilty, my lord.
—*Bill Kinsey*

At the outset, Judge Platt gave the assessors a brief explanation of what to expect and told them that they should talk to no one about the case during the trial. The assessors received no further instructions until the end of the trial, when the judge summarized the case and asked them to leave the courtroom and come back with a verdict. Each day during the trial, Gail Bagley drove to the court in the morning and drove back to the Agricultural Institute in the evening. When I spoke with him in 2012, he was ninety-one years old and living in Colorado. He said I was the first person to ask him about the case. No one talked to him about it after the trial—not the press, not the judge, not the Peace Corps.[1]

Once Judge Platt and the assessors were seated, a police officer escorted Bill Kinsey into the dock. Kinsey looked pale after five months in prison. He wore a single-breasted, light-weight green suit. Judge Platt read the charge of murder to him and then asked, "What is your plea?"

"Not guilty, my lord."

"Do you understand the charge?"

"Yes, my lord."

One newspaper account described Bill as a tall, slim, bespectacled young man who appeared calm during the proceedings, taking notes and passing them to his defense team.

Judge Platt then informed the assessors they were expected to listen carefully, decide issues of fact, and determine whether the accused was guilty or not guilty. They could consider only the evidence given in court.[2]

Next the judge addressed a procedural issue raised by the prosecutor, who objected to a defense medical expert, Dr. Tom McHugh, being present in the courtroom while the prosecution medical expert testified. Judge Platt had prepared a written analysis and decision on the objection and proceeded to read the document. He found that there was legal authority to allow the defense witness to be present and that it was a matter for the judge's discretion under Tanzania law. He ruled that the witness could be present, but that his testimony had to be carefully evaluated to ensure that he addressed only the medical issues that were directly asked of him.[3]

Interestingly, Tom McHugh lived next door to Judge Platt in Mwanza. The judge's house had a squash court, which McHugh had used on occasion prior to the trial. McHugh remembers going there most days after the trial proceedings and playing rigorous, exhaustive, aggressive squash against Byron Georgiadis. Although in Britain barristers from the same chambers may serve as prosecution and defense attorneys in the same trial, and there may be some connection between a sitting judge, a defense attorney, and a potential witness, in the United States it would be unusual and perhaps unethical for the attorney and a witness in a trial to use a facility for recreation at the judge's home. That the judge was an occasional, enthusiastic witness of the squash matches would raise even more ethical and procedural issues. McHugh and Georgiadis discussed the issue, but because the judge seemed untroubled, they decided to leave it alone.[4] Either the prosecution was unaware of these facts, or they chose to ignore them and continue the trial rather than challenging the proceeding as being tainted by a conflict of interest.

As the trial proceeded, the judge made handwritten, copious notes in the trial book, which made for a very slow process.[5] I have obtained a copy of the transcript of the PI, and I assume there was a transcript of the trial, but I have been unable to locate it. I did contact a friend in Tanzania, who contacted a High Court judge and was told that the files no longer existed. Therefore, my description of the trial and quotations from it come from what I have pieced together from news articles, the detailed notes Tony Essaye took, Georgiadis's later lecture on the trial, Peace Corps cables, and the PI transcript.

Once the court completed the preliminary matters, Senior State Attorney Effiwat made his opening statement outlining the prosecution case.

[The defendant] beat his wife to death with an iron bar and a stone, on March 27, the day after he made an entry in his diary which tended to say she had been unfaithful to him. . . . On or about March 26 defendant wrote in his diary, "She had been obliged to reply she could not really know if anything unusual had happened until about March 27."

On that "fateful day," [the] defendant induced his wife to go with him for a picnic, and in a picnic basket he had concealed a piece of iron wrapped in a towel. They had ridden their bicycles to lonely, rock strewn Impala Hill, two miles from their school.

Once there, Kinsey had taken his wife between two huge boulders where he had set upon her, beating her on the head with the piece of iron. There was fierce fighting between them but Peverley was soon overpowered. Apart from the piece of iron, he also made use of a stone against Peverley.[6]

(It was the police and prosecution position that Bill and Peppy never climbed to the top of the rock. All the action took place below where the witnesses saw what appeared to be a fight.)

The first witness called by the prosecution was the AMO for Maswa, Philip Mganga. Mganga's testimony generally followed the narrative he had supplied at the preliminary hearing in Maswa. When the prosecutor asked him about his medical background, he reported that he had no formal medical qualifications but had successfully completed an AMO course at the Muhimbili Hospital in Dar es Salaam and before that had attended the medical assistant's course at the Sewa Haji Hospital in Dar es Salaam from January 1946 to December 1948. He had then worked as a medical assistant with various government departments for seven years until he was promoted to senior medical assistant and held that rank until 1961. In 1961, he completed the AMO course and was promoted to AMO. He testified that he had been specializing in medicolegal work since 1961 and had been stationed at Maswa Hospital since June 1961.

Effiwat then asked Mganga to describe the postmortem he performed on Peverley Kinsey.

Mganga stated that on March 28, 1966, Inspector Kifunta and Father Charles Liberatore accompanied him to the Maswa Mortuary, where they identified a body as that of Peverley Kinsey. Inspector Kifunta presented Mganga with an order to carry out a postmortem. In his testimony, Mganga relied on the written report he had completed and signed shortly after completing the postmortem.

He described the wounds as follows:

There was a wound on right parietal region which was about 3" long and ½" deep, and which exposed the bone. There was another wound on the top of the head which was 2" long and ½" deep. There was another wound on the occipital region which was 3" long and ½" deep. There was a lacerated wound of irregular shape on the left temporal region which was about 2" long and 1" deep. There were two smaller wounds over the left side of the had-left [sic] temporal. The wound on the right parietal region was slanting upwards. The wound on the top of the head was across the top of the head going horizontaly [sic] across. The wound on the occipital region went from side to side and was mostly on the right side. The two wounds on the left side were above the left ear and were slanting, pointing upward.[7]

He went on to report that on the skull itself there was a fissured fracture about 4 inches long over the left temporal bone and extended on to the occipital bone. There was also a depressed fracture of the right temporal bone about 2 inches in diameter.

Mganga then testified that he examined the brain and found about 2 ccs of free blood within the skull. The blood was oozing from two small pin points on the top of the brain. He found blood in the subdural area of the left temporal region of the brain and subdural hemorrhages on the right temporal and right occipital regions of the brain. (Georgiadis later observed that because Mganga found so little blood, no one believed he could gauge or quantify it properly.[8])

The testimony continued with a report of additional wounds, including a 4-inch fissured fracture of the right frontal bone; a wound on the right eyebrow, which was about 3 inches long and ½ inch deep running from the socket of the eye upward; a small contused wound on the right upper eyelid and two superficial bruises on the right arm; and a superficial bruise on the back of the right hand. He also found that the right upper central incisor tooth was missing, and there was some blood in the socket.

After the completion of this account, Prosecutor Effiwat asked Mganga if he had come to any conclusions about how the injuries would have come about. Mganga was silent for a moment while he reviewed his notes from the postmortem. He then responded that he had come to some conclusions.

He began with some body measurements:

> The body was well built and well nourished. She would have weighed around 120 lbs. She was 5'2" tall. I took no other body measurements. [Dockeray found she was 5 feet 7 inches tall.]
>
> With these injuries, and considering her general build, I should think that if she were physically to [have] exerted herself in any manner she would have passed out within a very short time of receiving the injuries, but I cannot give an estimate in minutes. Had she fallen down or sat down intently [sic] after receiving the injuries, she could not, in my opinion, in view of the extent of the injuries and injuries to the brain have stood up as she would not have been able to co-ordinate her activities. She could have called out names or shouted for help and would, until she had passed out, be oriented towards places and persons immediately near her. There would be a numb feeling that would over come [sic] her the instant she receives those injuries. That numbness would gradually merge with a state of unconsciousness. For a few minutes the subconscious would work and she would possibly cry out or mention names until she passes into a coma.[9]

He thought she might have been beaten, perhaps by a blunt stick, club, stone, or iron bar. He continued:

> I would say no to the question; [w]hether these injuries were caused by anything sharp or pointed. To cause those fractures a fairly good amount of force was used. I do not think that these injuries all occurred at the same time, but I think occurred one by one. These injuries are not compatible with a fall. The reason is that a fall would cause a gross fracture at one place and the surrounding area of the skull bone would show depressed contused fractures. The head falling on a rock surface would produce a contused wound and a contused fracture because in a fall, if the fall is continuous, the area of the head coming in contact with the rock surface, would be small and pass over quickly. She died as a result of a cerebral hemorrhage resulting from a fractured skull.[10]

After the iron bar and stone had been introduced into evidence and shown to Mganga, he responded that the bar could have caused the injury to the head, and the rock could have caused the injuries on the side of the head. He felt the injuries were caused by "violence" and by a fairly strong force. He considered that there was no other possibility. Mganga said he had seen injuries caused by a fall. In such case, he would expect gross injuries to one side, especially over the most prominent areas of the body—top of the head, the shoulders, and the side of the body.

Mganga went on to testify that when later that same day he examined Bill Kinsey, he found bruises on the knees, a bruise on the left leg, scratches on the palm of his hand, and a bruise in the lumbar region. He also testified that during the exam the accused did not seem excited. In conclusion, he opined that the injuries likely occurred within one or two days of the exam.

Effiwat said he had no further questions.

The judge then asked Mganga to tell him the number of fractures.

Mganga stated, "There were three fissured fractures and one depressed fracture."

Defense counsel Georgiadis began his cross-examination by asking Mganga to again review his medical qualifications. Mganga described the courses he had taken and the various medical positions he had obtained.

Georgiadis: "So you have no medical degree whatsoever. In fact, you are neither a doctor nor a pathologist. Is that correct?"

Mganga: "Yes, that is correct."

Georgiadis proceeded carefully to take Mganga through each of his findings from his postmortem. In doing so, Georgiadis laid the groundwork for later undercutting the accuracy of Mganga's testimony.

During the cross-examination, Georgiadis challenged a number of Mganga's findings and his anatomical descriptions. In particular, he asked Mganga about his description of fractures and said, "Were these not in fact sections of the brain which had sprung apart rather than fractures?"

Mganga acknowledged that this was likely the case.

Georgiadis asked him about the discrepancy between his measurement of Peppy's height and Dr. Dockeray's measurement.

Mganga responded, "She might have been curled up."

Georgiadis asked him about a number of other injuries and bruises found around the mouth, nose, and right eye. Mganga admitted that he might have missed these items.

Georgiadis then said, "I put it to you that you don't know what you are talking about."

Mganga replied, "I might have forgotten my anatomy."

Georgiadis went on to ask whether the head injuries could cause a victim to become violent.

Mganga agreed that a violent reaction would be possible.

Georgiadis asked, "Could not the cause of death been from shock and concussion to the brain as a result of head injuries, and not, as you had earlier stated in your postmortem, from cerebral hemorrhage?"

Mganga answered, "Yes, that is possible."

Georgiadis asked, "Isn't it likely that the injuries were caused by falling on the rocks?"

Mganga said, "No, they were probably inflicted by a blunt instrument as I had said before." That ended Mganga's testimony.[11]

That same day Dr. Tom McHugh provided defense counsel with a detailed point by point analysis of Mganga's testimony. Fortunately for the defense, Judge Platt had permitted McHugh to remain in court while Mganga testified. McHugh's clear, well-reasoned, and comprehensive approach is evident in his analysis, which ran to more than eight pages, with thirty-four separate comments on Mganga's testimony. I provide the most relevant sections here.

1. He [Mganga] testified that there was a fissured fracture 4" long over the right frontal bone.

There was a fracture of approximately 4" length in the line of the right fronto-parietal suture, ascending from the side of the head to the midline, not, as he has said, ascending from the right eyebrow toward the vertex. I would guess that he may have seen the fracture under the right eyebrow and postulated that it ran up the exterior aspect of the skull. Or, this may be a fabrication of his. Very careful examination of the frontal bone has revealed no fracture and no other marking, aside from the suture separation. . . .

7. He says that a fall would cause injuries of one area or over one side of the body. This may be so but a fall is a pretty random thing which may cause injury anywhere. Also, the injuries do not have to be confined to one part of the body. Beside the position of the body, the topography of the area will be an important factor in determining the location and the severity of the injuries.

8. Asked what kind of injuries would result from a fall he answered that the injuries would include gross contusions, large area bruises, and large area fractures.

Contusions and bruises are the same thing. Fractures may be, in my opinion, of any type and severity, depending on the positions, stresses, etc. I would say that any type of injury from superficial to mortal from slight to severe, would be possible following a fall. . . .

16. He states that the scratches on the palm(s) of Mr. Kinsey's hand(s) would have been the result of "a hard object which chaffed the hand" or "scratches from fingernails."

I agree with his contention that they could have been resultant from contact with a hard object which chaffed the hands. However, their punctate (with dots or points) nature rules out a skidding type of contact. It also rules out a wrenching type of contact such as might be seen if a rock twisted in the hand during landing of a blow or if the lipped end of a pipe was held in the hand and twisted due to the same reason. The injuries are more in keeping with falling on a rough surface, as from a standing position—with little forward momentum. The scratches are hardly compatible with injuries sustained from being scratched with fingernails. . . .

17. The Judge asked the number of fractures. He answered that there were three fissured fractures and one depressed fracture.

He has said that there was one depressed fracture. I assume that he is referring to the depressed fracture found in the right temporal region. If this is so, that accounts for my fractures 3 and 4. Then I cannot account for his finding of three linear fractures. I would call the springing of the fronto-parietal suture a single fracture from its farthest right to its farthest left extreme. I would call the linear fracture of the left temporal and parietal bones a second fracture. However, he denies that the suture was sprung or fractured. He cannot easily refer to the fracture of the right orbit and orbital plate as one or two fractures. In the first place, he denies that they exist. In the second place, they are of the penetrating or depressed variety.

He claims a fracture of the right frontal bone, extending superiorly from the right orbital ridge and, presumably underlying the incised wound of the right mid-frontal area. (I claim from my examination of the skull that this fracture did not exist). If he claims this as a second linear fracture, then he has still not accounted for one fracture. The only possibility I can think of is that he has counted one of the fractures defining the depressed fracture as being one linear fracture. A fracture cannot be fitted into more than one category at a time. . . .

22. He gave the height of the body as 5' 2". He says that he measured this with a tape measure. When pressed he states that he only estimated the dimensions of the head wounds because he did not have a measure.

A curious inconsistency. He was wrong by 5" in his measuring of the height of the body with his tape measure. I don't understand why he did not think to measure the wounds of the head with the same tape measure with which he determined the length of the body. . . .

24. He says that the sutures of the top of the head are natural and that there was no fracture along the suture line.

He is obviously mistaken as the fronto-parietal suture is well sprung for almost the entirety of its length as it crosses the skull from one side to the other. I am afraid that the trouble lies in the belief by Dr. Mganga that the suture line is normally lying open so he has not recognized this very gross fracture for what it really is. . . .

28. He was asked how much blood he found clotted in each of the hemorrhage sites. For each of the subdural clots of the left and right temporal and occipital areas and for the epidural clot in the vault (top) of the skull he estimated 2cc.

This is an unimaginative and uninformed answer from a man unwilling to say I don't know and unwilling to be forced to guess. These amounts are virtually insignificant as far as the normal functioning of the brain is concerned. . . .

This amount could be all that there was in each of these locations. Significant and mortal changes in brain function can probably result from blows to the head with no intracranial blood loss, but it is not common. . . .

In common clinical useage [sic], 2cc of blood would not be considered to fit the definition of hemorrhage. . . .

34. He stated that in his opinion, shock and concussion and hemorrhage are all one in the same thing.

This simply is not so. I would attribute this mainly to a man who is down and knows it and simply no longer cares.[12]

Much of Dr. McHugh's analysis was included in the memos he authored for the defense before the trial. Since Mganga's testimony at trial in large measure followed his testimony at the preliminary inquiry, McHugh had been able to base his earlier analysis on this testimony. The memo he created on August 26 came after Mganga's testimony on the first day of the trial, and it would be very helpful to the defense in constructing their questioning of Dr. Dockeray, Dr. McHugh, and an additional head-wound specialist and to allow the defense to rebut and cast doubt on Mganga's testimony.

It is curious that the first witness for the prosecution was the AMO, whereas at the PI Inspector Kifunta was the first witness. It would seem logical and more persuasive to start with Kifunta, so that he could recount the events on Impala Hill, and then follow up with the medical testimony to demonstrate the results of the alleged beating. Even though the PI case was presented by a police officer rather than a state attorney, that officer chose what seems the more compelling narrative by beginning with Kifunta.

Father Charles Liberatore was sworn in as the next witness, and he testified that he had gone to the hospital and identified the body.

Corporal Silashi was called and described how and where he had found a blood-stained stone in a crevice under some bushes near the site of the incident. He had to cut down the bushes in order to get the stone out. He was shown the stone, he identified it, and it was introduced into evidence. Silashi was also asked to identify photos taken by Peter Katiti, the CID regional director. Silashi made the identification, and the photos were marked as exhibits. Sergeant Thomas was also called as a witness to describe how and where he had found a blood-stained piece of pipe at the scene of the incident. He was shown the pipe, which he identified, and it was introduced into evidence. At this point, the court adjourned for the day.[13]

The trial was not immune from the Cold War conflict between the Soviet Union and the United States, as shown in a report, dateline Moscow, filed on August 26 by the United Press International:

UPI—37

(PEACE CORPS)

MOSCOW—THE TANZANIA TRIAL OF PEACE CORPS WORKER WILLIAM HAYWOOD KINSEY, CHARGED WITH BEATING HIS WIFE TO DEATH, "WAS THE LAST DROP IN THE BUCKET FOR THE TANZANIANS INCENSED BY THE

NUMEROUS CASES OF DISGRACEFUL CONDUCT BY 'PEACE CORPS' VOLUNTEERS," TASS SAID TODAY.

UNDER A DAR-ES-SALAAM DATELINE, TASS SAID THE NEWSPAPER ZANZIBAR VOICE WROTE THAT THE U. S. ADMINISTRATION HAS BEEN TRYING TO CONVINCE THE AFRICAN COUNTRIES THAT THE PEACE CORPS IS AN INSTRUMENT OF AID TO DEVELOPING COUNTRIES.

"IN REALITY, HOWEVER, 'PEACE CORPS' VOLUNTEERS LACK ELEMENTARY EDUCATION AND TRAINING TO BE OF ANY HELP," TASS QUOTED THE NEWSPAPER AS SAYING. IT REPORTED THE NEWSPAPER SUGGESTED REVISING THE ATTITUDE TOWARD THE PEACE CORPS AND ASKING THE VOLUNTEERS "TO CLEAR OUT OF THE COUNTRY."

8/26—TD1037AED[14]

A somewhat similar charge had been reported in Tanzania newspapers when my own Peace Corps group of teachers arrived in Dar es Salaam in December 1964. An article in the *University Echo,* a newspaper produced by students at University College in Dar es Salaam, claimed that most Peace Corps volunteers were members of the CIA.[15] One method the United States employed to counter some of the anti-American sentiments was to send famous American jazz musicians to tour around Africa in what became known as "jazz diplomacy."[16] While I was in Mwanza in 1966, Woody Herman and his big band, the Herd, appeared at a local venue and played to a sold-out audience.

21

Trial Day Two

Saturday, August 27, 1966

Kinsey Had Blood Stains on Clothes, Says Witness.
—*Nairobi Sunday News*

At the opening of the session on Saturday, August 27, the judge informed counsel that the court might call its own expert witnesses if deemed necessary. He also asked the prosecution and defense to agree on medical sources that the judge and the assessors could consult.[1]

CID inspector Martin Kifunta was the first witness to be sworn in that morning. (Although this chapter covers the same testimony as provided in chapter 13, there are important differences, especially in the prosecution's examination, which did not take place at the preliminary inquiry.) The prosecuting attorney asked Kifunta to describe the events on the day Peppy Kinsey died. Kifunta testified that an African had come to the police station and told him a woman was dead on Maswa Hill, so he went there, and when he arrived, he found about one hundred people surrounding the defendant. When Kifunta asked him about his clothes, Kinsey said that his wife had fallen from a rock and that his clothes became bloodstained when he tried to help her. After this explanation, Kinsey led Kifunta to the body, which Kifunta found covered with a green towel and near a number of objects: a bottle, a book, a bottle opener, some cigars, and a headband. These items were produced in the courtroom, marked as exhibits, and entered into evidence. The book found was *Little Big Man,* and it was bloodstained, with the pages stuck together. Kifunta went on to testify that he and several policemen searched the area, where they found pieces of a beer bottle and a small pool of blood near where Kinsey said his wife had fallen. They also found a metal pipe with blood and what looked like some tufts of hair on it. Kinsey told him that the pipe was part of some camera equipment he was assembling, but that he did not know how it had become bloodstained.

Kifunta said that he had taken the defendant back to Maswa and searched his house. After the search, he took Kinsey's bloodstained clothes and left him with the local priest, Father Bob Lefebvre, with whom Kinsey spent the night. Kifunta told him to report to the police station in the morning, where Kinsey showed up with Father Bob at 8:00 a.m., at which time Kifunta arrested him and told him he believed Kinsey had murdered his wife.

To appreciate the nature of the prosecution's development of its case, it is useful to provide a portion of the examination of Inspector Kifunta. A transcript of his direct examination by the prosecution includes the following questions and answers:[2]

Q: How long have you been an [sic] Maswa Police Station as an A. S.
P. (Assistant Superintendent of Police)?

A: Since December 1964.

Q: How long have you known the deceased?

A: Since 1965 as a teacher in Binza School in Maswa.

Q: Did you see the accused on March 27th, 1966?

A: Yes.

Q: Under what circumstances did you see the accused?

A: I saw the accused on a hill where I was summoned, where a fight
had taken place.

Q: In what part of the district was this?

A: This was in the Maswa district about two miles from the village
of Maswa.

Q: Who told you to go to this place?

A: Corporal John, a police officer called me out and asked me to go
to this place. I called all available officers together and we went.

Q: Did you go alone, that is, were there any other civilians there that
went with you?

A: Yes, a Roman Catholic priest, Father Charles was at that time in
the office and he and another man, a Padre Masunsu, were also
there. . . .

A: I arrived at the hill about 5:30 . . . and I saw a group of Africans.

Q: What is the name of this place?

A: The name of the place is Malampala Village.

Q: How many people did you see when you arrived at this place?

A: There were about 100 people or over at this place.

Q: What were they doing?

A: They were looking after the accused and waiting for the police. . . .

Q: What did you do when you met the accused?

A: I asked him where is your wife?

He said, over there and led me to her.

Q: Since when did you know her?

A: I knew her . . . since 1965 when they moved to Maswa.

Q: In what state did you see Mr. Kinsey's wife?

A: She was dead with her head leaning on a rock [demonstrating]. . . .

Q: Apart from the body, what else did you see?

A: I saw a basket near the body and in it there was an empty beer bottle and opener, reading book, a packet of cigars, and a green headband. . . .

Q: Where did you take them? Where did you put them, keep them?

A: I kept them in the police store until the P. I. when I produced them in the court in Maswa. . . .

Q: Did you make an examination of the hill?

A: Yes, I made an examination of the hill. I went to the second place after I saw the body, where I was sent by the accused. I was directed by the accused to this place.

Q: Did he say why you should go there?

A: Yes, he said it was where his wife had fallen.

Q: Did he tell you what sort of a fall it was?

A: Yes, he said she slipped off the edge of the rock and fell down. . . .

Q: Did you see the rock from which he at that time said that his wife had fallen?

A: I did.

Q: Were you able to examine the rock?

A: Yes.

Q: Can you describe it to the court?

A: The place where the accused sent me is on top of the rock. It is a flat rock. It is roughly flat on top of the rock and has a sudden depression in the direction where the wife fell. There is a sudden drop on the edge of the rock.

Q: Did you take the circumference of the rock?

A: No.

Q: Can you compare it with something?

A: I think it had a diameter of 5 to 6 feet.

Q: How was the top of the surface?

A: It was a smooth surface. . . .

Q: At this time, although it was growing dark, what were the rest of the officers doing?

A: I made an order to have them look around to see what we could find which may relate to the incident. After about 8 minutes search, Sargent Thomas made an alarm in Swahili. "Sir, here is a piece of iron." So I went to the place where he was standing with a piece of metal pipe in his hand. I looked on the pipe and I noticed that it was covered with fresh blood and some thred [*sic*] like things that looked like hairs were sticking to the blood. The accused was present and I asked him if he knew anything about that.

Q: Did he give an answer?

A: Yes, the accused said that the pipe was part of his camera stand. I asked him further as to how and why blood stains and he said "I wouldn't know." I then marked the place where the detective picked up the metal so I could measure the distance later.

Kifunta took Bill and several officers back to the scene the next day to continue the search. The examination continued, focusing on the second visit to the hill:

Q: Was anything discovered in the search?

A: Yes, Corporal Silas[hi] made an alarm in Swahili saying, "Yes sir, here is a piece of stone with blood on it." I went there immediately. He pointed to a stone and I looked at it, there was a small stone of this size. It was at a space between two rocks, covered in red black blood. I told Corporal to take and give it to me. Corp. Thomas [*sic*] picked up the stone and gave it to me. When I examined the stone, I saw fresh blood and threads like hair over it.

Kifunta told the court that after the search on the hill they returned to the Kinseys' house, where he searched again. During the latter search, he found a diary that Bill had kept. He took the diary with him when he left.[3] At this point, the court adjourned for the day.

In his notes for the trial, Tony Essaye wrote a reminder to himself to warn defense counsel about a potential charge of interference with the police based on Sack and Dockeray's meeting with Kifunta and going to Impala Hill with him, a further indication that the Peace Corps continued to assist the defense rather than remaining neutral.[4]

The prosecution's examination of Kifunta is in a fairly unimaginative form, developing the story one step at a time. One question we might ask is how much time, if any, the prosecution spent in preparing Kifunta for his examination. Had the prosecution known any of the defense case, they could have, if they had time, prepared Kifunta so that his testimony could anticipate questions likely to be posed during cross-examination. In such a way, they could weaken the defense case. However, the prosecution lacked such knowledge, and it is unclear whether they spent time preparing Kifunta.

22

Trial Day Three

Monday, August 29, 1966

That's what's good about the good old days, the other fellow got the girl.
　　　　—Bill Kinsey's diary

On Monday, August 29, the trial resumed with Inspector Kifunta still on the stand. Much of the day was taken up with a review of Kifunta's sketch of the scene after the prosecution had asked that the sketch be identified and introduced into evidence. Judge Platt ruled the sketch admissible, marked as Exhibit L, but reserved the right for the defense to attack it later.

In the sketch, Kifunta, with help of the eyewitness Maganda Vilindo, had marked relevant sites on the rocks where Peppy had died, including measurements between the various points. He identified specific sites—for example, where Peppy fell, where her body was found, where Bill carried her, where objects were found, where various witnesses told him they stood when they saw the events, and so on. In addition, he identified where the witnesses' vision might have been obscured by bushes and where they would have had a clear view of what was happening. Kifunta testified about the distances between where the witnesses watched and where actions they could see took place. These distances ranged from about 60 to 100 feet. The sketch also located where the bloodstained iron pipe and the bloodstained rock had been found.

Kifunta's sketch became an important document for assisting the court and the assessors to understand the rather complex layout of Impala Hill, although later the judge would severely criticize a number of features of the sketch. When coupled with the photographs supplied by both the prosecution and the defense, a fairly clear picture of the scene could be obtained. In addition, when the court and participants later visited the area in person, the details became even clearer. During that visit, Judge Platt pointed out that it was now the dry season, six months after Peppy died, so view-blocking shrubbery might look very different.[1] During the rainy season in Tanzania, foliage is lush and abundant, whereas in the dry season much of the foliage dies, and it is easier to see through and around such shrubbery.

When Kifunta was asked what medical involvement he had requested, he responded that he had Kinsey examined on Monday, March 28, and a blood sample taken at that time. He also ordered a postmortem to be conducted on Peppy's body, blood samples and samples of her hair be taken for analysis, and a piece of the towel that had covered her be taken for analysis as well. After the postmortem, he arranged that the stone, the bar, the bit of towel, the hair sample, the blood sample of the accused, and the clothes of the accused be packed and sent to Dar es Salaam for analysis by the government chemist. Sergeant Mohammed took these items and Peppy's body to Dar es Salaam. Kifunta then took Kinsey before Justice of the Peace A. S. Swai and told him that if he had any statement to make, it should be done there. Kinsey did make a statement at that time.[2] The court then adjourned for lunch.

After lunch, Kifunta continued his testimony and was asked about the weight of the pipe and when he had taken statements from various people who were not eyewitnesses. The judge also asked him to clarify certain statements he had made about where items were found and how well they could be seen.

The prosecutor showed Kifunta a diary, which Kifunta identified as the one taken from Bill Kinsey's house when it was searched after Peppy died. State Attorney Effiwat then asked him to read the sections of the diary that he thought were relevant to the case. Kifunta noted that the important section was dated March 26, the day before Peppy's death, and he read several paragraphs verbatim:

What a friggin' bore is it to get to know people. Don't you think they're nicer before you know them.

That's what's good about the good old days. The other fellow got the girl.

You scared off your own kind. I'm scared they might be real. I mean realer than I am.

Why he wondered reaching for the girl did things coming towards him seem to break into pieces and things that receded into

159

the past seemed to make sense. When she had asked her if anything unusual had happened Etoile had been obliged to say that it might have but she wouldn't really know until about the 27th of the month.[3]

The diary extracts continued for several more paragraphs, and Kifunta read them all. Effiwat went on to elicit Kifunta's conclusion that the excerpts were evidence that Bill planned to murder Peppy.

At this point, the prosecution ended its questioning of Kifunta, and the defense took over. Georgiadis aggressively cross-examined Kifunta on the pipe and the rock. Where were they found? Could they have rolled away from other spots? What did he do to protect them? When questioned about the bloody stone, which was not found until after Kinsey was charged the next day, Kifunta admitted that he had not placed a guard on the site overnight and that it was possible that one of the one hundred or so spectators who had been milling around could have kicked the stone. Kifunta admitted that he had found two other stones with blood on them but left them by a tree after the PI. The judge ordered him to go get them, which he did after his first day of testimony.[4] The stones would be brought in on the fifth day of testimony. He also admitted that he had not thought it necessary to retain Peppy's clothes to be used as exhibits. Georgiadis remarked: "Fortunately the defence [sic] has preserved them and they will be produced later."[5]

Georgiadis pressed Kifunta on his interaction with Bill on the day of Peppy's death and ensuing days. Kifunta responded that Bill had been cooperative throughout the investigation and had "consistently told the same story."[6]

Several times during his cross-examination, Georgiadis accused Inspector Kifunta of improper handling of the investigation: "Because of various derelictions of duty, we have been placed in a position of having to do lots of police work in this case."[7]

Late in the afternoon, the court adjourned with the cross-examination of Kifunta not yet finished. By this time, Kifunta had spent more than ten hours in the witness box. The court had been in session that day from 8:30 a.m. to 12:30 p.m. and from 1:30 p.m. to 5:30 p.m.[8]

Years later, Georgiadis would report on one of his wily efforts to unsettle Prosecutor Effiwat by often mispronouncing his name.[9]

23

Trial Day Four

Tuesday, August 30, 1966

"Dramatic Turn in Kinsey Murder Trial"
—Dar es Salaam Standard

Tuesday began in dramatic fashion as Georgiadis entered the courtroom with a parcel wrapped in brown paper. He untied the string holding the package, opened it to reveal a number of copies of a paperback book. He handed copies to the judge, the prosecutor, the two assessors, and Inspector Kifunta, who for yet another day sat in the witness stand. The book was *Ceremony in Lone Tree* by Wright Morris.[1] Georgiadis then walked Kifunta through the book, telling him to open to a specific page and read a specific section on the page. The sections read were essentially word for word the same as the parts of Bill's diary that the prosecution alleged illustrated Bill's belief in Peppy's infidelity and provided the motive for her murder. For example, the prosecution had pointed out that Kinsey had written the passage reading "Etoile had been obliged to say that it might have been but she wouldn't really know until about the 27th of the month" on March 26 and that since Peverley had died on March 27, the passage demonstrated his plan to kill her.

Similarly, the other passages written in the diary on March 26 were the same as passages from *Ceremony in Lone Tree*. On being pressed by Georgiadis, accusing him of gross dereliction of duty "for not asking Bill about the diary entries," Inspector Kifunta agreed that the passages might have come from the book, that he had no idea the book was one selected by the Peace Corps for volunteers, and that "the book could put an entirely new light on the case."[2] (The book was included in the Peace Corps Book Locker, which each volunteer

161

received shortly after arriving at his or her assignment. The Book Locker is more fully described in chapter 24.) Had the defense been required to present its case at the PI, the prosecution would have found out about the connection between the diary and the book and been able either to prepare Kifunta or to decide to withdraw the charge. It seems a dangerous tactic for the defense not to reveal the connection and potentially resolve the case at an early stage. Of course, the eyewitness testimony, the postmortem report, and the alleged murder weapons might still have compelled the prosecution to proceed anyway.

Georgiadis then asked whether there was a scintilla of evidence that Peverley had been unfaithful. Kifunta agreed that the connection to the book suggested a very different posture for the case and that he had found no other evidence of infidelity or problems in the marriage. Georgiadis demanded that the prosecution and the inspector make a complete apology and withdraw any such accusation. Georgiadis said: "I would think if you had any shred of decency . . . ," but the judge intervened at this point, and Georgiadis withdrew his demand.[3]

Georgiadis produced a statement made by Kinsey to the district magistrate in Maswa on March 29 and asked Kifunta to read it aloud. Kifunta proceeded to do so. Once the revelation of the source of the quoted passages from Bill's diary was made, requiring Kifunta to read Bill's statement to the magistrate would underscore the likely veracity of Bill's story and put Kifunta's entire investigation in question.

Georgiadis went on to question Kifunta on his report, which included a statement that he had found "books" at the scene. Kifunta said that must be an error because he had found only one book. He said he may have mistaken the cigar box for a book. Further questions focused on when Kifunta had taken the Binza School headmaster's statement and where various bike pumps had been found. Kifunta replied that a pump had been attached to the green bike and that he found a pump in a basket of letters at the accused's house. After these questions, Kifunta was allowed to step down from the witness box.

By the end of the cross-examination of Kifunta, the defense had substantially undercut the quality of his investigation. He admitted to a number of failures: not securing the site, not retaining various items of clothing, throwing away bloody stones, and, most important, not investigating Bill's diary more thoroughly. The judge would also later criticize Kifunta's sketch of the site.

Prior to independence in 1961 and for some time afterward, the Tanzania CID was under the command and control of experienced British policemen.

Even at the time of the Kinsey case, at least one British policeman served in Mwanza. Kifunta would have been trained by such officers, so it is surprising that his investigation was not more impressive. In his defense, it should be said that most British officers had left the country by this time, and the resources available to the CID were very limited. Interestingly, despite the serious flaws in Kifunta's investigation, at the end of his testimony Judge Platt "told him that he had stood his evidence and cross-examination very well."[4]

In the afternoon, Constable Thomas was sworn in and took the stand. He testified that a man called "Padre" had come to the police station and told him that a "European" had murdered his wife. Thomas testified that when he arrived at the site where the body lay, he could see her face. (Inspector Kifunta had testified that there was a towel over her face when he saw her.) Thomas also testified that he found a piece of iron hidden in the grass near the stones not far from where the wife "fell down." The rocks were put in the back of the Land Rover with the body, and there was blood on the floor of the Land Rover when the body was taken out, he continued.[5] Thomas's testimony further demonstrated the failure to secure the evidence properly because some of the blood found on the rocks may have been deposited during the time they were in the Land Rover.

The next witness was the junior laboratory assistant Raphael, who described the technical procedure used to examine the various bodily fluids.[6]

The prosecution then called one of the eyewitnesses, Humbi Sayuda, an elderly woman around seventy years old and resident of the nearby village who was working in her *shamba* (garden) at the time of the incident. When the judge asked her how old she was, she replied, "I have lived so long that I do not know my age."[7]

Humbi testified that she heard a yell and thought that it was her son. She then saw a "European" man walking up the hill. She followed him, but he seemed to be waving at her and forbidding her to come in that direction. (The judge would later observe that she may have misunderstood Bill's gesture because Africans generally use a gesture different from Europeans and Americans when encouraging someone to come to or to go way from them. An African will gesture with the palm of the hand down rather than with the palm up to get someone to come toward them.[8]) She thought that one of her children might be in danger, so she shouted an alarm. In answer to the alarm, Maganda Vilindo and another man came up to her. She said the men didn't talk to her but made a search up the hillside. She did not follow them. When asked about

163

the European man, she told the court that he was a tall young man wearing a coat that flapped when he was waving at her. He was about 50 yards away from her.[9]

Humbi reported in her testimony that the police did not interview her at that time but came to her home that same evening. The police interviewed her there at home, so she never took them to the place where the cry came from or where she was when she heard the cry. The failure to have her show the police where she stood will eventually lead the judge to deem Kifunta's testimony about her position inadmissible, with the result that the court was unable to rely on her testimony.[10]

Humbi was the last witness for the day, and court adjourned.

The prosecution was beginning to see that what appeared to be a very strong case was now in danger of leading to an acquittal. The defense had not only pointed out several failures in the police investigation but seemingly removed the impact of the diary as suggesting a motive. Humbi had responded to a cry but had seen neither a fall nor Bill doing anything to Peppy, so her testimony was not crucial to the prosecution's case, although it was important to lay the groundwork for the testimony of the other eyewitnesses.

24

The Peace Corps Book Locker

No one is quite sure where the idea for the Peace Corps Book Locker came from. One seemingly well-founded rumor has it that Eunice Shriver, Sargent Shriver's wife, came up with it. Wherever it came from, it generated warm support from all the volunteers in the field who received the locker. The Book Locker was a black two-sided case made from very heavy cardboard, with hinges on the end so that the case could be opened and closed to form a small, portable library. Despite its popularity among volunteers, by the end of the 1960s the Book Locker was gone, and volunteers were left to their own devices for their research, personal reading, and books to give to their students and friends in the host country.

This was not the first time that the U.S. government had provided books to Americans working overseas. During World War II, with backing from President Franklin D. Roosevelt and the U.S. government, the American Library Association launched the National Defense Book Campaign, followed by the Victory Book Campaign and finally the Council of Books in Wartime, which, with funding from the armed services, produced more than 120 million books by the end of the war. Made small enough to fit into a pocket, the books were provided to the men (although rarely to the women!) in the various services. This massive effort was instigated not only to entertain the troops suffering in distressing conditions but also in response to the Nazis' book banning and burning. An account of the World War II program is titled *When Books Went to War*.[1] The story of the Peace Corps Book Locker might be called *When Books Went to Peace!*

Sargent Shriver wrote to the volunteers in the early days of the Peace Corps describing the Book Locker and its potential use. He pointed out that it consisted mainly of paperbacks of both classics and modern writings by American and foreign authors, historians, political scientists, poets, and many others. In addition, it contained books with simple English, called Ladder Editions, which could be used to help children and adults to learn English.

The books were divided into categories: literature, nonfiction, reference, learning English, and regional lists for the area where the book locker would be used—that is, Africa, Latin America, Asia, and so on. Lockers with slightly different contents would be sent to volunteers in the same area so they could trade books.

Included in the lists of books were *Moby Dick* by Herman Melville, *Brave New World* by Aldous Huxley, *Ceremony in Lone Tree* by Wright Morris, *Invisible Man* by Ralph Ellison, *Thunderball* by Ian Fleming, *Silent Spring* by Rachel Carson, and the *Burl Ives Songbook*. Reference works included maps, a *Thorndike-Barnhart Handy Dictionary, Baby and Child Care* by Benjamin Spock, and books related to the region where a volunteer was stationed.

Although compiling the titles for the Book Locker was an interesting and pleasurable experience, it was not without its controversies. The locker compiler for 1964, Jack Prebis, later reported on the battles he had with the State Department and the U.S. Information Service over certain titles: "After some concessions on their part over a few titles, there remained two objections: *No Exit* [by Jean-Paul Sartre] and *Catch 22* [by Joseph Heller]. Finally, I agreed that we didn't need to export the Communist line, but contended that *Catch 22,* in spite of depicting the U.S. military in a less-than-complimentary light, likely would not get wide distribution among host country nationals, but would be good escape reading on quiet nights." Prebis went on to discuss the arguments he had with friends and colleagues over what to include. "Debated along the way: Was Henry Ford a suitable example of American industrialization and the free enterprise system? (more or less). Or, would Ayn Rand stimulate depression and early terminations? (One couldn't be too careful.)"[2] Few of those individuals involved in developing the Book Locker would ever have thought that it might become a key factor in a celebrated murder trial.

Ceremony in Lone Tree by Wright Morris was published in 1960 by the University of Nebraska Press. Morris had previously won the National Book Award in 1957 for *The Field of Vision,* and *Ceremony* uses many of the same characters found in that book. The "ceremony" in the book is the ninety-second birthday of Tom Scanlon, who lives alone in the fictional town of Lone Tree, probably in Nebraska. In the book, Scanlon family members gather and review their past, present, and future as well as what might have been. It is a spare view of life in the Midwest that reviewers have seen as following on from Faulkner's writings about the South. Wright Morris was born in 1910 in Central City, Nebraska, and lived there for several years. Six days after he was born, his mother died. Much of his writing focuses on the landscape and lives of the inhabitants of middle Nebraska. In the early 1960s, *Ceremony in Lone Tree* was popular among college students and often found its way into classes of contemporary literature. Morris won the National Book Award for his last and best-regarded book, *Plains Song* (1980).[3]

25

Trial Day Five

Wednesday, August 31, 1966

When the court reconvened on the morning of August 31, Maganda Vilindo, a farmer in Maswa and a member of the Sukuma tribe, took the stand. (Maganda Vilindo and the next witness, Padre Masunzu, were sometimes identified by first name and sometimes by last name. I use their last names throughout.) As mentioned previously, Vilindo was listed as "pagan" by the court and so affirmed his testimony rather than swearing on a Bible. He appeared in an ankle-length gown known as a *kanzu* in Swahili. The *kanzu* was commonly worn by African men throughout East Africa. Vilindo was a vital witness for the prosecution, perhaps the most important, because he had witnessed the alleged beating. However, by damaging his testimony, the defense might create sufficient uncertainty to lead to an acquittal. When the prosecutor asked Vilindo about the events on March 27, he testified that he had seen two people fighting on a hill near his *shamba* (farm). He said he heard a cry from a neighbor named Humbi, and so he ran to her because he thought people tending to the cattle had been attacked by wild animals. When he met Humbi, she said her daughter was being attacked and asked him to go in the direction where she heard a scream.[1]

When Vilindo got near the place, he saw two people fighting:

When I saw them fighting one another I could not go near because I was afraid and I took the bushy side to see exactly the end of the

168

fight and I saw a woman down and a man on top of her beating. One held the other while the other was raising his hand frequently. The one who was raising and lowering his hand was the man and the person who was holding the forearms was the woman and the man was striking like this (here he demonstrated several blows on the fore-head). I cannot tell exactly on which part of the body the man was hitting the woman but I could see from far away that the man had a black tool and as I saw him from far away he was beating her on her forehead. As a result of that hitting the woman fell down and I passed the bush side while raising the alarm. The woman fell down with her head slanting to the right side. She fell on her right side and the legs were pointing to the North and the head was pointing to the South.[2]

Vilindo said he was standing about 126 paces (140 yards) away from the woman and man and in the middle of a maize field. He identified Bill Kinsey, sitting in the dock, as the man he had seen. When Vilindo saw the woman fall, he called for others to come near. (At this point, the interpreter, who was translating from Sukuma, was asked to lie on the ground so Vilindo could demonstrate what he saw.) Padre Masunzu arrived first and asked him why he had called out. Vilindo told him to look over there and see two Europeans fighting. They then went to the south side of the rocks to see better, and Vilindo told Masunzu to go get the police.

Vilindo continued that the man sat on the woman for a considerable time. He then saw the man get up, climb down the hill, and get on his bike. At this point, Vilindo and the others rushed over, surrounded him, and took the bike from him. Kinsey's clothes were heavily stained with blood, Vilindo testified, and by this time the police had arrived, and the entire group went to where the body lay.[3]

Byron Georgiadis then took up the cross-examination of Vilindo. He first pressed him on how far away he was, and Vilindo admitted that it was perhaps as much as 150 yards. When Georgiadis asked about the weapon, Vilindo said he had not really been able to see the tool. "Why then have you told the court untruth, that you had seen him use a black tool?" Georgiadis asked. Georgiadis then asked how many times Vilindo had seen the man hit the woman.

"She was hit only once and at that the man came on top of her," Vilindo replied. He confirmed the distance from where he had first observed the fight (some 126 paces) but went on to explain that he could not properly see the instrument with which the man had beaten the woman and on further reflection thought it was a whitish object about a foot long and not a black one. He said he was sure of seeing only one blow with some object on the forehead, after which the lady fell down. At first he said the fight went on for a long time, but on further reflection he said it was a short time. When he was cross-examined on the statements he had made at the PI, he admitted that he went to the second place to the south in order to see more clearly but also because he gained courage from the other men who had joined him. He had at first said that from this second place he had seen that when the man left the woman, he rushed to his bicycle. But it became clear under cross-examination that this was not accurate, and in fact he had seen the man carrying the woman and placing her on another part of the rock without trying to hide her. Vilindo apparently did not observe the man do anything else—that is, he never saw him with a pipe or stone or basket. He admitted that at this stage he could not see very clearly how the man was carrying the woman, but he did observe that he bent over her at one point. Vilindo had been raising the alarm all this while, so a large crowd of people had gathered, and they followed the man until they eventually prevented him from going away.[4]

At this point, it was discovered that the translation from Sukuma might have been incorrect, and a new interpreter was sworn in in an effort to clarify matters. The change did not seem to help, but it did demonstrate the difficulty of obtaining accurate testimony when translations must pass from Sukuma to Swahili to English and back again.[5] The same issue was present during the testimony of Humbi and Masunzu. Although such a procedure was not uncommon in a country with more than one hundred tribal languages in addition to Swahili and English, it remained difficult to ensure that important information was not lost in translation. Even in America the issues of translation in court has been a vexing one, and not until fairly recently have courts been forced to obtain trained and certified interpreters.

By the end of this cross-examination, Byron Georgiadis had managed to highlight not only a number of inconsistencies within Vilindo's own testimony but also possible differences with the testimony to come from the other primary eyewitness, Padre Masunzu. At this point, Vilindo was excused from the stand. Georgiadis's success in demonstrating inconsistencies was obviously helped enormously by his opportunity to review before the trial Vilindo's testimony at the PI.

In the afternoon, Assistant Superintendent Kifunta was recalled to the stand. During cross-examination earlier in the week, Kifunta had admitted that he had collected two stones as possible exhibits but had put them under a tree near the court in Maswa, where the PI had been held. Judge Platt ordered Kifunta to bring the stones to court, and he did so at this time. They were then identified and introduced in evidence. Such an oversight was surely embarrassing for Kifunta and added to the growing list of missteps in his investigation—errors that, as Tony Essaye observed in his notes, were "quite unbelievable."[6]

Later in the afternoon a government chemist from Dar es Salaam took the stand. He testified that he had received a tuft of hair and a vial of the deceased's blood, but the police had not given him enough details for him to be able to say that the blood and hair on the iron bar and the stones came from Peverley Kinsey. There were twenty-seven hairs in the cracks at the flat end of the pipe. The blood on the pipe was not on the end. The average length of the hairs was 8 inches. He found thirteen hairs on the stone. The largest was 5 inches long. Microscope examination showed that they could generally be classed as "European race hair" but nothing further could be stated apart from the fact that they were red in color.[7]

The court also heard argument on whether they should visit the site of the incident on Impala Hill near Maswa. Judge Platt said he would consult with the assessors and make a ruling later. The court then adjourned for the day.[8]

One must wonder how many of the inconsistencies Georgiadis established in Vilindo's testimony arose from the tedious translation back and forth between the several languages. Vilindo's lack of sophistication may also have been a factor: he would surely have been intimidated by appearing in the courtroom and largely being surrounded by Europeans. Although he had the experience of testifying at the PI, that inquiry had taken place near his home in Maswa, and that court was filled with Africans. He may never have traveled as far as the "big city" of Mwanza, a factor likely adding to his anxiety. Anyone who has appeared in court as a witness to face the usual grilling by opposing counsel can well sympathize with Vilindo and appreciate the ease with which a skilled attorney could make his testimony look bad.

It should also be pointed out that despite the belief that eyewitness testimony is highly reliable, "in fact, research shows that eyewitness identifications are highly unreliable, especially where the witness and the perpetrator are of different race."[9]

26

Trial Day Six

Thursday, September 1, 1966

The woman was being throttled.
　　—*Padre Masunzu*

I loved my wife.
　　—*Bill Kinsey*

On Thursday, September 1, the trial began with the testimony of Padre, son of Masunzu (known as Padre Masunzu), the second primary prosecution eyewitness. Masunzu testified that he had heard some shouting near his *shamba* around 4:00 p.m. He thought perhaps some wild beast was attacking his animals, so he walked toward the hill, where he saw people ahead of him moving toward the shouting. (It was not uncommon for livestock to be attacked by lions, leopards, cheetahs, or hyenas in this area.) Vilindo was on a rock in the maize field near the hill. Masunzu estimated the distance from where he stood to the hill as about the same as from the witness stand to the lakeshore outside the courtroom (about 66 paces, according to the judge). Masunzu said he couldn't see anything going on from this place. He quickly reached Vilindo, who was standing on a stone in a field of maize, and asked him why he was making so much noise. Vilindo said there was a person on the hill killing another person. Masunzu asked him where. Vilindo said they should go around the south side of the hill and see. So they did. There they climbed on a big rock, and Vilindo pointed to the hill, where Masunzu saw the people. A woman was down, and the other person was on top of her. The woman was being throttled. The body was down flat on its back, with the man on the left side of her, both hands around her neck, and he kept looking around. Vilindo asked Padre if he had a bicycle. When Masunzu said yes, Vilindo told him to go to the police station because it was a "big" matter. Masunzu went to the police station, told them what was happening, and led them back to the scene.[1]

On cross examination, Masunzu repeated that he was at home when he heard the shouting. When he reached Vilindo, the two women he had seen in the field were far behind Masunzu. Humbi was not one of these women. He was asked about the testimony he gave to the magistrate in Maswa, which was different from his testimony in court. He said he told the magistrate the same thing, but the magistrate may have written down something different. The point focused on was whether Masunzu and Vilindo could see anything from where they were standing in the maize field. Masunzu said he could not see what was happening on the hill from this place in the field (whereas Vilindo testified that from there he had seen the fight taking place). That is why they went around the rock to see better. He also stated that he didn't tell the magistrate that one person was on top of the other but that one person was beside the person on the ground. Since Masunzu could not see what was going on with the two people when he first met Vilindo in the maize field, he was unable to corroborate Vilindo's testimony about there being a fight. Only when he came to the area on the south side of the hill could he see the people. He then testified that he saw the man "throttling" the woman.[2]

In his court trial testimony, Masunzu said the man was "throttling" the woman, but on cross-examination Georgiadis read his testimony from the PI, where he made no mention of "throttling," and asked him about the inconsistency. Masunzu was at a loss to explain it. He thought perhaps the magistrate at the PI had not written down what he said. However, his testimony at the PI had been read to him, and he had signed it at the time, acknowledging its accuracy. Georgiadis reviewed several other points in Masunzu's PI testimony that were at odds with his testimony in court, such as the distance between various places. Again, Masunzu could not explain the inconsistencies. When Georgiadis asked Masunzu what he could see from the spot where he first met Vilindo, Masunzu responded that he couldn't see anything where Vilindo was pointing. This testimony conflicted with Vilindo's, who said he could see the couple.[3] The impact of the mounting number of inconsistencies, both between Vilindo and Masunzu as well as between their testimony at the PI and their testimony at the trial, began to make all of their testimony suspect.

Georgiadis's well-prepared, skilled cross-examination demonstrated the inconsistencies within both Masunzu's and Vilindo's testimony.[4] By this time,

Georgiadis's cross-examination had substantially diminished Masunzu's credibility as a witness. Interestingly, neither of the East African newspaper accounts of the testimony on September 1 discussed Masunzu's testimony. It is unclear whether this was because the newspaper editors felt the testimony was so weak and deflated by cross-examination or because Bill's testimony was so important that it demanded the full space allotted to the trial in the day's papers. However, in his notes on the trial, Tony Essaye used two full pages of single-spaced, small print to summarize Masunzu's testimony and cross-examination. Obviously, in a murder trial witness testimony must be carefully examined, and inconsistencies may be crucial to the final decision. However, given the difficulty of verifying testimony translated through three languages as well as the witnesses' presumed unfamiliarity with court procedure, one must ask whether the differences mentioned are really that significant—that is, whether Bill was on top or to the side of Peppy, what color the bar was, and so on.

The last prosecution witness was A. S. Swai, justice of the peace in Maswa, who was called to place Bill's statement, made before him on March 29, 1966, in evidence. The prosecution also placed in evidence the record of Bill's bail hearing, apparently to be used in future cross-examination of defense witnesses.[5]

Although Bill had been cautioned about his right to remain silent at his arrest, before Justice Swai he had chosen, without a lawyer at his side, to describe exactly what happened. His consistency and the openness with which he told his story throughout the many interrogations and hearings would eventually become a substantial source of credibility for him before the judge and the assessors.

Even though Britain didn't (and doesn't) have a written bill of rights, prior to Tanzania's independence the British urged Tanzania to include such protection—for instance, the right to remain silent—in the Independence Constitution. Tanzania declined at that point, but such a right had made its way from British common law into the India Criminal Code and so eventually into Tanzanian law. Tanzania would not embed the right to silence in a bill of rights in its constitution until 1984. In this constitutional provision, the law limited the value of the right to remain silent by establishing a rather broad set of circumstances in which the court or the prosecution or both could draw adverse inferences from the failure to testify. Under British common law, adverse inference could be drawn only under a very limited set of circumstances.[6]

Once Swai finished his testimony, the prosecution closed its case after some thirty-six hours of testimony, having called twelve witnesses. Before beginning the defense, Georgiadis reminded the court that he was still waiting for the prosecution to withdraw its "hideous accusation of unfaithfulness."[7]

One question that might be raised about the eyewitnesses' testimony is whether the prevalence of eye disease in Tanzania might have affected their vision. Barbara Doyle, who was a Peace Corps volunteer teacher in the Mwanza area at the time of the trial, told me in an interview that a large number of her students had eye disease.[8] Such problems continue today. Norwegian relatives of my wife who are on the faculty of the Medical School at the University of Bergen and specialize in eye disease have been traveling to Tanzania annually for several years to perform surgery at a hospital not far from Maswa. They discovered some years ago that eye disease is quite common but that it often can be readily treated by rather simple surgery. However, it can also be argued that Tanzanians in the rural areas in the 1960s were accustomed to seeing over long distances in order to track wild animals and to round up their own domestic animals.

Before resuming testimony, Justice Platt delivered his ruling that the court, including assessors, counsel, and so on, would visit the scene of the incident in Maswa.[9]

Although the defense had demonstrated major failures in the investigation by Inspector Kifunta and in the postmortem by AMO Mganga as well as significant inconsistencies in the testimony of eyewitness, later in the afternoon the judge announced that he considered there to be a sufficient case to answer, and he would not dismiss it for lack of evidence. He then told Bill Kinsey that under Tanzanian law Bill had three choices: first, give a sworn statement from the witness box and then submit to cross-examination; second, make an unsworn statement from the dock (where the accused sits) without cross-examination; or, third, make no statement.

Bill chose the first option.

The judge asked him what kind of statement he would like to make. Kinsey replied, "My Lord, I would like to cross over to the witness box and make a sworn statement."[10]

Bill then crossed the courtroom and was sworn in. Under Tanzanian law, "if a defendant testifies, he must be the defense's first witness."[11]

When Bill entered the box, the courtroom was packed and quiet. He began by saying that he loved his wife and that he had never at any time wanted to cause her any harm. They had met on August 31, 1964, at Syracuse University, where they underwent Peace Corps training before coming to Tanzania.

They were married ninety-four days after that first meeting. Bill continued that they had no children but expected to start a family after traveling through Europe once their Peace Corps service was completed. He said they had no sexual difficulties, that he had no reason to believe his wife was unhappy or unfaithful, and that he had never at any time wished to cause her harm or to hit her.

Bill told the court that he was interested in photography and owned two cameras, several lenses, and a bulky tripod. He was planning to construct a lighter and more transportable tripod, using a bicycle pump and a piece of metal piping. When he was shown Exhibit L, a piece of metal with blood on it, he said, yes, that was the metal for the tripod. When he was asked if he knew how blood could have gotten on the pipe, he said he didn't know. Bill stated that he and Peppy had been marking students' exams for most of the morning on the Sunday of the incident and then decided to have a picnic on Impala Hill, which was a short way from their home. Because it was then a bit late for the picnic, he decided to leave his camera and other equipment at home. He could not explain, however, how the piece of metal came to be in the picnic basket. He and Peppy had been taking a number of drugs at the time of the incident, he added—malaria medication and a drug for a skin condition. Peppy was also taking medication for an infection.

Both he and Peppy were avid readers, he said, and they had taken two books with them on the picnic, *Little Big Man* and *Ceremony in Lone Tree*. He went on to testify that the notes he had made on March 26 and that the prosecution alleged showed motive were taken from *Ceremony in Lone Tree*. He often copied similar passages into notebooks because he found them to reflect a character in the book or were particularly descriptive or were humorous. He had made many similar entries over the years and had found it useful from his college training, sometimes using such passages in his writing.[12]

Bill had been on the stand for one hour and twenty-five minutes when the court adjourned for the day, and he would continue his testimony the following day.

27

Trial Day Seven

Friday, September 2, 1966

"Wife's Dying Word Was My Name—Kinsey"
—*Dar es Salaam Standard*

On Friday, the trial continued with Bill Kinsey in the witness box. Defense counsel Georgiadis began by asking Bill to describe the events on March 27 at Impala Hill. Although Kinsey had given a statement to the magistrate in Maswa a few days after Peppy died, he did not testify at the preliminary inquiry, so this would (unfortunately) be the first opportunity for the prosecutor to hear him tell his story. Bill first described the 2-mile bicycle ride from Maswa to Impala Hill, where he and Peppy finished their lunch. Newspaper reports continue the testimony:

> They climbed a rocky hill, drank some beer and read for a while. It was fairly windy and when they began to get cold they decided to climb a high rock for a better view of the surrounding countryside.
>
> Peverley had carried her bottle of beer up the rock with her. They were standing on top of the rock when he heard the sound of breaking glass. The first thing that flashed into his mind was that his wife had thrown the bottle at a rock rabbit [probably a Hyrax, a small rodent-like animal which is prevalent on the rock Kopjes in the area. Despite their small size, they are related to elephants], but when he turned round he found she had fallen some 20 feet.[1]

"I crawled on my hands to the edge of the rock and saw her legs moving below. I rushed down. When I came round the rock, I found

177

my wife standing, supporting herself with one hand against the rock—there was blood on one side of her face and blouse.

"When she saw me, she reached towards me and screamed my name and fell forward. I fell to her side on my knees and tried to help her."[2]

She continued flailing her arms, so he held her head to keep it from smashing against the rocks, and then he pinned her down with his knees to protect her.

Peppy calmed down a bit, so he placed a towel under her head. He got up and went toward the south side of the rock but saw no one. He returned to where Peppy lay and saw a woman in a maize field. He shouted at her in Swahili and gestured to her to come, but she didn't move. He then picked Peppy up and carried her, but he fell twice; first, where the second pool of blood was found and again farther on in the narrow corridor between the rocks, where he left her. When he first left her and ran back for help, he saw no one to the south, but when he returned to her, there was a crowd of men in that direction. He shouted for help, but no one came, and so he picked Peppy up again and continued on. He started to walk down the hill, but after he fell several times, he put her down and spoke to her; she seemed not to hear anything and said nothing. Bill then ran down the hill to his bicycle to ride to the village to get help, but several people stopped him. They showered him with sticks and stones, and finally two men grabbed his bicycle. He then tried to run to Maswa, but a large crowd surrounded him, and someone hit him on the back with a club.[3]

The Binza School headmaster and the police soon arrived, and at this point the police handcuffed Bill and took him back to the hill. When Inspector Kifunta arrived, for some unknown reason he asked, "Where is the knife?" Kinsey replied that he didn't have one.

Georgiadis asked Kinsey how the piece of metal and rocks had become bloodstained. Kinsey said he didn't know. However, during the struggle he had used something to elevate her head, but he couldn't remember what. He went on to say that he never hit her with any of these things. When Georgiadis asked him about the medications that he and Peppy were taking, he responded that they both had become dizzy in the past when they had taken pills for their skin condition.

When Georgiadis was finished, Prosecutor Effiwat began his cross-examination, which lasted some two hours. Effiwat aggressively challenged Bill with the accounts by the previous witnesses, who testified that Bill had struck, beat, and pushed Peppy down. Kinsey responded in an unruffled manner, denying these accounts and reiterating that everything he did was in an effort to help Peppy.[4]

The following reconstruction of part of the cross-examination and Kinsey's responses is derived from the notes taken by Tony Essayo at the trial. The prosecutor's questions were sometimes but not always included in the notes, so I have added my best guesses based on the responses.

PROSECUTOR (EDEDEN EFFIWAT): What medications were you taking, and when did you take them?

KINSEY: We took one tablet of Benadryl sometime after 2:30 p.m.

PROSECUTOR: Why did you go to that hill?

KINSEY: Because it was the nearest hill to our house.

PROSECUTOR: Who packed the basket?

KINSEY: I packed the camera equipment. The basket was empty at the time. Peppy did not know the pipe was in the basket until we got to the hill.

PROSECUTOR: The court has been told that your wife had a bad reaction and passed out from taking Benadryl on a previous occasion. How did you determine that, and when did she take the Benadryl?

KINSEY: I found her passed out on the kitchen floor, but I don't know when she took the Benadryl.

PROSECUTOR: What did you do with the basket after the fall?

KINSEY: I don't think I touched it after the fall. At least I didn't consciously notice it.

PROSECUTOR: Did you go with the police to the site of the body?

KINSEY: No, I wasn't with them then. There was a crowd of people around where she lay when I got there.

PROSECUTOR: Were you at the place where the pipe was found when they found it?

KINSEY: No. Inspector Kifunta held the pipe up when he was about 40 feet away. I didn't see blood or hairs on it at that time. I wasn't told there was blood on it until the next morning. The next morning it was on Inspector Kifunta's desk, and he asked me how the blood and hair came to be on it. I saw the blood but not the hair. Inspector Kifunta did not give me the pipe, and I didn't ask for it.

PROSECUTOR: Where did you see blood at the scene?

KINSEY: The first pool of blood was where Peppy lay. When I saw the police measuring it, it was downward to a place on the same rocks, but Inspector Kifunta did not show me the place. I inadvertently saw the measurement.

PROSECUTOR: Please tell the court how the pipe was to be used.

KINSEY: On the camera. It was to be a camera support. I took it to see if it was usable and what would need to be done to fix it. I planned to use it for wildlife photography and wanted to design it to be most useful on rocks.

PROSECUTOR: How much time passed between when the deceased fell and before you reached her?

KINSEY: It was about twenty or thirty seconds before I sat on her.

PROSECUTOR: Did you notice injuries on the deceased?

KINSEY: I only saw some blood and swelling in the area of the right eye. I didn't notice a missing tooth.

PROSECUTOR: What was the deceased doing when you reached her?

KINSEY: She was flailing. Her arms were out in front of her or on the side. She pulled herself up using me, and I think that she pulled on my clothing.

PROSECUTOR: What did you do then?

KINSEY: I elevated her head with something, I think, but I can't exactly recall what it was, and then I ran to get the towel.

PROSECUTOR: Isn't it true that you knew the deceased would be weak and powerless because of the drug?

KINSEY: [Answer unavailable.]

PROSECUTOR: Did you see people in the area?

KINSEY: I saw an old woman. Probably Humbi. I shouted at her, and she shouted back.

PROSECUTOR: Did you see the witness identified as Maganda?

KINSEY: I don't recall seeing him then. He looked familiar at the preliminary inquiry.

PROSECUTOR: Do you agree there were scratches on your hand? How did you get them?

KINSEY: Yes, there were scratches on my right hand. I am right-handed, and I got the scratches from sticks and from warding off blows. I showed them to the magistrate, but I wasn't sure I had been arrested at that point. I also had blood blisters and scratches on both hands.

PROSECUTOR: How were you situated after you found the deceased on the ground?

KINSEY. I was kneeling next to her and looking around, one way and then the other. This is probably what Padre saw.

PROSECUTOR: How much do you weigh? Why did you kneel beside the deceased?

KINSEY: When I weighed myself in March, I weighed about 185 or 190 pounds. I was aware that a concussion or spinal injury or broken rib could be made much worse by movement.

PROSECUTOR: What quotations were you most interested in? Weren't they all indicating something unpleasant?

KINSEY: I don't think so.[5]

When the prosecution concluded, it was clear that little if any damage had been inflicted on Bill's testimony. In fact, looking at the line of responses and likely questions, the prosecutor's focus seems weak in the extreme and showed little preparation. One would expect from a more skilled prosecutor a careful building up of the facts, which the defendant could not easily fend off. The questions instead essentially walked Bill through the same answers he had given previously. Of course, a major hurdle faced by the prosecution was the lack of opportunity to hear Bill testify before this point, although they did have access to the written statement he had given to the magistrate as well as his answers to Kifunta's questions. As one of the reporters described Kinsey's testimony, "Kinsey was unruffled by a two-hour cross-examination by the prosecutor, Mr. Ededen Effiwatt. He denied the account of a previous witness that he felled his wife with a blow and sat on her with his hands around her neck."[6]

The judge asked some questions about what Bill had seen and heard at the time of Peppy's fall. The judge first observed that, as reported by Bill, Peppy was on top of the rock facing east the last time Bill saw her. He was 6 to 8 feet away. The judge asked Bill what he heard. He responded that he heard nothing until the sound of breaking glass. The judge asked if he could hear someone walking on the rock. Bill responded "no" because it was very windy. The judge went on to opine that normally in an accident you would expect the person to call out. Is it possible, wondered the judge, for someone to fall without a sound?[7] The judge was obviously troubled by Bill's failure to hear anything when Peppy fell.

181

Inspector Kifunta testified that he did not think that Bill and Peppy had gone up to the top of the rock at all, so there was in fact no fall, only the alleged beating of Peppy at the lower site where the blood was found. His view was supported by the eyewitnesses, who saw only the alleged beating but no fall. Of course, the fall might have occurred prior to their looking at the scene on the rocks.

Bill Kinsey was then excused, and the court adjourned for the day.

On that same day, PCDC cabled staff in Tanzania that the Peace Corps Act Amendment authorizing retroactive payment of legal fees had passed both houses of Congress.[8]

28

Trial Day Eight

Saturday, September 3, 1966

"Mystery Move in Trial"
—*Dar es Salaam Sunday News*

On Saturday, the trial was scheduled to continue; however, the prosecutor arrived thirty minutes late, and he and defense counsel immediately went into Judge Platt's chambers. After about ten minutes, Platt returned to the bench, and Mr. Effiwat requested that the hearing be adjourned and continued to the next convenient time. Effiwat said he was trying to find out about certain matters, and he did not think the issues should be discussed in open court. Defense attorney Georgiadis replied: "I have no objection to my learned friend's application." Georgiadis went on, however, to request that if Effiwat's inquiries were completed by the end of the day, testimony from one witness (Dr. Dockeray) should be taken the next day because he was scheduled to return to Nairobi and then to proceed overseas. Judge Platt adjourned the hearing until 9:00 a.m. the following day, a Sunday. It was unprecedented for a murder trial to sit on a Sunday.[1]

Perhaps with free time afforded by the early adjournment, the press managed to track down an encouraging omen for the defense:

Kinsey Arrived in Court Today in a Police Wagon from Mwanza's Butimba Prison on the Shore of Lake Victoria. He Is Lodged There with an African Prisoner in Cell Number 7, from Which Tradition Has It No One Accused of Murder Has Yet Been Convicted.

183

"It's a Good Omen," Said Attorney Carroll Brewster, of New Haven Conn., Who Is Keeping a Watching Brief at the Trial for the Kinsey Family.[2]

What Effiwat did not reveal was that two Peace Corps couples had requested to intervene in the case in order to provide testimony about Bill and Peppy's relationship. One of the couples, Pam Engle and her husband, John, were members of the Tanzania IX group of primary-school teachers who had arrived in Tanzania in 1965 and were assigned to a Muslim school in Mwanza. Both John and Pam were from New York State; Pam was a graduate of Sarah Lawrence College and John of Bentley College in Massachusetts. Although they had met the Kinseys only once, they were very interested in Bill's trial, and because they taught near the court, they were able to attend the trial with some regularity. At one of the court sessions, they met Phil and Ann Ellison, the Peace Corps couple working at the Upper Primary School at Sayusayu near Maswa, who had become friends of the Kinseys. The Ellisons were concerned about the course of the trial and sought to provide testimony about problems between the Kinseys.[3]

When the couples met at the trial, they got into a discussion about what to do. Although the Ellisons had been shocked when Bill was charged, had described the Kinseys as a couple without troubles, and had visited Bill in prison, by July they had become convinced that he had killed Peppy. Their decision was based on conversations with Peppy before she died, on the weapons involved, and on reports by people in the area about how Peppy's head and face had been injured, which made them conclude that her death could not have been an accident. In a letter home, they described their change of heart: "Kinsey's trial is this Friday and you'll probably read about it. The lawyers were out yesterday to talk to us—maybe to feel us out if they want us to testify but seeing we think he's guilty didn't ask."[4]

The Engles suggested that the Ellisons go to the judge and ask his advice, which they did. The judge said he couldn't talk to them, so they should go to the prosecution or the defense attorney. It is surprising that the judge sent them away because a provision of Tanzania law at the time appeared to impose a requirement on the judge to bring the Ellisons into the trial and examine them as witnesses: a court is empowered "at any stage of the proceedings to summon and examine any person as a witness." It also imposes a duty to do so "if his [the person's] evidence appears to be essential to the just decision of the case."[5]

The four Peace Corps volunteers then went to Ededen Effiwat, the state attorney, and told him what they knew. He listened to them, took notes, but later told them it was too late, and he could not use their testimony. After that, they decided there was nothing further to be done and abandoned their effort to intercede in the trial. They were also concerned that Poppy Kinsey's mother would testify in the next few days, and whatever the Ellisons had to say would likely embarrass her.[6]

At around 1:30 a.m. (yes, a.m.) on either Saturday, September 3, or Sunday, September 4, Paul Sack and Jack McPhee went to the Engles' home to talk to them about the other couple and what was happening. The Ellisons reported later that they felt they were being threatened and would possibly be sent home for their involvement in the episode; however, nothing further happened. In the end, the Ellisons returned to Sayusayu, concerned that they were in trouble with the Peace Corps.[7]

While Sack and McPhee's visit may have been meant simply to obtain information, it led these couples to feel that the Peace Corps was not maintaining a neutral posture on the case but were supporting Bill and challenging anyone who pressed for a guilty verdict. But Peace Corps officials did have an interest in and an obligation to find out what volunteers under their supervision were doing and could claim that the visit was simply doing that, although why it was necessary to make the visit in the middle of the night remains unclear.

An Ellison letter home at the time also explained why the villagers had so aggressively surrounded Bill and kept him from running away: "The reason they did this was that several years ago a man of this area (who was a policeman with a gun) found his wife with another man and was so incensed that in the course of a few weeks he shot and killed 36 people. When they saw Kinsey's act they didn't want another carnage to begin."[8]

29

Trial Day Nine

Sunday, September 4, 1966

"Legal Clash at Mwanza; BULLYING CHARGE DENIED"
—*Nairobi Daily Nation*

The trial resumed on Sunday, September 4, with several battles between the prosecution and defense. The day began with a charge by the prosecution that defense attorney Georgiadis had at 1:30 a.m. gone to the home of a Peace Corps couple (presumably the Ellisons) and bullied them about information that might be useful to the prosecution.

Georgiadis agreed that he went "to see them to find out what information could possibly assist this court, either the defence [*sic*] or the prosecution." There was no rule or authority forbidding such procedure.

> I did not bully as my learned friend said. I merely asked that if they had any information to disclose they should please do so, either to the prosecution or the defense or the police.
>
> What I did say was that they should not go behind the backs of everybody making allegations and suggestions without being prepared to back them up in a proper way by making statements and allowing the prosecution or myself or the court to call them in evidence.

Judge Platt said he saw no injustice in Mr. Georgiadis's action and had no intention of sitting in judgment on his professional conduct. "If it was in favour [*sic*] of the prosecution let us just consider that he [Mr. Georgiadis] asked them to disclose it. Is there any injustice in that."[1]

Perhaps because of these "mysterious" developments and the clash of attorneys, the courtroom was now regularly filled to overflowing, and the reporters exhibited heightened interest, although government-linked and Swahili-language newspapers seemed to be ignoring the trial.[2]

The next incident arose when the defense objected to the presence of officers armed with guns both inside and outside the court. As Georgiadis described the situation forty years later, "I found a large sinister looking Tanzanian with a submachine gun . . . in camouflage sitting directly behind me. . . . I moved to the window and looked out and saw the courthouse surrounded by paramilitary toting guns. I decided I was having none of this and marched Mr. Effiwat into the judge's chambers." The judge quickly ordered the officers to leave. After they left, three policemen remained standing behind the accused, where formerly there had been only one guard.[3] In his talk about the case in 2007, Georgiadis reached back to a quote from the Roman philosopher, Pliny the Elder, to describe his surprise: "Ex Africa semper aliquid novi" (There's always something new coming out of Africa).[4]

Peace Corps officials had come to understand that prosecuting attorney Effiwat believed that the U.S. government would send a squad of soldiers to Mwanza to rescue Bill and take him back to the United States before the trial was completed. It is not clear whether the presence of the soldiers in the courtroom at this time was a response to that belief. Effiwat's concern was perhaps not unfounded. According to Paul Sack, Jesse Helms, then a radio and television executive and later a U.S. senator for North Carolina, approached the State Department with the proposal that U.S. marines be sent in to grab Bill and take him out of Tanzania.[5] Peppy's sister, Charlotte, remembers her uncle marching about the house insisting that marines should be sent in to grab Bill from prison. He even called Sargent Shriver, the former Peace Corps director, to express his feelings.[6] Given the history of U.S. intervention in other countries—for example, in Cuba, the Dominican Republic, Iran, Chile, and Haiti—such a suspicion on the prosecution's part was not necessarily misplaced.[7]

Meanwhile, Bill Kinsey seemed to be maintaining an optimistic outlook. On September 4, in a reply to a message from his family, he said, "All I can do is echo what others have already said. Things are going well and we are looking forward to a favourable [sic] conclusion. I'll be seeing you shortly. All my love, Bill."[8]

The defense then resumed its presentation by calling to the witness stand Dr. Gerald Dockeray, the Nairobi pathologist, whom the defense believed was perhaps their most important witness. Sensing his importance although not privy to the details of his expected testimony, the prosecution argued vigorously that Dockeray should not be allowed to testify because he had not obtained the required Tanzanian coroner's permit before performing the Kinsey autopsy. After arguments in court, a two-hour delay ensued while Judge Platt went back to his chambers to review the law. The judge returned to the courtroom and announced that he had determined that the permit was not needed under Tanzanian law; therefore, Dockeray could testify. "In addition, the Magistrate at Maswa is a coroner and he authorized Dr. McHugh and a 'specialist' to examine the body after the official postmortem had been carried out."[9]

It was fortunate that Bill's Tanzania attorneys had the foresight to seek the relevant orders for further examinations from the magistrate in Maswa at a time when the pathologist was unknown or even if there would be such a pathologist. The judge might have been persuaded to permit the testimony anyway, but the order he mentioned gave him a very credible basis for his decision. Had Dockeray been kept out of the case, the defense would have been in serious trouble.

Despite Dr. Dockeray's impressive credentials (see chapter 4), or perhaps because of them, he looked on the witness stand very much like a character from a Somerset Maugham short story set in one of Britain's colonial outposts. He projected a tired-of-the-world, seen-it-all, and slightly surly demeanor. However, his presence on the witness stand conveyed a very powerful expertise.[10]

Dockeray testified that he had carried out a postmortem examination on Peppy Kinsey on the evening of March 29, two days after her death. The examination had taken place at Mwanza Hospital, with Dr. Tom McHugh and Dr. Salu, a medical assistant at the hospital, present. Nancy Churchill, the Peace Corps volunteer nurse, also attended and served as scribe.

When asked by defense attorney Georgiadis to summarize his findings, Dockeray essentially followed his written report of the examination performed in March. He reported that he had found a number of lacerated wounds mainly on the top and the right side of the head around the ear. He also found a one-inch vertical laceration at the corner of the right eye, which he called a penetrating wound reaching to the orbital plate of the front part of the base of the skull. (The orbital plate is essentially the eye socket.) He emphasized the paper-thin nature of the orbital plate. The orbital plate "was broken over an area measuring about the size of a fingertip, and from this impact area fractures radiated in several directions." He initially had thought the injury might have been caused by a twig or root, but after visiting the scene of the death, he decided that it was probably caused by a small stone. He did not think that Dr. Mganga could have seen that injury. There was a depressed fracture, made up of two fractures, to the right parietal bone and extending into the suture line, which had been sprung (separated) from the right side of the skull over the top to the left side of the skull. There was a lacerated cut above this fracture, which he thought led to the fracture below the cut. On the left side of the skull, he found a fissured fracture leading from the parieto-temporal suture to the back of the skull but not reaching the occipital bone at the rear of the skull. Dockeray found no fractures to the occipital bone or the frontal bones. There was a star-like fracture to the orbital plate, but the orbital bone itself was not fractured.[11]

At this point, the trial was recessed, with Dockeray scheduled to continue his description of his postmortem on the following Monday.

30

Trial Day Ten

Monday, September 5, 1966

"Injuries Bear Out Kinsey's Evidence of Fall—Doctor"
—*Nairobi Daily Nation*

On Monday morning, September 5, the trial resumed, with Dr. Dockeray still in the witness box and continuing his summary of the postmortem. Much of his time there was spent describing Peppy's external injuries.

Although his findings have been discussed previously, it is important to restate them in the context of the trial, where there was the opportunity for cross-examination and for the judge to ask his own questions. Dockeray found on the top of the head two parallel cuts about 1¼ inches long. On the left side of the head were two wounds and a cut 2½ inches long above and behind the left ear. He found at the back of the head a 3-inch cut. Dockeray then described various injuries to the rest of the body. He found no bruises on the shoulders but three bruises on the back of the left shoulder, several small abrasions on the lower back, and no bruises on the buttocks or back of the legs. On the left arm, he found a small bruise below the left elbow and bruises on the left fingers and wrist. On the right arm, he could see a large bruise on the back of the right hand and an abrasion like a skid mark below the elbow along the ulna. He found a 5-inch bruise on the right knee and a 3-inch bruise on the left knee. (However, in his written report on his postmortem, he asserted that these bruises developed after the first postmortem.)[1]

Dockeray testified that Peppy's injuries could have been caused by a fall and that they were consistent with the account Bill had provided. When asked by defense counsel whether these injuries suggested a fall from a height of 20 feet,

190

Dockeray responded that he would have expected such a fall to cause more extensive damage, but the lesser level of injuries was not a surprise. "People have fallen from enormous heights and broken only an ankle," he told the court. "The absence of other serious bodily injuries does not rule out the theory that she fell and landed on her head." When asked about the cause of death, Dockeray responded that the principal injury was the extreme blow to the right side of the head, causing separation of the bones of the skull, and it was the likely cause of death.[2]

Dockeray reviewed a drawing of Peppy's skull and analyzed the separation of the fronto-parietal suture. He observed that it wouldn't be fully ossified at her age; however, it would require a very considerable force to separate it. He went on to describe his findings of several small fractures as well. He thought these fractures per se were not important. Such head injuries would cause shock and damage to brain cells but would not create sufficient damage to cause death. He concluded that the separation of the suture line was caused by a severe force and that it was this injury that had caused Peppy's death.[3]

Georgiadis showed Dockeray the piece of pipe and a bloodstained stone that the prosecution had introduced into evidence with the allegation that they were the murder weapons and asked him his opinion whether they could have caused the injuries described. Dockeray didn't think the pipe would cause the injuries in question—that is, the two fractures and the suture separation. As to the rock, he didn't think there could be enough force generated to cause the injuries if the person being hit were standing erect. If she were lying down, the rock might cause the injuries, but he would expect more brain damage in such a case. He did not try to explain the police report, which stated that the two items had hair matted on them.

When Dockeray was asked about the scalp injuries, he reported that there were twelve in number, which might have been caused by hitting the rocks in her fall. He went on to testify that none of the lacerations had characteristics suggesting they occurred while she was warding off an attack. Dockeray opined that these injuries were more consistent with Peppy having struggled to her feet after the fall or struggling with anyone who might be trying to restrain her. "She could have been knocked immediately unconscious but she might have been capable of quite a lot of semi-automatic movement without being aware of what she was doing," he added.[4]

The prosecution were unable to diminish the strength of Dockeray's testimony in their cross-examination. An embarrassing moment did arise when Mr. Effiwat asked Dr. Dockeray if he was familiar with the thirty-second edition of *Gray's Anatomy*. Dockeray responded that he was but that he was actually more familiar with the latest edition published in 1962.[5] The incident provides further evidence of the prosecution's lack of resources, especially current forensic medicine materials.

Effiwat complained that Dr. Dockeray did not tell the police about his postmortem or send them a copy of his report. He got Dockeray to admit that the stone could have caused the injury on the right side of the head and that the hair could have been deposited on the stone from the accused's hands. When asked about the fall and whether a sound should have been heard by the accused, Dockeray responded that it "could" have been heard but that saying "should" or "would" "was going too far." He observed that the sound of the wind could have a substantial muffling effect.[6]

Dr. Dockeray's eminence and widely established reputation in East Africa continued on after the trial when he was requested in September 1967 to determine whether the chimpanzees at Gombe, the world-famous research center founded by Jane Goodall, were suffering from leprosy. He determined they were not.[7]

After Dockeray was excused and before the day ended, Dr. Tom McHugh was sworn in and began his testimony, although the court would soon recess, leaving much of his testimony for the next day. McHugh was the Peace Corps staff doctor in charge of volunteers' health in Northwest Tanzania, including those in the Maswa District. He had been in Tanzania for a little more than a year at the time of the trial. Since the judge had allowed McHugh to remain in court while the prosecutor presented his case, McHugh was in a particularly good position to be familiar with the testimony and to be able to refute aspects of the prosecution medical evidence. McHugh was not only the Kinseys' doctor but also a friend, having stayed with them on occasion; he could therefore testify both as an expert medical witness and as a person who knew the Kinseys and about their relationship.

It is unusual in a murder trial to allow witnesses to be in court prior to their appearance in the witness box. The issue had been argued at the beginning of the trial, but the judge had ruled that McHugh could be in the courtroom prior to his testimony, one of a number of rulings that seemed to favor the defense.

Under questioning by defense counsel Georgiadis, McHugh began with a description of his meeting and interview with Bill in Maswa on March 29, 1966: "Kinsey's reaction was marked relief at seeing us . . . . Immediately he shook hands with me, and did not let go of my hand for one and a quarter hours. He was on the verge of tears, trembling, pale, drawn and shaken. I considered his state to be one of a high degree of anxiety and emotional upset medically known as normal grief reaction."[8]

McHugh testified that he had a conversation with Bill somewhat later in which Bill expressed his concern that some of his actions attempting to calm Peppy might have exacerbated her injuries or caused other ones. McHugh also gave his opinion that the Kinseys seemed to be a happy couple and that he knew of no discord between them.[9]

As the Peace Corps doctor, McHugh treated the Kinseys for various ailments and prescribed preventative medications, which he described, along with their likely impact, particularly on Peppy. They were taking Benadryl to relieve a rash probably caused by a plague of caterpillars. McHugh himself had had problems with Benadryl causing drowsiness, and since the Kinseys had drunk some beer, which would have increased the drug's effects, such common effects as vertigo and dizziness were likely to occur. Georgiadis told McHugh that there had been testimony about Peppy being found on the floor in their kitchen, suffering from dizziness. McHugh said he was aware of the incident at the time and had concluded then that Benadryl was the likely cause.

McHugh described the experiment he had conducted at the top of Impala Hill when he visited it with Gurbachan Singh. With McHugh staring out toward Sayusayu and Singh standing behind him and to the right, as Bill had testified, he could barely see Singh. Georgiadis asked him whether someone could collapse from a standing position without a sound. McHugh replied, "It is possible and frequently occurs." He said that in his opinion the shattering of a bottle, which Kinsey said he had heard, would have blocked any other sound and that some of the injuries might have been caused by glass from the broken bottle. When asked about the lacerations, McHugh responded, "I believe that some of the lacerations could have been caused by a length of pipe but I would have expected that at some point the pipe would have inflicted a t-shaped wound. There was none."

McHugh also testified that Bill had told him about his dissatisfaction with the improvised tripod sometime before Peppy died. Later in his testimony, McHugh stated that he had visited and stayed with the Kinseys on occasion, and as far as he could tell, there were no marital problems; they were a happily married couple. At one point, they had had some troubles with the school administration and had asked for a transfer, but those issues were resolved, and they withdrew their request.

The trial would continue on Tuesday.

31

Trial Day Eleven

Tuesday, September 6, 1966

At the opening of the session on Tuesday, September 6, Judge Platt announced that the court would visit the scene of the incident on Impala Hill near Maswa. Because it was important to visit the scene at approximately the same time of day as the incident took place, they would travel to Maswa either the next afternoon or on Thursday afternoon.[1]

Testimony continued with Dr. McHugh on the stand. When Georgiadis questioned McHugh about Peppy's injuries and how they might have come about, McHugh responded that they were definitely compatible with the kind of fall that prior testimony indicated she had experienced. Only an accidental fall, landing on her head, was likely to have caused the extreme force resulting in the separation of the parietal suture. He went on to state that the kind of behavior Peppy exhibited after the fall was consistent with the type of head injuries she received. In his experience, it is not unusual after such a fall for a person to resist and actually fight against efforts to help. It might require a number of people to restrain a patient in an emergency-room situation before doctors can evaluate the conditions after an extreme head injury. When asked about the damage to Peppy's face and right eye, McHugh speculated that it might have been caused by Peppy falling on a part of the beer bottle, such as the neck, which she might have still been holding. McHugh also supported Dockeray's testimony that neither the pipe nor the stone would likely have caused the star-shaped fracture next to the right eye.[2]

Once the defense finished its questioning, the judge also questioned Dr. McHugh.

JUDGE: Could a fall occur without visible damage to the brain?
MCHUGH: Yes.
JUDGE: Would head injuries have occurred from thrashing and no
    others?
MCHUGH: Possibly.
JUDGE: Could she have damaged herself much between the fall and
    Bill reaching her?
McHugh: [She] could have.[3]

Prosecutor Effiwat cross-examined Dr. McHugh at some length about his medical qualifications and whether the qualifications of the several medical experts were important. However, he made little effort to counter the medical evidence McHugh provided. None of his questions appeared to damage either McHugh's or the other medical witnesses' testimony. After the cross-examination and a brief redirect by Georgiadis, McHugh was excused.[4] It is surprising that Effiwat did not press McHugh on the lack of wounds to Peppy's body, which the prosecution believed indicated that a fall had not occurred.

A second expert medical witness called by the defense was Peter Clifford, a consulting surgeon in charge of head-and-neck surgery at Kenyatta National Hospital in Nairobi. Dr. Clifford testified that it was quite possible that Peppy's injuries were caused by a 20-foot fall. He wouldn't expect other types of injuries in such a fall. The skull absorbed the force of the fall. The wounds were more likely from forceful contact with rocks or debris in the landing area than from blows. In addition, he testified that he thought Dr. Mganga's view that the injuries could not have been caused by a fall was quite wrong.[5]

Judge Platt observed that it seemed to him unlikely that a separated suture would be caused by a fall like this. Dr. Clifford responded that, on the contrary, in a person of Peppy's age the suture is not yet very tightly ossified, and so a separation could easily occur. Although he hadn't seen such injuries from a fall, he had seen them in similar situations, such as a car accident or a pedestrian or cyclist being hit by a car. The force is the same. The judge seemed unable to believe that Peppy could have fallen without incurring other injuries or bruises. Dr. Clifford said yes, it could have happened without other injuries.[6]

The court adjourned at the completion of Dr. Clifford's testimony.

Judge Platt seemed troubled and perhaps unconvinced on two key points arising from the medical testimony and the allegations of the prosecution. The prosecution maintained that the Kinseys had not climbed to the top of the rock, so all the injuries were incurred at the lower level and without a fall. So, first, Platt pressed the expert witnesses with the view that the injuries were not extensive enough to derive from a fall alone. He thought a person suffering a 20-foot fall would show injuries all over the body, and if some injuries to the head occurred after the fall through thrashing around, why didn't the thrashing cause injuries to other parts of the body? Similarly, he questioned Dockery's and McHugh's finding that despite the long fall there was no visible brain damage. Second, the judge found it difficult to believe Bill's story that he heard nothing during the fall, further supporting the prosecution's position that no fall had taken place. Since McHugh had testified about his re-creation of the incident on Impala Hill, Platt pressed McHugh on his belief that noise from the wind and Bill's placement vis-à-vis Peppy made it likely that Bill did not hear the fall. To all these questions, the defense medical experts maintained their professional belief that Bill's description of the events was medically possible.[7]

The second crucial aspect of the medical testimony concerned whether the alleged "weapons" could have caused the injuries to Peppy. The defense doctors asserted that the iron bar was too light to cause fractures of the skull or the incised cuts, that the stones could not have caused the incised wounds, and that neither the bar nor the stones could have caused the stellate fracture of the right eye, which Dockeray felt was the likely cause of death and which Doctor Mganga probably did not see.[8]

32

Trial Day Twelve

Wednesday, September 7, 1966

"Kinseys Never Had a Cross Word—Mother-in-Law"
—Nairobi Daily Nation

Marianne Dunn, a Peace Corps volunteer formerly stationed at the Sayusayu School, was the first witness when the trial resumed on Wednesday, September 7. Dunn was asked how well she knew Peppy, and she replied that she was Peppy's closest friend in Maswa. When asked about the relationship between Bill and Peppy, Dunn responded that Peppy had said she wished Bill were more affectionate but that she never doubted that he loved her. Peppy had told her they were sexually compatible and happy. "She spoke to me quite freely and confidentially about everything," said Dunn.

Dunn produced a letter Peppy had written to her in early March 1966; by that time, Dunn had transferred to another school. Dunn stated that in the letter Peppy "talked about how well things were going at the school and said Bill was now more affectionate and she had never been more happy in her life." Dunn also testified that in May 1965 she had gone on a picnic with the Kinseys and others to a hill near Maswa. At the picnic, she heard Bill say that he wanted to get a less-bulky tripod for his large telephoto lens.[1]

Marianne Dunn was the only volunteer called to testify in the trial. Her testimony gave credence to the defense argument that the Kinseys were a happy, compatible couple. Obviously, the defense would not seek out anyone with conflicting testimony. However, did the Peace Corps have an obligation, moral or otherwise, to canvass other volunteers about the Kinseys' relationship? Had Peace Corps officials done so, they might have found Aileen Dower,

197

Delores Ledbetter, the Ellisons, and possibly others with conflicting information. If so, the Peace Corps would presumably have given the information to the prosecution, but Peace Corps officials and the prosecution seemed to have no contact. Given the limited resources available to the Tanzania state attorneys and their lack of knowledge of Peace Corps operations, it is not surprising that they made no efforts to find witnesses among the volunteers. In his decision, the judge would make the point that the only testimony from a volunteer demonstrated a "normally happy marriage."[2]

One of the most dramatic moments in the trial came when Charlotte Dennett, Peppy's mother, took the witness stand following Marianne Dunn. Mrs. Dennett, age fifty-two, had flown out with her sister from her home in Connecticut. The two sisters had stayed for several days in Nairobi at a comfortable hotel arranged for them by Peace Corps Kenya before arriving in Mwanza so that their appearance in East Africa would come as a complete surprise to the prosecution. As Mrs. Dennett took the stand, she probably couldn't help noticing on the table in front of her Peppy's blood-stained skirt and blouse as well as the pipe and rocks that the prosecution alleged had been used to kill her.[3]

Mrs. Dennett testified that she had received many letters from Peppy; never had Peppy mentioned any problems or strife between her and Bill. In fact, she received a letter a week after Peppy's death that Peppy had written the day she died. When Mrs. Dennett was asked if she might read it, although obviously in distress she replied, "I am all right. I can read it." Georgiadis, however, took the letter from her and read it to the court. Peppy apologized in the letter for not writing more often and said how busy they were. "We haven't a minute to be bored," she wrote. Peppy went on to say that later in the day they planned to ride their bikes to a nearby hill for a picnic.

Mrs. Dennett said that she, along with her sister, had traveled to East Africa the prior year to visit Peppy and Bill. They toured Kenya and Tanzania together, and she never saw a sign of trouble between them. "There was never any hint of trouble in their marriage. When I got home I told a friend of mine it was a very comfortable relationship, which seemed good for a young couple after a year of marriage. I think they enjoyed doing things together immensely."[4]

A witness such as Mrs. Dennett presented an enormous challenge to Prosecutor Effiwat. Any effort to attack her testimony could easily backfire and make a more powerful case for Bill's innocence. An older woman, mother of the dead woman, voicing strong support for Bill's innocence, she would arouse great sympathy in the court. Any vigorous cross-examination attempting to rattle her might make the assessors and the judge inclined to view her as a more important and credible witness. So Effiwat proceeded with caution and asked her whether it was not uncommon for people to appear happy when they were not. She responded that this was certainly so, but she didn't believe that applied in her daughter's case.

"Are you aware that well-brought-up people do not wash their dirty linen in public?" asked Mr. Effiwat.

"Yes I am aware of that," responded Mrs. Dennett.[5]

After a few more gentle questions, the prosecutor finished his cross-examination, and the court adjourned the trial for thirty minutes to allow Mrs. Dennett time to talk to Bill. She crossed over to the dock, and he leaned down to embrace her. They talked for a short while, and then Mrs. Dennett was taken from the court and left immediately for the United States. Reporters tried to interview her, but to no avail.[6] In offering the adjournment, the judge also allowed the opportunity for the defense to signal the closeness of Mrs. Dennett and Bill, further strengthening her credibility as a character witness.

Earlier that day, PCDC called the office in Dar es Salaam with two messages from Bill Kinsey's father, one to Charlotte Dennett and one to Bill:

"Called morning you left. Missed you by minutes. May God bless you for efforts behalf Bill and ourselves."

"We are encouraged as news of defense case reaches our papers. Looking forward your return with God's help."[7]

Paul Sack, the Peace Corps country director, was also called to testify about his conversation with Bill on March 29 and his visit to the scene on Impala Hill. The gist of his testimony confirmed that Bill had told him the same, consistent story at that time. Sack had a photographer take photos of the scene, so he could also identify the photos and they might be offered into evidence.[8]

With the passage of legislation permitting the Peace Corps to pay for Bill's defense, PCDC informed its counterpart in Dar es Salaam that the full cost of the defense would be covered. Its estimate of the fees up to that point was $15,000, and it requested an estimate of the costs for the remainder of the case.[9]

33

Trial Day Thirteen

Thursday, September 8, 1966

"Murder Trial Goes to Death Scene"
—*Nairobi Daily Nation*

In the morning on Thursday, defense counsel Georgiadis reported to the court that his missing witness, the photographer who had taken photos of the crime scene, had still not appeared, so he suggested that the court travel to the scene in Maswa that day with the hope that the witness would appear in the meantime. Because the witness had previously been served with a summons to appear, Judge Platt issued a bench warrant for his arrest.[1] Without the photographer to authenticate his photos of the scene, it would be difficult to introduce them into evidence, although Paul Sack's identification might be sufficient.

The court then adjourned to travel the 90 miles from Mwanza to Maswa, the town where the Kinseys taught and where Peppy had died. Bill traveled in a Land Rover escorted by four paramilitary Field Force members armed with automatic weapons. Court officials, the defense, the prosecution, and Judge Platt traveled in Land Rovers as well. Judge Platt appeared in civilian clothes rather than in his wig and scarlet gown. The judge wished to survey the scene at approximately the same time the incident occurred, so they planned the trip accordingly.

Impala Hill (a kopje, as described earlier) looked over a group of African "mudhuts and dusty maize and cotton fields [that] could be the backdrop for a western movie. Huge granite boulders perch[ed] miraculously on top of each other high on the slopes. The rock at the base of which Peverley Kinsey died jut[ted] out like a knuckle on a fist."[2] Once there, the judge and the assessors

200

climbed to the top of the rock Bill said his wife fell from. According to one newspaper report,

> Platt took off his shoes to scale the rock and scramble down again to the spot to which the defense claims Peverley fell and where the prosecution charges Kinsey beat her to death with a length of iron pipe.
>
> Then the judge and the two assessors, Gail Bagley, an American, and Fred Mugoxbi [*sic*], climbed over the tangle of rocks, and wild sisal plants to where African witnesses testified they watched Kinsey struggle with his wife.[3]

The judge viewed photographs produced by the defense and a map prepared by Inspector Kifunta. Although Judge Platt asked no questions during the tour, he was particularly interested in observing the shrubbery and how it might have affected the witnesses' view. However, he would later point out that the court visit came at a drier time of the year, and so the shrubbery would be less dense and lush than in the spring. The group also visited the site where witnesses said they had seen Bill beating his wife. Shards of a bottle were found at the scene, perhaps confirming both Bill's testimony that the bottle of beer Peppy had been drinking was broken and the police failure to properly secure the evidence. This visit to Impala was made almost six months after the event, so perhaps the glass came later from someone else's bottle.

After about an hour at the site, the group traveled back to Maswa, where they stopped at the Kinseys' little red-roofed home while they taught at Binza School, then on to a shop for cold drinks. Judge Platt stood a few yards from Bill as he chatted with local friends. The caravan then headed back to Mwanza.[4]

One wonders what went through the judge's and the assessors' minds while they were surveying the scene of Peppy's death. Certainly, it would give them a better sense of the terrain, the distance between relevant sites and objects, but did it sway their views in any way? Did they come away with a greater sense of Bill's guilt or innocence?

34

Trial Day Fourteen

Friday, September 9, 1966

All that is left is sheer blind unreasoning prejudice.
—*Byron Georgiadis*

Presentations by the prosecution and defense came to a conclusion on the fourteenth day of the trial; each side was then called upon to summarize its case. First, Judge Platt ruled that the photos taken by Mr. Virji Natha Taank (hired by the defense and discussed further in chapter 35) could be admitted without the photographer's presence.[1]

Defense attorney Georgiadis began with a two-hour summing up of the relevant law and the facts of the case. Focusing his attention on the assessors, he stressed that the prosecution needed to prove Bill was guilty, not that the defense needed to demonstrate his innocence. The assessors must ignore rumors, gossip, and stories. "This is a small town, and like all small places, it can be rife with gossip and rumor. This has been an intriguing case and the alleged facts have been bandied about." Georgiadis warned the assessors that they must consider only the evidence produced in court and must ignore anything they heard outside the court. There were three things they needed to consider:

1. Whether Bill caused Peppy's death
2. Whether it was an unlawful act or omission
3. Or (and?) whether there was malice aforethought

Georgiadis then proceeded to review the prosecutor's case. He argued that there were at least twenty-three incidents of failure on the part of the police and the prosecution, which he proceeded to recount one by one—for example, the area was not secured, photos were not taken of the site, rocks were tossed aside, Peppy's body was placed in the Land Rover along with evidence, and so forth. The police investigation had been wholly inadequate and single-minded in an effort to prove Bill guilty. Inspector Kifunta had formed an early opinion of the case, and evidence that supported the defense was discarded, while anything that might prove Bill's guilt was carefully retained. What happened to Peppy was a tragic accident that, through the failures of and incompetent investigation by the police, was turned into a travesty.

The medical testimony provided by Mr. Mganga, an unqualified doctor, was contradicted by the testimony of two eminent and well-qualified doctors. The assessors must ignore the medical testimony offered by the prosecution because it was so obviously wrong. The defense expert medical witnesses had determined that the metal rod and the rocks that the prosecution alleged were the murder weapons could not have caused Peppy's injuries.

As to the accusation of infidelity as a motive for murder in the case, Georgiadis said, the fact that the sections in Bill's diary had been copied word for word from a book he had been reading should totally negate the persuasiveness of this theory. In addition, both Peppy's mother, Mrs. Dennett, and Peppy's friend Mary Anne Dunn had testified that the marriage was a happy one and Peppy was well satisfied.

The testimony of the prosecution witnesses Humbi Sayuda and Maganda Vilindo, stated Georgiadis, was unreliable. Humbi was almost senile and incapable of an accurate description of events, and Vilindo had contradicted himself when he was on the witness stand.

Georgiadis pointed out the unlikelihood that Bill would have chosen an open spot where many nearby villagers could see them as a place for a murder if he had planned it in advance. Bill's account of the events had been perfectly consistent, and it would strain credulity if he were able to concoct his story at the time of the incident and have it later confirmed by medical evidence.

Although Georgiadis attacked the prosecution case with vigor, he seemed to admit that the evidence was not completely one-sided and that, in fact, there might be some validity to certain prosecution assertions. He went on, however, to stress how such a result still called for an acquittal: "You may feel that in many questions there is a fine line to be drawn. Sometimes that line is blurred and in many respects may seem a question of guess-work. But if you find yourselves guessing and say to yourselves you can't be sure, the only course open is acquittal," he told the assessors.

In concluding, Georgiadis argued that since the prosecution had utterly failed to prove Bill's guilt, they must find him innocent and decide that a tragic accident had taken place. Bill was the "victim of circumstances caught in a web of investigative ineptitude."[2]

Senior State Attorney Ededen Effiwat then proceeded to make the case for a finding of guilty as charged. He began by explaining why certain evidence was missing. When he saw the results of the PI, he noticed that some evidence had been left out—for example, certain police photos. He had prepared to reopen the PI, but the director of public prosecutions in Dar es Salaam had informed him that the defense counsel objected to the case not proceeding in August because he would lose material witnesses. Effiwat said he then agreed to proceed with the case as is and did not object to the admission of photos that were properly identified. Under Tanzania law, the prosecution was required to present its entire case at the PI, so when Effiwat noticed evidence was missing, he could not simply present it at trial. He might have been required to reopen the PI, obviously a difficult procedure and likely to be fiercely fought by the defense.

Effiwat went on to argue that the story Bill had told was simply untrue. If Bill did not hear or see Peppy fall, then the fall did not happen at all. If the accused was looking toward the mission at Sayusayu, then the deceased must have fallen in front of him, yet he claimed to have seen nothing. Effiwat argued that Kinsey took the metal rod on the picnic because he planned to use it to kill her and that the pipe had nothing to do with camera equipment, nor could he offer any reasonable explanation for taking the bar to the scene or how the blood and hair could have been found on the rock other than that it was used to strike Peppy.

Effiwat reminded the court that two eyewitnesses, Maganda Vilindo and Padre Misunzu, saw Bill beating Peppy, so there was no question of circumstantial evidence but in fact clear proof of the charge of murder. These witnesses could easily have seen what they described, and there was no reason to disbelieve them. Any inconsistencies in their testimony was minimal and should not diminish its creditability.

As to the medical evidence, Dr. Dockeray was unregistered in Tanzania, so his postmortem was illegal, and the testimony from it should be stricken. Dr. McHugh's testimony should be stricken for the same reason. Therefore, the testimony of Dr. Mganga was presumptively correct and under section 13 of the Tanzania Evidence Code must be followed. Effiwat said that even though the extracts from Bill's notebook might have been taken from a book, they had been carefully selected and showed his morbid state of mind, a state that should be seen as evidencing malevolence toward and unhappiness with Peppy. It was also a compelling coincidence that the diary entry in question was dated March 26 and that Peppy died the next day. Effiwat pointed out that Kinsey quoted only "cynical" sections of the book and not beautiful sentences "about romance and religion."

Even Mary Anne Dunn's testimony about the happiness of the Kinseys' marriage, stated Effiwat, was qualified by her testimony that Peppy was unhappy because Bill denied her companionship and failed to show affection in public. Similarly, Mrs. Dennett admitted that it is not always possible to know what is going on inside a marriage.

Effiwat also pointed to the drugs taken by Peppy, which showed that Bill intended to knock her out or at least make her dizzy when coupled with the beer he gave her.

The defense claimed that there was more than one fall, but Bill said he saw only one fall. (This statement seems to confuse the fall from the rock and the fall when Bill was carrying Peppy.) It was not believable, Effiwat argued, that such a fall would not result in other injuries to the body. The prosecution had presented sufficient evidence to prove the case beyond any reasonable doubt. "The accused had, at the material time, become dissatisfied with the deceased and he planned to murder her. He carried out his plan on March 27," Mr. Effiwat concluded.[3]

Once Effiwat finished, the court adjourned until the following day, Saturday, when it was expected that the judge would instruct the assessors.

PCDSM established an elaborate procedure to ensure that news of the verdict would reach Washington, D.C., as soon as possible. However, given the vagaries of telephone and telegraph connections in East Africa, PCDSM sought several different paths for the communications—for instance, sending messages both to Nairobi and to Dar es Salaam as well as requesting use of a special "flash" format for such notices.[4]

35

Trial Day Fifteen

Saturday, September 10, 1966

Judge Platt was expected to instruct the assessors on Saturday, September 10, but he postponed it until Monday. No explanation was given. He did, however, rule that under Tanzania law, the defense medical testimony should be admitted.[1]

After adjourning for an hour, the court took up the issue of the missing photographer, Virji Natha Taank. Taank had taken photos for the defense, which they had planned to introduce into evidence, and he had been served with a summons but failed to appear on time. Despite not having the photographer available to verify the photos, the judge had allowed the photos to be used as evidence through verification by another witness (presumably Paul Sack) but had also issued a bench warrant for Taank's arrest. At this point, however, the judge found that the original summons was improper, so he withdrew the warrant and released Taank as a witness.[2]

As the trial came to an end, and a decision seemed imminent, PCDC and staff in Tanzania began to worry about what to do at that point, particularly if Bill were found guilty. Communication facilities between Mwanza, Dar es Salaam, Nairobi, and Washington, D.C., were extremely limited, and PCDC worried that a press report of the verdict might surface before the Peace Corps had time to prepare a response. In the event, the judge's final decision was delayed by a week, so the Peace Corps continued to assess various methods to transmit reports to PCDC. In Tanzania, Peace Corps staff lacked their own telecommunication facilities, so the likelihood of getting ahead of press reports was marginal at best.[3]

PCDC asked that an open line be established between Mwanza and either Nairobi or Dar es Salaam and cables prepared for urgent transmission to assure clear language was used to describe a decision of either "guilty" or "innocent." Once the decision was announced, PCDC would ask for an immediate telephone conference to discuss next steps and, if the verdict were guilty, what to do. At the same time, Peace Corps officials recognized that these procedures might be wholly unfeasible given the level of communication facilities available in Tanzania. In addition, Tony Essaye planned to schedule calls to PCDSM and Nairobi at likely times and would relay the verdict to whichever office he reached first. He would make his calls from Mwanza if possible, but, if not, he would forward the news to PCDSM for forwarding to PCDC.

Much cable space was also given over to the impact of a not-guilty verdict, particularly on Bill's plans. Bill had earlier stated that he would like to continue his term in Tanzania. Peace Corps officials expressed great concern about such a course, with respect both to Bill and to the government's and the Tanzanian citizens' response to his continued presence there. "Should the Court find Bill guilty, Bill's attorneys planned to appeal immediately to the East African Court of Appeals. Grounds for such an appeal could not only include the common basis found in American Law of prejudicial error, but also on the basis that the verdict was contrary to the accumulated weight of the evidence. The attorneys were confident of a successful appeal on the latter ground. It was also clear that the prosecution was prohibited by law from appealing an acquittal."[4]

36

Trial Day Sixteen

Monday, September 12, 1966

"Assessors Say Kinsey Not Guilty of Killing His Wife"
—*Nairobi Daily Nation*

During his instructions to the assessors, which lasted more than one and a half hours on Monday, September 12, Judge Platt pointed out various discrepancies in the evidence provided by certain witnesses and drew their attention to crucial facets of the case. They were to advise him as to the defendant's guilt or innocence only on the evidence before them—that is, what the witnesses said, the documents introduced, and the visit to the site. He stressed that if they had any doubts, they must acquit Mr. Kinsey.[1]

Continuing with his review of the law, he summarized it as follows:

The main issue is whether the accused is guilty of murder. The ingredients of murder are:

1. Did the accused cause her death?
2. Was it by unlawful act or omission?
3. Was it with malice aforethought?

He explained that "malice aforethought" would include intent to kill or a knowledge that death will probably occur or an intent to cause grievous bodily harm or an indifference as to whether death would occur. "Grievous bodily harm," he went on to say, is defined as any harm that would amount to the destruction of an internal or external organ. The judge stated that the prosecution's proof must be beyond a reasonable doubt, but if there is doubt, it must be genuine. If the assessors believed the death was an accident, then they must find the accused not guilty. This would also apply to each of the three parts of the definition of murder. The prosecution must prove its case beyond reasonable doubt on each aspect of the case, whereas the defense need only raise a doubt.[2]

Review of Site

Judge Platt then summarized the prosecution's case, starting with a review of the site. The photos gave a good idea of what the geography and landscape looked like. Inspector Kifunta's sketch mixed vertical and horizontal aspects and would have been clearer if the two views had been given separately. Some of the photos were misleading because of foreshortening. He pointed out that the passage between the rocks ran from north to south and that if one stood on rocks looking from the south, the view of the platform where Peppy lay was clear. Maganda was alleged to have stood on these rocks. The rocks, however, were difficult to climb. When the court visited the scene, it was different from the day of Peppy's death—for instance, some brush had grown, some had been cut down—so the photos taken near the date of the incident became more important. (Platt's ruling allowing the photos to be placed in evidence without authentication by the photographer became more significant.)[3]

Eyewitnesses

Judge Platt concluded his review of the scene by attempting to identify where the various witnesses stood and analyzing the consistency or lack thereof in their testimony. As to witness Humbi, the judge thought that it was very difficult to tell exactly where she was at the time of the incident. He advised that she might have misunderstood the sign the accused gave to her—that is, whether it meant to come to him or to go away. Maganda Vilindo and Padre Masunzu indicated they were in the field when they first became aware of the incident. It appeared that they would not have had a very good view from their locations. Inspector Kifunta agreed that the view from their locations was not clear. The judge pointed out that Vilindo's testimony was disjointed and contained discrepancies—for example, the color of the object used to strike the blow or blows; the number of blows (at one point he said several, but at another he said only one); and whether a basket was being held during the struggle or not. Masunzu said the accused was throttling Peppy and kneeling at her side, but at the PI he said the accused was on top of her. The judge told the assessors that they could accept the evidence if they felt the discrepancies were unimportant, but if they felt the discrepancies were important or the witnesses were confused, they could reject the testimony.[4]

The Parties' Arguments

The positions of the prosecution and of the defense were not reconcilable—not just the difference of one blow, Judge Platt observed. Under the defense version of the incident, Vilindo and Masunzu could not have seen the struggle because the fight was over by the time the accused saw Humbi. Vilindo and Masunzu did not arrive on the scene until after Humbi raised the alarm.

As to the metal bar, Inspector Kifunta said it could not have gotten there by accident. The assessors must decide whether they thought the rock was used as a weapon or as a pillow. The location of the rock was another issue they needed decide. Was it where the police said they found it, or had it been moved by someone during the investigation?[5]

Medical Evidence

Turning to the medical evidence, the judge said AMO Philip Mganga was sufficiently qualified to perform a postmortem and to provide evidence. Nevertheless, the assessors need not accept his evidence. He pointed out that some experts are more qualified than others. If the assessors accepted Mganga's evidence, then in the judge's opinion the wounds would not have come from a fall but likely from an assault. The other doctors were of the opinion that the wounds were consistent with a fall. In the end, if the assessors had a doubt, they should find that the medical evidence supported the accused.[6]

A Possible Fall

The judge next reviewed the facts concerning whether there was a fall or not. The accused testified that he couldn't see or hear the fall. The assessors could decide whether to believe him or not. It seemed that Peppy could not have fallen straight down, said the judge. There was testimony that the deceased had taken Benadryl and drank some beer. Would that have caused her to slip and fall? But the prosecution argued that there was no fall at all. No one knew exactly where she fell, the judge stated, but it appeared that it was in the region of the first pool of blood. Had the defense raised a doubt or just told a story?[7]

Motive

As to motive, were the entries in the diary an unfortunate coincidence? It was up to the assessors to decide. Was the marriage compatible? They should not speculate.

If the assessors were satisfied with the testimony of the witnesses that an assault took place and that the bar and stone were used in the assault, then they must find the defendant guilty.

However, if they found the evidence of the eyewitnesses unsatisfactory, then it was a case of circumstantial evidence. In such a case, to determine guilt they must find that the circumstantial evidence leads irresistibly to such a conclusion.

If they found the defense argument correct that the death was an accident, then they must render a verdict of not guilty.

If they felt that both the prosecution and defense might be correct and that there was a real possibility that the defense was correct, and if they had doubts about the prosecution case, then they had to find the defendant not guilty.[8]

The Assessors' Decisions

Once his summation was concluded, the judge turned to Gail Bagley and asked him to give his verdict. In a clear, firm voice, Bagley said he found Bill not guilty.

"My opinion is that it was an obvious accident beyond any doubt."

When the judge questioned him, Bagley said he preferred to believe the two defense medical witnesses that Peppy's injuries were consistent with a fall and unlikely to have been caused by the iron bar or the stone. He went on to say that the metal rod could have been at the scene by mistake, as Bill had testified, and that the bloodstained rock could have been used as a pillow for Peppy's head. The marriage appeared stable, and he found no credible evidence for infidelity. Maganda Vilindo and Padre Masunzu misunderstood what they saw. Efforts made by the accused were meant to calm down the deceased and to prevent further injuries. He was not striking her. One witness also seemed confused as to the color of the rod. It seemed more likely to Bagley that the stone was used as a pillow, so that is how the blood came to be on it. The location of the stone was not important—it could have been tossed by people the night of the event or the next morning. The accused's testimony that the pipe was brought to the picnic—as he said—to make a tripod support was believable. The notebook was truly a notebook, not a "diary." There was no basis for implying a motive from the entries.[9]

"I believe the accused not guilty of the charge," declared Fred Mugobi, the Tanzania economist and second assessor. Mugobi went on to say that he felt the fall took place as the accused had described and that the prosecution had failed to prove any infidelity, which might have provided a motive. Mugobi believed the testimony that the marriage was a happy one. The eyewitnesses, he reasoned, misunderstood what they saw. Vilindo was far away and needed to go to a different place to see better. Masunzu didn't see what had happened prior to what he called "kneeling" and "throttling." It was more likely that the situation was as the accused testified, that he was trying to restrain and calm the deceased. The defense medical evidence was more reliable, and a fall was a more likely explanation for the death. Blood and hair probably got on the pipe during the struggle and on the stone when it was used as a pillow. Mugobi thought the death was clearly an accident and that there should be an acquittal on that ground.[10]

When I interviewed Gail Bagley, he told me that he was very concerned during the trial whether Bill would be found guilty. He felt the prosecution had a very strong case, but in the end the testimony did not support the prosecution's case. He and Mugobi did not discuss the case until the end of trial, and he felt Mugobi was at a bit of a loss and so simply followed Bagley's decision. Bagley never asked any questions during the trial, although he believed it was permissible for him to do so. In his mind, one of the most difficult aspects of the trial was the need to translate from Sukuma to Swahili to English and back again.[11]

Once the assessors had rendered their decisions, Judge Platt announced that he would render his verdict on Saturday, September 17. Under Tanzania law, the judge need not follow the assessors' decisions.[12] "In a murder trial it would be unusual, but not unknown for a judge to reach an opposite decision to his assessors. When he does, it generally is recognized as grounds for appeal."[13]

Despite the great concern expressed by Peace Corps officials in Tanzania that limited communication facilities might prevent them from getting the assessors' decision to PCDC in a timely manner, in the end they were able to send the news to Washington, D.C., before the wire-service reports reached the United States.[14]

Even though the judge's final verdict was yet to be rendered, it seems Bill could and did become optimistic regarding a favorable outcome because he asked Peace Corps officials to cable the following message to his parents on September 12: "EXPECT FINAL JUDGMENT SATURDAY WHEREUPON I SHALL EMPLANE FOR STATES ASAP. PROBABLY WILL SPEND ONE NIGHT IN RIVERSIDE [Peppy's mother's home], THEN HOME. WILL INFORM YOU DETAILS LATER."[15]

37

Trial Day Seventeen

Friday, September 16, 1966

On Friday, September 16, Judge Platt announced that he would not issue his decision the next day as originally scheduled but would give it on Monday. No explanation was given for the delay.[1]

Meanwhile, PCDSM provided an update of the estimated costs for the defense:

Singh fee	$4,500
Singh expenses	$1,000
Georgiadis fee	$3,750
Georgiadis expenses	$500
Dockeray fee and expenses	$1,000
Clifford fee and expenses	$400
Mwanza Hotel costs for Brewster, Georgiadis, Dockeray	$700
Shorthand secretary for trial	$500
Brewster fee, $150/day	$7,000
Brewster expenses	$2,000
Total estimate	$21,350 or $22,000–23,000[2]

The total in today's dollars would be about $164,000.

Although the Kinsey family had originally agreed to cover the cost of the defense, by this time legislation had passed whereby the Peace Corps was enabled to pay these expenses. The increase in costs over earlier estimates seemed commensurate with the length of the trial and the need for additional witnesses.

In addition, Peace Corps Tanzania staff forwarded a nine-point comparison of Tanzania law and U.S. law (presumably prepared by Tony Essaye) that found few if any differences between criminal law in the two countries.[3] It is curious that the author of the comparison (Essaye) did not focus on the significant differences between the procedure for a PI in the United States and the procedure in Tanzania. It may be that because each U.S. state establishes its own procedures and the federal rules apply only to federal cases, the author felt that a simple comparison could not be made, or perhaps the choice was made to show how similar the two systems were in an effort to diminish any claim that Bill did not receive a fair trial.

Peace Corps officials became worried about an article in the press that reported on arrangements having been made even before the verdict was announced to fly Bill out of Mwanza. They were afraid that this report might have an effect on the judge's decision and wondered how the reporter could have known about these plans. Dar es Salaam officials responded that a reporter was at the airport when travel arrangements were being made by staff and may have been the source of the article.[4]

38

Trial Day Eighteen

Monday, September 19, 1966

> Every judgment in every trial in every criminal court shall be in writing, shall contain (a) the point or points for the determination, (b) the judge's decision thereon, and (c) the reason for the decision, and shall be read . . . in open court in the presence of the accused.
> —*Tanzania Criminal Code*

On Monday, September 19, the eighteenth day of the Kinsey trial, Judge Platt issued his judgment, spending almost two hours reviewing the evidence and the law and reading his twenty-two-page, single-spaced decision. The document contains many typos and cross-outs, suggesting it might have been typed by the judge himself. Only after the lengthy review of the case did he finally pronounce the judgment. During those two long hours, Bill Kinsey sat grim-faced with rapt concentration on the judge and his words. The packed courtroom was also quiet, and the tension was palpable.[1] Although much of the detail in the judge's decision has been supplied previously, it is instructive to see how the judge developed his thinking, so in this chapter I summarize the document in some detail.

Summary of Arguments

Judge Platt began with a review of the prosecution's charges and its description of the events on the day Peppy died, saying that "the prosecution set out to prove that the accused had planned to kill his wife during the picnic and had in fact concealed a metal pipe in the picnic basket for this purpose." Platt then examined the prosecution's portrayal of the events leading to Peppy's death, generally following the same narrative he had provided to the assessors.

In contrast, he said, the defense contended that it was all an unfortunate accident, arguing that the eyewitness testimony was unreliable and that the better medical evidence supported a finding that the injuries resulted from a fall, not from a blow. "It was alleged that the direct evidence given by the so-called eye-witnesses was too conflicting to be relied upon and that the remainder of the evidence, being only circumstantial evidence, it was capable [o]f innoqnt [sic] explanation and therefore could not lead irresistibly to a conclusion of the guilt of the accused."

Platt then referred to the assessors' conclusion that Peppy's death was an accident and that therefore the defendant was not guilty, but he went on to say: "It remains for me to decide whether upon the evidence adduced in this Court the prosecution had indeed failed to establish the charge of murder against the accused. It will be found that the evidence is intriguingly elusive and that the decision is most difficult, resting as it does, upon a narrow margin of circumstances."[2]

Interlocutory Orders

At this point, Judge Platt reviewed several interlocutory (preliminary and not final) rulings made during the trial and concluded that they were correctly made under the law and that he saw no reason to change them. Among the rulings he mentioned were the admissibility of Inspector Kifunta's sketch of the scene, the presence of Dr. McHugh in the court while the doctors were testifying, the calling of the government chemist, and so on. He also suggested that the Tanzania authorities might wish to issue instructions about proper methodology in undertaking the investigation of a murder. Although this latter suggestion could have provided a hint to his ultimate conclusion, it also apparently led to Inspector Kifunta and Dr. Mganga being transferred far away from Maswa and suffering major setbacks to their careers.[3]

Prosecution Evidence

Judge Platt then summarized the evidence of what took place on the day Peppy died, as presented by the prosecution. The witness Humbi was working in her *shamba* when she heard a cry. She thought one of her children might be in danger, so she cried out in alarm, and witness Maganda Vilindo appeared. Maganda (Judge Platt referred to him as "Maganda," whereas I have usually called him "Vilindo") saw the accused strike a woman and fight with her. He was joined by Padre Masunzu (whom the judge called by his first name, whereas I have usually called him by his last). The two of them went to the other side of the rock, and Maganda said he saw the accused sitting on the woman, and Padre said he saw him kneeling beside her. Both demonstrated to the court that the accused's hands were at the woman's neck, and Padre said he was throttling her. Padre then left to call the police. At this point, the accused picked up his wife, moved her to another part of the rocks, and descended to his bike. He was met by an angry crowd. He tried to talk with them in Swahili, but apparently they understood only Sukuma. Finally, someone came who understood him and immediately left to bring the headmaster. The headmaster and some students arrived, discovered the situation, and immediately sent word to the Catholic mission and to the hospital. The accused returned to the hill when two priests from the mission and the police arrived. Police inspector Martin Kifunta listened to the accused's account of the events and then began a search of the site. During the search, he found a bloodstained pipe with hair on it near a pool of blood. Kifunta kept the pipe, a picnic basket, and the other articles. He gathered statements from the witnesses before taking the body to the mortuary. The accused was released to the priests for the night. Before leaving with the priests, the accused was taken to his house for a change of clothes, and Inspector Kifunta took the clothes he was wearing to the police station.

The next morning the accused returned to the station, where he was charged with murder. He made a statement to the police under the usual caution about self-incrimination. The police then returned to the scene for further investigation. At the scene, Inspector Kifunta took measurements, made notes of various points at the scene with the help of the witness Maganda, found a rock with blood on it, and took it with him as an exhibit. From the scene, the police traveled to the accused's house for a search. At the house, camera equipment, various papers, and the "diary" were taken as potential evidence. On the same day, the accused was taken to the hospital and examined, and a blood sample was drawn. Kifunta also issued an order for a postmortem examination. In the absence of a coroner, the examination was performed by Dr. Mganga.

On March 29, the accused made a statement to Mr. Swai, a justice of the peace. On that same day, the accused's clothing, the pipe and stone, and samples of the deceased's hair and blood were sent to Dar es Salaam, accompanied by Constable Mohammed. A week later the constable returned with the exhibits, and shortly afterward the government chemist's report arrived. It concluded that the blood samples were human blood type O, which was the blood for both the accused and the deceased. The chemist also confirmed that the hair samples from the pipe and the stone were of the same "European" type as the samples taken from the head of the deceased.[4]

Defense Activities

The judge next described what the defense did while the police investigation proceeded. On March 29, Dr. McHugh, Paul Sack, and attorney Parekh flew to Maswa by charter plane. Both McHugh and Sack separately interviewed the accused, Bill explaining to each one that what happened to Peppy was an accident. McHugh was granted permission to examine the body, which he did and then flew back to Mwanza with Constable Mohammed and the body. Before leaving Maswa, Parekh and McHugh obtained authorization for a "specialist" to examine the body. At Mwanza, Dr. Dockeray performed a postmortem assisted by Dr. McHugh.

On March 30, Paul Sack returned to Maswa and was shown the scene of the incident by Inspector Kifunta. Sack and a photographer returned to the scene, where they took fifteen photographs. Among the fifteen, twelve were accepted as accurate and entered as exhibits in evidence, and three were marked as Exhibits number 9, 13, and 15 but were rejected as evidence.[5]

Description of the Scene

As the judge read on, he began to describe the scene and the various items that had been found there. He turned to the map that Inspector Kifunta had prepared, which had been marked with letters at various points to assist in describing the scene. The photos taken by Paul Sack and his photographer were correlated with the points on the map. The judge described where the various *shambas* were in relation to the map sites and where Maganda had gone around the hill for a better look. He observed that at several points the view of activities on the hill would have been obscured to the witnesses. The place where the bloody pipe and the bloody rocks were found was identified on the map. The judge reviewed Bill's testimony about where certain events happened on the hill.

He pointed out that Bill had testified that the articles he and Peppy had taken with them to Impala Hill had been spread out where they had been sitting, but he also noted that Inspector Kifunta had found the objects near Peppy's body.

Judge Platt spent some time analyzing the witnesses' ability to see the events owing to distance, shrubbery, and other factors. He observed that the events took place at a wetter time of the year than when the court visited the scene, so the shrubbery would have been denser because of the rains. The photos had been taken a few days after the event and would provide a more accurate depiction of the scene than what they had observed on their visit during the trial. However, the defense had pointed out that even the photos would vary from the scene on the actual day of Peppy's death because the police had cut down and flattened some of the shrubbery before the photos were taken. There remained considerable confusion as to where people were standing at various times, in particular Bill and Peppy at the time of the fall, which led the judge to express great skepticism about Bill's claim that he did not see Peppy fall, if she did fall.

"In concluding the description of the scene it is necessary to observe that the witness Humbi could not remember having shown (him) her shamba from which she raised the alarm to Mr. Kifunta and so that that part of his evidence became inadmissible and accordingly point 'I' on the sketch plan cannot be taken into consideration. The result is that it is not known exactly where Humbi was."[6]

Eyewitness Testimony

Humbi Sayuda's Testimony

Next the judge reviewed the testimony of the eyewitnesses. Humbi, age seventy, heard a cry, and she saw a European man on the hill. (In Tanzania at the time, all white people were called "Europeans.") The man motioned to her, and she believed he was motioning her away. She raised the alarm. Maganda and another man, who was not called as a witness, arrived. Maganda understood that Humbi's child was in trouble, so he went to look. The accused testified that he had seen a woman and motioned to her to come and help. He was not sure that the woman he saw was Humbi. Africans and Europeans (and Americans) differ in the way they make motions for someone to come or to go away, and the judge relied on this difference to explain the possible misunderstanding.

He also pointed out that Humbi's vision was perhaps not too reliable because she was unable in court to identify Bill as the man she saw.[7]

Maganda Vilindo's Testimony

Judge Platt felt Maganda Vilindo's testimony was extremely important to the prosecutors, and so he quoted it verbatim:

> When I saw them fighting one another I could not go near because I was afraid and I took the bushy side to see exactly the end of the fight and I saw a woman down and a man on top of her beating. One held the other while the other was raising his hand frequently. The one who was raising and lowering his hand was the man and the person who was holding the forearms was the woman and the man was striking like this (here he demonstrated several blows on the fore-head). I cannot tell exactly on which part of the body the man was hitting the woman but I could see from far away that the man had a black tool and as I saw him from far away he was beating on her forehead. As a result of that hitting the woman fell down and I passed the bush side while raising and [sic] alarm. The woman fell down with her head slanting to the right side. She fell on her right side and the legs were pointing to the North and the head was pointing to the South.[8]

The judge pointed out that by the time Maganda's cross-examination was concluded, a number of inconsistencies were found in his testimony. Maganda confirmed that he was about 126 paces away from the scene when he first observed the fight, but he could not see the object the man used to beat the woman. At first, he thought it was black but on reconsideration thought it white. He stated that he had seen only one blow, and then the woman fell down. He admitted he went to the second place to see better but also to get the support of other men who had arrived by then. He first said the man rushed to his bicycle but then changed his story to say the man first carried the woman to another place. He didn't see the man with a pipe, stones, or a basket. However, he was able to identify Bill in court as the man he observed at the scene.

Padre Masunzu's Testimony

Padre Masunzu testified that he also answered Humbi's alarm. He joined Maganda in the middle of the field, but they could see nothing at that point, so he and Maganda went around to the south, where Maganda showed him two Europeans (Bill and Peppy). The judge's decision described Padre's testimony as follows: "The man was kneeling beside the woman, who was lying on her back and the man had both hands around the neck while peeping back on both sides. He explained that the woman was being throttled." Maganda urged Padre to go fetch the police. Which he did.

The judge continued with a very damning review of the inconsistencies in the eyewitness testimony. His decision is quoted at length because it marks such a defeat for the prosecution case.

It is not easy to explain the discrepancies between the evidence of these two men. Of course, one may make allowance for the disjointed nature of the narrative and perhaps for their nervousness in carrying as they did, the main weight of the prosecution. But, nevertheless, despite their favourable demenour [sic] there are inconsistencies of importance which cannot be passed over for these reasons. It is difficult to tell why Padre could not have seen anything from where Maganda was standing. But Mr. Kifunta agrees that from the place pointed to him by Maganda, the view was obscured by shrubbery. If this is so, it appears that Padre's evidence is strengthened on this point while Maganda's evidence is weakened. It is possible that Maganda may have seen something which suggested a fight to him and that the woman had fallen down before Padre arrived. In that case it would appear that these witnesses did not observe the accused on top of the deceased until they climbed the rock to the South. Looking at Maganda's evidence, this may well be so. There is, therefore, only Maganda's word for it that there was an assault. His evidence on this point was considerably weakened by the changes in his story. First, there were many blows, then only one; first it was a black tool like object and then a whitish object, then he did not know on which parts of the body the blows had fallen and then it was one blow on the forehead. . . . . One should not criticise [sic] witnesses too severely for differences in the estimating of the distance, but Maganda quite deliberately [sic] chose an object in estimating the distance which was a very much longer way off than that chosen by Padre and, having in mind his evidence which frequently states that he was far away, it is yet another matter which must be considered in estimating the accuracy of his observation. On any view of the evidence one can only conclude that he could see with difficulty from the maize shamba. Indeed, the Assessors were not satisfied that his observation was reliable from this point. There is again inconsistency in the comparison of the evidence of Maganda and Padre in what they saw from the southern ock [sic, rock?]. Mr. Kifunta's estimate that this was about 100 ft from the scene seems to be right. Although the witnesses could see quite clearly from this point, they described the actions of the accused in a suspicious but conflicting manner, either the accused was sitting on the deceased or he was kneeling beside her. It is difficult to say which one was exaggerating on this point. As far as the throttling is concerned, this point was not really stressed by Maganda although Padre did so. But it is to be observed that in the lower court neither of these witnesses made this point. Padre who disagreed with the record of his evidence in the lower court, although it was read over and acknowledged by him, can only be said to have changed his evidence. He disagreed with several points recorded by the committing magistrate and, therefore, his evidence became unreliable and I must treat the observation of throttling as an exaggeration.[9]

Bill Kinsey's Testimony

Judge Platt continued with the observation that the accused testified that he knelt down and picked up his wife before carrying her around the ledge. He had been sitting on her at an earlier stage. When the prosecution cross-examined him, he conceded that the witnesses accounts could reflect his actions but that they misunderstood them. Although the defense downplayed the differences, Judge Platt found them more profound, and he quoted from Bill's testimony to underscore this conclusion:

I sat on her until she had calmed down and would not injure herself and would get up. I then thought I had to do something to get help. I got up and went back around the ledge where I saw nobody at all on that side, but I could hear people shouting. I went and returned to the spot where my wife is [sic] lying. I saw a woman coming from the right passing through a maize field[.] I shouted at her in Kiswahili. I gestured at her to come[.] But she continued going from right to left.

I thought she was going to some place so she could climb up the rock to come. I waited there for just a few minutes. I could still hear shouts. So I went back in that direction. I saw men at a distance. I don't know how many. So I shouted to them in Kiswahili also. They shouted back as well. They stood where they were. What seemed like to me a long time passed and I thought I had to do something. I went back to where my wife was lying, I picked her up and went again round the ledge carrying her.[10]

Judge Platt concluded that the story told by the accused was in direct conflict with the villagers' testimony. "If the accused's story is correct, it would appear that Maganda and Padre had jumped to the conclusion that there had been a struggle on seeing the deceased being carried by the accused, both of them covered with blood. Having seen the villagers, it seems, that it would be remarkable that they had imagined as much as this and the question is which of the two stories is the more reliable."[11]

Motive

At this point, Judge Platt turned to the alleged motive for the crime, observing that if the villagers' testimony was correct, motive was an essential factor. The "diary" had been marked as Exhibit W and admitted into evidence. The prosecution pointed to several sections of the diary entered the day before the incident and claimed that they showed the accused believed his wife had been unfaithful and something would happen on March 27.

The defense produced evidence that this item was not a diary but a journal containing passages from books read by the accused. The prosecution apparently was unaware of the source of the quotation before trial but accepted that they were from a book called *Ceremony in Lone Tree*. However, the prosecution argued that even if they were quotes from a book, they reflected the accused's state of mind at the time and still provided evidence of a motive. The prosecution was unable to provide any direct evidence of a motive on the part of the deceased, and the testimony of Dr. McHugh, Miss Dunn, and the deceased's mother, Mrs. Dennett, supported the idea that the Kinseys were a happy couple.

The judge then set forth the quotations in question, each coming from *Ceremony in Lone Tree* and copied into Bill's "diary":

The first quotation is a trite remark about the bore of getting to know people. A character in the novel asks "Don't you think they are nicer before you know them?"

"That's what is good about the good old days, the other fellow got the girl."

"You scared of your own kind?" "I'm scared they might be real, I mean realer than I am."

Then perhaps the most important quotations follow:

"When he asked her if anything unusual had happened Etoile had been obliged to say that it might have but she wouldn't really know until about the 27th of the month."

"It was on his mind until it happened, then it was on his mind because it had."

"It is from the first of these latter quotations that the connection was drawn between the entries in the notebook and the events of the 27th March 1966. The second of these quotations was suggested as showing that the accused had something on his mind and had, so to speak, warned himself of his feelings after the intended event."

The quotations then continue:

"You want to know why?" she yelled. "It is because nobody wants to know why, it is because nobody wants to know *anything*. Everybody hates everybody but nobody knows why anybody gets shot."

"In the middle of life Morgenstern Boyd had everything to live for, everything worth living for having eluded him. He was that rare thing, a completely self-unmade man."

"Oh crying out loud why not admit it? What so wrong if you say so. Almost everything your feelings would be showing." [*sic*]

"Her father lived by himself so he could believe the stories about himself."

"He had always picked up the tab so to speak without the fun."[12]

The quotations in the judge's decision end here and mirror the prosecution's evidence. The judge found that these selections did not lead directly to the conclusion that the accused had a motive for killing the deceased. It didn't seem unusual for a student of literature to copy such passages, and the "notebook/diary" contained other similar examples of selections from books and personal observations. In the end, the weakness of this part of the prosecution case is revealed in Inspector Kifunta's statement that had he known the source of these quotes at the time, he might very well have treated the case differently.

Judge Platt concluded, "There was no proof of motive for the alleged crime."[13]

The Pipe and the Rock

Judge Platt was especially troubled by where the pipe and rocks were found and how that might or might not fit into the accused's testimony that he had left them with the picnic basket, but they were found near the deceased and near pools of blood. The judge also seemed to think it unlikely that a murderer would hide the objects so close to the scene when there were other excellent hiding places nearby. It was clear that the hair and the blood most likely came from the deceased. Although the defense had posited that a likely scenario was that a bystander had come into the area before the police arrived and had moved some of the objects, Judge Platt found that suggestion unpersuasive:

> Summing up this part of the evidence then, it can be said that both the pipe and stone were stained with deceased's blood and a part of her hair attached to both. It was possible that after being involved in the incident either as weapons or in some other way that they had been placed at the places they were found by the accused, but on the other hand in the case of the pipe, it was not quite certain that it could not have rolled or been propelled to its resting place in the grass innocently, especially, having in mind the unlikelihood of an accused trying to hide a weapon there. In the case of the stone it was much more likely to have been hidden but due to the uncertainty as to whether anybody had interfered with the site which may have accounted for the removal of the picnic articles, there is just a possibility that the stone may have been dislodged accidentally. According to the evidence of Maganda, it is not easy to see that the accused had the opportunity of disposing of these weapons. But it must be said that if the accused did use the metal pipe, it would be consistent with what Maganda first described; namely a black tool. On the other hand, it is very difficult to see how it could have been whitish, as he later corrected himself.[14]

Medical Evidence

Judge Platt reviewed Dr. Mganga's (the judge spells the name "Maganga" throughout his decision, although everywhere else it is spelled "Mganga") medical evidence, relied upon by the prosecution, for accuracy and credibility. He first disposed of the defense argument that Mganga was unqualified. He found that Mganga had completed the required training and was therefore a qualified doctor under Tanzania law. Similarly, he denied the prosecution's objection to Dr. Dockeray's testimony based on the fact that Dr. Dockeray was not on the list of registered medical practitioners in Tanzania. Judge Platt commended the defense for providing eminent medical practitioners, Dr. Dockeray and Dr. Clifford, and pointed out that the prosecution could also have obtained more accomplished experts had it chosen to do so.

Because the competing medical evidence was so central to the case, Judge Platt used five pages of single-spaced text to analyze in detail the various medical findings. AMO Mganga and Drs. McHugh, Dockeray, and Clifford were brought into the analysis.

> There is no doubt that the deceased died through the injuries which she sustained to her head, externally, there were multiple lacerated wounds and one contused sort of wound while underneath the latter wound there was a depressed fracture on the right side of the head and two other linear fractures. According to Dr. Maganga [sic], there was subdural haemorrhage [sic] under the depressed fracture. In his opinion, death was due to cerebral haemorrhage due to the fractures of the skull. In Dr. Dockeray's opinion, the amount of haemorrage [sic] estimated by Dr. Maganga was not sufficient by itself to cause death and he preferred to base his opinion as to the cause of death on injuries to the brain. Whichever it was, scientifically speaking, there is no doubt that the blows to the head which had caused the head wounds and fractures of the skull had caused the death, however, this force was applied.[15]

The nature and extent of the head injuries were disputed in part by the medical experts who examined the body. Dockeray's testimony provided more detail and demonstrated a closer examination than Mganga's. The various wounds were described in the judge's decision as to size, placement, how they might have interacted with other wounds. The judge reviewed the descriptions of the bruises and lacerations on other parts of the deceased's body for differences and similarities between the doctors' reports.

> From this evidence, several deductions may be made according to the examination preferred. The Assessors preferred the evidence of Dr. Dockeray and on reviewing the evidence as a whole, I think it must also be admitted that his evidence is the sounder of the two. I do not think there is any need for me to demonstrate this in detail, but I need only say that the methods used by Dr. Maganga to observe the body and measure the wounds as well as his method of removing the scull [sic, brain?] were not the most satisfactory. One should not estimate where measurement is possible. Dr. Maganga's general knowledge was faulty. I think it was generally agreed that while Dr. Maganga had carried out quite a fair post-mortem examination, Dr. Dockeray had carried out a more thorough going and exact examination. Suffice it to say, therefore, that I think the Assessors were quite correct in choosing the evidence of Dr. Dockeray.[16]

Dr. Dockeray and Dr. Clifford agreed that one blow to the right side of the head could have caused the depressed fracture on that side of the head. The judge examined the likelihood of the flanged pipe being used to strike the deceased on the head. Which end of the pipe used was important because if the flanged end struck the head, there would be a T-shaped wound on the head. There was no such wound.

> On the whole, therefore, while the stone and the pipe could have caused some of the wounds to the head, it was difficult to see that they could have been [sic] caused them all. On the other hand, if the prosecution case is right [that] these weapons did cause all the wounds, although Maganga only observed one blow to the forehead, there was a cut just inside the hair-line just above the forehead which might possibly be reconciled with his observation. On the side of the defence [sic], it was suggested that all these wounds on the head could have been caused by the various occasions in which the deceased's head came in contact with rock.[17]

Turning to the question of the likelihood of the fall causing the relevant injuries, Judge Platt described the wounds, lacerations, and bruises and whether their occurrence and nature were consistent with a fall. Both Dr. Dockeray and Dr. Clifford testified that they were very consistent with a fall, and although Judge Platt seemed skeptical on some of their points, he felt that their expert testimony could not be denied. "What the defence says with some force is, that the accused had been consistent throughout in his explanations as to what happened and that from the beginning he had given an explanation which very well fitted with concussion to the brain. I think it must be said that this part of the story does appear to be remarkably clever if this is fabricated evidence. The defence, therefore, certainly appears to have considerable weight on this point."[18]

Judge Platt indicated that the prosecution argued vigorously that the story of a fall was unreasonable. The accused testified that he and his wife were on the rock, and she was six to eight feet away from him, looking to the east. He was looking toward the northeast. He heard the sound of something like a bottle breaking. He turned, and she was not where he last saw her. He crawled to the edge of the rock, peered down, and saw her below. The judge seemed skeptical that he would not have heard her fall.

The defense, stated the judge, offered several explanations for this mystery: a small sound is often missed when a person is concentrating on something else; he might not have seen her fall if his peripheral vision were not wide enough. Both the accused and deceased had been taking Benadryl for a skin rash, and they both had drunk some beer. Benadryl had produced dizziness in the accused previously, and as Dr. McHugh suggested, the alcohol may have intensified the dizziness caused by the Benadryl. If that were so, it seemed odd to the judge that they would have been scrambling around high on these rocks, although the assessors seemed satisfied with these explanations.

Judge Platt opined that the strength of the defense lay in its consistency, but its weakness lay in a series of coincidences and the accused's inability to explain the pipe, the stone, and the nature of the fall. The assessors also accepted the accused's explanation that the pipe was to construct a tripod, as Dr. McHugh and Marianne Dunn had reported. The prosecution's attacks on these points seemed quite reasonable, however, and so Judge Platt could not agree with the assessors' view that Peppy's death was an accident.[19]

The prosecution's evidence relied almost entirely on Maganda's testimony, but his testimony not only had internal inconsistencies but also differed from the testimony of the other primary eyewitness, Padre. The defense's medical testimony presented a more reasonable description of the injuries being caused by a fall. The problems of the condition of the pipe and the rock with blood and hair remained difficult to explain away, as the defense argued. Similarly, that the accused did not see or hear the fall was difficult to believe.

> In this welter of conflict and speculation, the weight of the evidence seems to me to be fairly evenly divided. I think it would be wrong to say that there was not a genuine doubt that the deceased's death could have been caused by accident rather than assault. It may be that with more astute investigation the accused would have been found guilty, but then, on the other hand, it is possible that it might have been proved to be a clear case of accident. Having given anxious thought to the evidence in this case, I am of the opinion that the charge has not been sufficiently proved against the accused so as to enable me to find that he is guilty beyond reasonable doubt. While the accused must, therefore, carry with him the suspicion that he may have been responsible for his wife's death, he must, in justice, be acquitted and set free unless held for any other lawful cause. And I so order.
> Delivered in Court at Mwanza on 19 September 1966.[20]

Once the decision was read, the judge talked to Bill and urged him not to return to Tanzania because there were people who thought he was guilty and had gotten off by bribery or on some other pretext.[21]

Despite concerns about communication difficulties and likelihood of delays, PCDSM was able almost immediately to send the following cable to PCDC: "KINSEY INNOCENT repeat KINSEY INNOCENT."[22]

Conclusion

Once Judge Platt had finished reading his judgment, Bill Kinsey was taken back to Butimba Prison, and Peace Corps staff expected to pick him up and fly him home. However, his long ordeal was not yet over. The Tanzania authorities still held his passport, and the prosecutor was unwilling to release it. When Peace Corps officials went to the prison to get Bill, he told them he had found some drugs in his clothes. The officials were concerned that he was being set up and would be charged with another crime.[1] Fortunately, no charge was ever brought, and the issue disappeared.

Gurbachan Singh, Carroll Brewster, and Tony Essaye drove immediately to the prosecutor's office, where Mr. Effiwat became furious and threatened to arrest them if they didn't get out of his office. He even picked up the telephone and called the police, so the Americans left, went back to Jack McPhee's house, and called the Peace Corps office in Dar es Salaam.[2]

Peace Corps assistant director Gene Mihaly immediately contacted James Curran, economic officer at the U.S. embassy in Dar es Salaam. Based on a call from Mihaly and urging from the embassy information officer, Phil Cohan, at about noon Curran called Tanzania attorney general Mark Bomani. Cohan was very keen that Bill not talk to the press in Mwanza and so wanted him out of town as soon as possible. Bomani was in a cabinet meeting then at State House. At about 3:45 p.m., Curran reached Bomani at his home. Bomani told Curran that he "did not understand how or why the Ministry of Justice would want to hold Kinsey (was also curious as to why PC would want to rush Kinsey away so hastily)." Bomani called Effiwat and told him not to interfere. At 4:15, he called Curran back and told him "as far as this particular case is concerned, Justice has no reason to delay Mr. Kinsey."[3]

Peace Corps staff had chartered a plane to fly Kinsey to Nairobi after the decision; however, the flight was delayed a day while Kinsey's passport was obtained. The passport was finally returned, and on September 20 Brewster escorted Bill to Nairobi, where the plane was met by Peace Corps deputy director Dick Richter. Richter arranged for the pair to have lunch with him and his wife and then be taken secretly to a hotel for the night. The U.S. embassy in Nairobi had arranged with British Overseas Airways Corporation to get Kinsey and Brewster to the airport and onto a plane in secret so that they would not be found by the press. The company flew them to London and then to the United States.[4]

Bill's Future

On Sunday, September 18, a day before the verdict was rendered, Carroll Brewster and Paul Sack had spent two hours at Butimba Prison talking with Bill about his future. Bill indicated that he would like time to think out his plans—Continue with the Peace Corps? Get a job? Enter graduate school?—but not rush to decide. He felt a strong obligation to complete his Peace Corps service contract, but he also understood the potential embarrassment arising from the doubts of people in Tanzania about Peppy's death. Paul Sack wrote that his office felt that Tanzanians' reaction was "one of uncertainty whether crime or not." He felt that the expatriate European community, Asians, and Africans around Mwanza and Maswa probably thought it was a crime, which was also the attitude that most government officials held in private. However, he believed that most Africans in Tanzania were unaware of the case because there had been so little coverage in the Swahili press and radio.[5]

By the time the cable was written, Bill had been found not guilty, so Sack recommended against Bill returning to Tanzania because of all the reminders of the trial, time in prison, his life with Peppy, and so on. He also reported that Gurbachan Singh and Judge Platt "advised against return on purely legal grounds." They pointed out that if Bill were to have any further legal entanglements, his "position would be very bad." In the end, Sack recommended that PCDC work with Bill to find alternatives within the Peace Corps and/or late entry into graduate school.[6]

Sack described Bill as a "very impressive volunteer" and mentioned that were he to participate in Peace Corps volunteer training at Syracuse University, his expertise might provide an "inspiring example of fortitude under stress." His fluency in Swahili would also allow him to teach the language to trainees.[7]

By the middle of October, Bill's future, at least for the short term, seemed to be set. On October 19, Sack wrote to him with an update on how things looked in Tanzania. The letter recapitulated the discussion that had taken place at Butimba Prison and indicated that the situation was not much changed. Sack felt that it would be uncomfortable for Bill to return. "Tanzania cannot help but remind you constantly of your months with Peppy and the whole dismal course of events this year." He also mentioned that they had not approached the Tanzania government for a re-entry permit, which could be a serious impediment, depending on the government's current view.[8] Sack's letter was followed by a letter from Tony Essaye to Sack on October 25 reporting that Bill had accepted a position as assistant to the editor of the Peace Corps newsletter "until February, when he will start graduate school."[9]

Tanzania CID Begins Investigation of the Case

That same month Tom McHugh wrote to Carroll Brewster about further repercussions from the Kinsey trial. The Dar es Salaam CID had undertaken an investigation into actions by various participants in the case. Among the people McHugh mentioned being interviewed were Dr. (Mrs.) McMahon, Dr. Salu, Miss Roberts (matron of Mwanza Hospital), Dr. Datar (RMO), Dr. Nicholson (doctor at Butimba Prison who gave Bill medications), and two medical wardens at Butimba Prison. Curiously, all of the interviewees were medical personal rather than state attorneys or local CID staff. Others may have been interviewed, but as a doctor McHugh likely focused on the health workers to the exclusion of others. He did say that there was nothing secretive about the CID investigation and that the investigator "made no attempt to keep his activities from public notice. The questioning was all concerned with facts and appeared to be conducted entirely without bias." According to McHugh, one of Bill's local attorneys, Mr. Parekh, believed that the investigation was "mounted to either look into the handling of the case by officials or to check for dirty dealing on our part."[10]

However, the most likely basis for the investigation was the judge's decision, in which he suggested "that the authorities concerned may wish to reconsider the course of the trial with a view to issuing instructions as to the correct steps to be taken during an investigation."[11] It might also have been Assistant

Attorney General U. V. Campbell's reported displeasure with the quality of the prosecution.[12]

As discussed earlier, Inspector Kifunta and AMO Mganga were transferred elsewhere, and their careers were apparently damaged.[13] My research has revealed no further mention of State Attorney Effiwat in any context, and he may have suffered a similar fate, perhaps even being discharged. Since he was a Nigerian national, such a result might have been more easily accomplished than if he were a Tanzanian citizen. However, this is mere speculation.

The fact that the government looked carefully at the lessons to be learned from the case does suggest that the case's outcome was not treated as matter-of-factly as CID deputy director Ijumba or Attorney General Bomani professed.[14]

In the same letter to Carroll Brewster, McHugh reported that he understood that Dick Brooke-Edwards was planning to write a book about the Kinsey case. McHugh said he would not make any of his files available to Brooke-Edwards.[15] In a final piece of business, in December 1966 Brewster reported to the Peace Corps that the insurance company had fully paid out to Bill the amount due under Peppy's Peace Corps life insurance policy.[16]

Analysis of the Trial

In retrospect after the trial, it might have been easy to charge the investigators and prosecutors with incompetence for their many errors. In fact, Byron Georgiadis did exactly that in a speech in London in 2007. He complained that the trial should never have happened. For example, he pointed out that AMO Mganga did not notice the stellate fracture of the orbit of the right eye, which Georgiadis considered "the most important injury." In addition, he argued that "any competent prosecuting person would query the police investigation and ask to see and evaluate *all* the exhibits found at the site and ensure their safe custody for production to the Court in due course. No serious prosecutor would have relied on investigating officer Supt. Kifunta's investigation of an alleged 'motive' from a notebook ('diary?') with disconnected sentences which amounted to a big zero."[17] A careful examination, however, suggests that many other factors likely moved the case forward.

If the defense was so sure that all evidence pointed to Bill's innocence, why didn't they ever raise that evidence with the prosecution early on, thereby saving Bill from months in prison, eliminating the expensive costs for the trial, protecting the Peace Corps from hostile scrutiny, and clearing the air for all? As Paul Sack wrote in his letters to volunteers and cables to PCDC, the prosecution case appeared quite strong for many months, and the defense would likely have been fearful of showing its hand. Although Georgiadis also later severely criticized the judge for his comments at the close of his decision, Judge Platt clearly felt it was a close case and deserving of a full hearing at trial.

How might the judge's conduct of the case be assessed? Judge Platt was an experienced, intelligent, and capable judge, or, as Byron Georgiadis later remarked about him, "left-over British Judiciary, good man, conscientious, upright and sound judgement."[18]

On the one hand, the judge's rulings in the case seem overwhelmingly in support of the defense. He allowed Dr. McHugh to attend the trial prior to giving his testimony. He accepted Dr. Dockeray's role as an expert witness despite his not being officially recognized in Tanzania and not having a coroner's certificate. He admitted the defense photographer's photos into evidence despite the photographer's not being in court to authenticate them. He refused to question Georgiadis on his late-night visit to the Peace Corps volunteers, which might have been seen as tampering with potential witnesses. On the other hand, a few of his rulings did support the prosecution. He admitted Inspector Kifunta's sketch into evidence, and he found that AMO Mganga had adequate credentials to provide testimony as a medical expert. Perhaps in the end his rulings were not so much a sign of bias but an indication that the defense provided the better arguments. The rulings as well as other facets of the trial suggest how a trial in Africa at this time might deviate from the orderly procedure in a case in Britain or the United States.

Nor did Georgiadis take into account in his later lecture the role of the high-powered defense team compared with the underexperienced prosecutor and sorely undersourced Inspector Kifunta. In America, where prosecuting attorneys generally have substantial resources, it may take a powerful, well-funded defense team to counter the prosecution. Although many public-defender offices have skilled, committed attorneys, they are generally underfunded, handle too many cases, often have limited access to such resources as expert witnesses and DNA and other blood tests, and lack travel funds for their witnesses.[19]

When defendants in America have the funds to pay for a sophisticated defense, they often are able to convince a jury that the prosecution's handling of the case includes many errors. One famous recent case demonstrates such a result, the O. J. Simpson murder trial.

The group of Simpson lawyers included some of best-known defense law-yers in America: Johnnie Cochran, F. Lee Bailey, Alan Dershowitz, Robert Shap-iro, and Dean Gerald Uelman of Santa Clara Law School. Supporting this "Dream Team," as the press called it, were pathology experts, medical experts, DNA experts, computer experts, jury experts, seasoned investigators, and others.

Despite the vast government resources mounted to convict Simpson, including experienced prosecuting attorneys, prominent expert witnesses, and the support of professional investigators from the Los Angeles Police Depart-ment (LAPD), the defense was able to demonstrate many errors in the prose-cution case—for example, pathology mistakes by the county coroner, errors by the LAPD in collecting and processing blood evidence, and deterioration of the blood evidence while it was being held by the LAPD. Perhaps most impor-tantly, the defense was able to show racial antipathy toward African Americans by an LAPD officer assigned to the case, which was discovered through a time-consuming, expensive search for evidence, including interviews with witnesses that revealed biased statements by the officer and proof that he had no hesita-tion in planting evidence, falsifying reports, or lying in court. Finally, when the prosecution team offered in evidence a blood-soaked glove they alleged Simp-son had used in the murder, the defense was able to show that it was too small for Simpson's hand, leading to the famous phrase from the defense: "If it doesn't fit, you must acquit."[20] (This feature of the trial is eerily reminiscent of the Kin-sey "diary," which turned out to be a collection of quotations from various books.)

In the end, Simpson was acquitted, raising a long-term controversy over the trial's result. Many books have been written, TV shows aired, and at least one documentary produced about the case.

Similarly, the Kinsey defense team included Byron Georgiadis, the pre-mier defense attorney in East Africa; Carroll Brewster, an experienced Africa hand and private attorney from Connecticut; Gerald Dockeray, an eminent pathologist; Peter Clifford, an expert head-injury physician; Tom McHugh, a Peace Corps doctor; and others. While the Peace Corps organization publicly maintained its neutral position, specific Peace Corps officials, including Tony Essaye, Paul Sack, Jack McPhee, and others at PCDC, supplied useful informa-tion for the defense. Eminent physicians at the Yale Medical School were also consulted.

Unlike the prosecution in the O. J. Simpson case, with its experienced attorneys, vast resources from the LAPD, and experts paid by the state, the prosecution in the Kinsey case was made up of an inexperienced attorney operating almost alone and speaking neither Swahili nor Sukuma, a police inspector with few resources, and a medical officer without a medical degree.

Although Tanzania was a poor country, it seems strange that the state did not make more resources available to the prosecution. It would have been relatively easy for the state pathologist to have performed a more professional autopsy in Dar es Salaam, especially since C. F. Ijumba, the deputy director of the CID, had indicated that one was to take place. However, it was not done. Perhaps, as Attorney General Bomani and Deputy Director Ijumba said, they were treating the case like any other. Perhaps the government did not make more resources available to the prosecution because it just wanted the case to go away and not become an international incident for this very young country.

Reactions to the Verdict

The Peace Corps reaction to the verdict continued to be somewhat muted. In Washington, D.C., Jack Vaughn "expressed gratitude that the first such trial in the five-year history of the Peace Corps had been 'eminently fair.'"[21] At the same time, Paul Sack urged Vaughn not to send a complimentary letter to Attorney General Bomani because some "Tanzanians, including members of the judiciary, took offense at Vaughn's statement in the press praising the Government's handling of the case." They apparently felt that the compliments suggested doubt that the case was "handled in a fair and first-class manner" and found such an inference offensive.[22]

An undated, unsigned memorandum entitled "The Kinsey Trial in Retrospect," apparently written by a staff member of the U.S. embassy in Dar es Salaam soon after the verdict, described the press coverage and the reactions of a number of Tanzanians to the verdict.[23]

Underscoring the intense focus on press coverage by the Peace Corps, the assessment quantified the number of times the case appeared in various newspapers, whether it was on the front page or inside, whether it was above or below the fold, and so on. For example, it reported that the *Tanzania Standard* "carried 13 stories on the trial and strongly reflected the faulty investigation and presentation of the prosecution. The East African Standard used 10 stories but relegated the case to lesser play. Nairobi's Daily Nation played the story 13 times—six on the front page, and the Nation's Sunday edition front paged the trial three weeks in a row." The report went on to mention that each of the three

Swahili newspapers printed only a single report on the trial and then only after the verdict.

The memo allayed the Peace Corps' early fear that the case would be sensationalized in the press and provoke strong anti-American sentiments. "The testimony was generally covered with restraint and there is a consensus among all levels here, that the reporting of the case was *less sensational than the evidence presented*."[24]

According to the memo, members of the Tanzania legal community seemed unhappy with the result. For example, Judge M. C. E. Biron, "a British expatriate and long term resident in Tanzania," expressed his feelings in no uncertain terms: "In his opinion there would never have been a verdict of acquittal had the prosecution been less inefficient and less negligent." Assistant Attorney General U. V. Campbell felt "that the manner in which the prosecution presented its case was embarrassing, and reflected upon the competence of his office." Campbell pointed out that the state attorneys' competence was presumed, so the Office of the Attorney General never interfered; however "there were several instances in which the State Attorneys should have sought assistance from the Office of the Attorney General."

Among younger Tanzania attorneys (unidentified in the memo), there seemed to be a feeling that the failures of the prosecution "rather than the innocence of the accused, or the superiority of the defense—although the latter is acknowledged, led to the result." In a curious summing up, the memo report mentioned "a tendency to look upon the trial as a sort of tragic comedy—in which the victims were the State Attorneys." This conclusion omits the obvious tragic results for both Peppy and Bill.

As to the general public, the memo concluded there was "either indifferent acceptance or concurrence with the verdict." However, some people suggested that a "conviction would have been political dynamite." Thus, "an acquittal was inevitable."

The memo ended with the observation "that neither the incident nor the trial will have a lasting, adverse affect [*sic*] upon either, the image of the Peace Corps or that of the US in Tanzania." Similar conclusions about the reactions to the case were made in a cable from PCDSM on September 21.[25] Although perhaps not directly a result of the trial, the memo's optimistic view was soon contradicted by deteriorating relations between Tanzania and the United States, culminating in a termination of the Peace Corps' presence in the country by 1969.

This memo appears to be the only effort to analyze the Kinsey case and its impact on the Peace Corps and U.S. interests in Africa. The lack of a more comprehensive review of the case by the Peace Corps and the State Department is curious. An event that was the first major test of how the Peace Corps would handle a potential crisis seemed to cry out for a detailed analysis of how the case proceeded, how the participants functioned, how a foreign government reacted, what lessons were learned, and much more. Jack McPhee's very detailed diary of the events in the early days after Peppy's death as well as the many cables, letters, and memos would have provided ample support for a careful analysis. But no such analysis appears in the record. The question of the Peace Corps' ability to pay for a defense was settled by legislation, but the questions raised in the general counsel's memo in preparation for the legislation remained unanswered: Would the Peace Corps pay for the defense of a volunteer who committed any kind of illegal activity? Would the Peace Corps pay for claims against others when a volunteer had been wronged or damaged? Would the Peace Corps arrange for an attorney?

The question of the Peace Corps' neutrality has not been officially examined, but it seemed to have arisen organically in the case and with little forethought. Should the Peace Corps have done more to protect Peppy's interests? Should the Peace Corps always maintain a position of neutrality, and what are the contours of such a policy? In the years ahead, it would not be uncommon for volunteers to be accused of drug crimes in various countries. The Peace Corps might have used the Kinsey case to project forward to other possible crimes and establish a framework for handling them.

How the host country perceived the policy of neutrality seemed to require some analysis. Peace Corps volunteers' situation of being subject to host-country laws was different from diplomatic and military officials' general exemption from such laws, but no effort was made to develop a framework for responding to legal cases involving volunteers. Perhaps the new policy of providing for the payment of a defense would undercut the Peace Corps policy of volunteers "living and working" like the citizens of the host country. Apparently, no review of the policy took place after the Kinsey case, but the Peace Corps continued to portray volunteers as living just like local citizens.

The Kinsey trial judgment did receive extensive coverage in the United States, with articles in the *New York Times, Time* magazine, and *Newsweek* as well as in hundreds of local newspapers around the country.[26] As discussed previously, press coverage and its potential for damage loomed large in much of the Peace Corps' view of the case. The *New York Times* coverage was short and sober, but *Time* and *Newsweek* carried longer, more detailed articles on the trial, with typically dramatic descriptions of the events and people involved. Prior to the judgment, *Time* carried a colorful report of the trial that included such colorful descriptive phrases as "the eerie screech of water birds," "solemn in his red robes," and "the ponderous coal-black prosecutor."[27] The most detailed and analytical coverage of the case, trial, and judgment was published in an article by Ruth Reynolds in the *New York Sunday News* on November 20, 1966. Reynolds regularly covered legal issues for the paper, and she provided a well-researched piece with many quotes from officials, witnesses, and the testimony at the trial. She had reviewed and synthesized the many newspaper reports on the case and ended her article with the following conclusion: "Maybe Kinsey isn't wholly satisfied with the outcome. Maybe Vilindo isn't either. But no one can say that the new republic of Tanzania didn't provide 'a very sophisticated legal procedure.'"[28]

On the other hand, Byron Georgiadis claimed in 2007 that the judge had done the "unpardonable" when he stated that "the accused must, therefore, carry with him the suspicion that he may have been responsible for his wife's death."[29] Georgiadis seemed to be continuing his advocacy more than forty years later.

The case has continued to appear in the press and books ever since 1966. Philip Weiss wrote in 2004 about the murder of a female Peace Corps volunteer by another volunteer in Tonga in 1975 and discussed the Kinsey case as a relevant precursor. He raised several questions that the Peace Corps had still not analyzed:

"Would paying for a volunteer's defense upset relations with the host government?"

"What if the Peace Corps had evidence touching on the volunteer's guilt—was it obligated to provide it?"

"What if a Peace Corps volunteer was the victim of a crime? Should the Peace Corps fund the prosecution as well as the defense?"[30]

There was little dispute about the evidence in the Tonga case. Dennis Priven, twenty-four, a volunteer science teacher, stabbed twenty-three-year-old Deborah Gardner, another volunteer science teacher from Tacoma, Washington, with his knife.

Stanley Meisler, in his book celebrating the fifty-year anniversary of the Peace Corps, examined the Kinsey case in some detail and concluded: "The

Peace Corps welcomed the verdict. It would have been a nightmare for the Peace Corps if a Volunteer had been sentenced to hanging or a long prison term in Africa while some Americans back home clamored for his release."[31]

The community around Maswa seemed to feel strongly that Bill was guilty. Some of the nearby volunteers shared the feeling that Phil and Ann Ellison had expressed. Even as late as 2010, one volunteer from the area, William Edington, stated in response to John Coyne's online posting describing the case, "Virtually every volunteer in the region, including me, believed that, in fact, Peppy was murdered by her husband." John Coyne, in his response, added to the accumulation of information about volunteers' feelings when he reported, "I was . . . in Ethiopia at the time and met a number of terminating Tanzanian Vols traveling north and they all believed Peppy was murdered."[32]

Other comments in the online exchange also complain about the lack of transparency by the Peace Corps. "The Peace Corps did not share any information about the case with [volunteers] and did not allow them to attend the trial."[33] The factual inaccuracy of such a claim is demonstrated in my earlier descriptions of and quotations from the several letters that Paul Sack sent to volunteers about the case as well as by the fact that I and other volunteers attended the trial. All of which may suggest that memories after forty-plus years are less than perfect. One must also question the reliability of claims of guilt by people who did not attend the trial or hear the actual exonerating testimony.

Peppy's Letters Home

I recently received a collection of letters Peppy wrote during her time in the Peace Corps to a good friend from college. These candid, detailed letters offer an excellent window into Peppy's relation with Bill and their lonely, isolated time in Maswa. Although there are only four letters, they cover the period from the end of 1964, when the Kinseys arrived in Tanzania, to the end of January 1966, only two months before Peppy's death.

In the letters, Peppy is quite open about the difficulties of life in Maswa and at Binza Upper Primary School. She and Bill felt isolated and rarely came in contact with other English-speaking people. The letters are frank and insightful both as to the struggles with life in Africa as well as to the common problems faced by spouses in the early years of marriage. They offer, perhaps, a more nuanced way of interpreting the comments Peppy made to other volunteers as well as a more realistic view than the one provided in testimony by Peppy's mother at trial. Charlotte Dennett said that there was never a bad word about Bill or the marriage in Peppy's letters to her. Although the letters to Peppy's friend Susan Stevens may not exactly include a "bad word," they do describe serious challenges in the relationship.

At the end of December 1964, while still in training in Mbeya, Peppy wrote that they had "an honest to goodness American Christmas dinner. It was divine after some of the food we have been having." The amenities in Mbeya were rather more comfortable than she had expected. "I spent most of my time by the swimming pool that the area has. True Peace Corps life. It even has a diving board and everything."[34] The letter contains no hint of the complaint about Bill's silences that she expressed to Delores Ledbetter. That omission does not mean they didn't happen, but the letter suggests Peppy is also enjoying her first taste of Africa.

By the middle of March 1965, they were settled into the routine of teaching and life in Maswa. Peppy reported on complex issues at the school and complained about Bill's stubbornness but ended, "Things are fine and I have absolutely no desire to be anywhere else." Their teaching life had been most complicated by the many changes of schedule as well as changes of headmasters. "We are on our fifth schedule for the year (only three month's [sic] worth). Bill's and my classes have been changed three times. . . . I am now teaching Math, English and Art, where previously I was teaching History and Geography."[35]

At the end of the term, their Peace Corps group was scheduled to meet in Dar es Salaam, which Peppy viewed with delight as a break from their isolated life in Maswa. "Being stuck out in the Bush or boonies as it is called, this will be a big treat."

Thoughts of the benefits to be found in the "big city" set Peppy off on a bout of philosophizing and offering insights:

> We literally don't see another English speaking native from one week to the next. I think the hardest part of being so isolated is since there are only two of us there is no one else to go to if one is in a bad temper or just uninterested. Being married makes one, me at least, doubly dependent on the other one and if something goes wrong there really is absolutely no one to talk to. Rationalizing helps a great deal, but what is really the best cure for temporary incompatibility is not

available. This is a new thought which occurred to me this morning when I felt energetic and ambitious and Bill was uncommunicative and lazy. We just weren't in the same moods, and that's all there was to it, but I couldn't find anyone to play with so I became a nuisance. This happens periodically, and there is nothing that can be done but to sit tight and let it pass. You mustn't think that I am complaining, because most of the time I am amazingly content.

She continued with further analysis of both her own and Bill's characteristics, observing that "I have married one of the most stubborn people in the world. I thought I was bad, but I had another thing [sic] coming." However, she closed with the quotation provided earlier that everything was fine and she wouldn't want to be anywhere else. The last sentence of the letter offers a sad preview of the later trial: she planned to "settle down to one of the 300 books the Peace Corps gave us."[36]

By August 1965, the Kinseys seemed to be at the lowest point of their first year, and Peppy described again the contrast between their situation and that of volunteers in more urban settings. They had recently spent time in Mwanza on a Swahili course and not only enjoyed time with their fellow participants but also joined a big party with beer, music, and dancing, "at which we saw more people than we have seen collectively in our 8 months in Maswa." Fun times in Mwanza only underscored their unhappiness in Maswa. She continued with a sense of desperation: "Return to our isolated existence has rather cooled us to the 'Bush.' This is the third term of school, and we are both *dying* to get out of here for an extended period of time." Bill urged her not to compare their bleak situation with that of other volunteers. She pointed out that they were among the few who had none of the amenities of other volunteers, such as "(1) electricity, (2) huge houses, (3) plumbing, (4) hot water, (5) pre-furnished houses, (6) neighbors they are friends with, (7) social life."

Despite the complaints about their situation, she described her relationship with Bill in a very positive light: "Speaking of Bill—we are on much better terms than last time I wrote you. Excellent ones as a matter of fact. Mark my words if you marry someone you aren't already 'used to' it takes a while to adjust. . . . At this point Bill is the only good thing about our life in the Bush."[37]

In a letter begun in November 1965 but finished on January 29, 1966, Peppy offered a much-improved view of their life in Maswa. The first part of the letter continues a theme from previous letters with a discussion of the lives of their friends in New York, and a primary focus is on relationships with boys, including an inquiry about a former boyfriend of Peppy's. However, none of the discussion suggests problems with the Kinseys' current relationship. Peppy wrote that "after a year here it has finally begun to seem like home." She described with great anticipation the impending visit from her mother and her aunt, which would include an extensive safari around East Africa. "Maybe we will even stay in a hotel with *hot* water—something I haven't experienced in over 10 months."[38]

When Peppy picked up in January, she wrote with enthusiasm, "Absolutely marvelous vacation—did all the things we planned. . . . Bill and I saw the other side of Africa for a change and it was a pleasure."

The combination of time passing, the pleasures of travel, and the improvements at school left Peppy in an almost euphoric state: "School this year is incomparable to last year. We have a great head teacher, new staff, etc. My outlook on the whole world has improved 500%. We had in case you didn't know, a lousy rotten situation as far as headmaster was concerned and crisis after crisis between staff, students, authorities, etc. So much for here. How is NYC?"[39]

These letters, together with previous comments from Tom McHugh about the Kinseys' desire to transfer out of the bad situation at school, make clear what a difficult situation they faced in their first year of marriage. However, the strains in their relationship that Peppy described do not seem all that unusual in the beginning of a marriage, particularly when the couple had known each other for such a short time. The letters seem to suggest that despite the lack of amenities and school issues, they were able to overcome many of the problems, and finally by January Peppy, at least, felt life had turned around.

Final Thoughts on the Peace Corps and Tanzania

As mentioned previously, it was also reported that Inspector Kifunta and AMO Mganga had been transferred, their careers in all likelihood damaged. The trial happened at a time when Tanzania was still struggling with improving its infrastructure, Africanizing its government officials, becoming more self-sufficient, and generally becoming a functioning state, still only five years old at the time. The fact that the principal players on the Kinsey side as well as the judge were white, whereas the prosecutors, police, medical personnel, and witnesses were black may also have made the case an embarrassment for the young country.

Although the Peace Corps weathered this potential disaster well, it was aided by luck and some clever early action by staff. Bill's conviction would have made for substantial international headaches as well as potentially causing many countries to withdraw their support for Peace Corps volunteers. In his speech in 2007, Byron Georgiadis claimed that a guilty verdict would likely have led to such an outcome: "President Nyerere had gone public and said, 'if convicted, the law will take its course and the Republic will hang him. Further the Peace Corps will be expelled from Tanzania.' Other African countries also said they would expel the Peace Corps. The presence of the Peace Corps in Africa hung by a thread."[40]

I have seen no such comment by President Nyerere in any of the documents I have obtained. When I asked Paul Sack and Tony Essaye if they knew of such a statement, both said "no" and that they would have been surprised if he had. However, Georgiadis's statement is very specific and thus unlikely to have been made up with no basis. Perhaps it appeared in the Swahili press and was never seen by others.

Possibly the most significant piece of luck was the fact that the Kinsey family was in a financial position to afford to pay the cost of Bill's defense. Many volunteers at the time came from families without such wealth. Once the Peace Corps determined that it was prevented from paying for the defense, Bill could have been left without a defense, or a significant fund-raising effort would have been required. Perhaps pro bono representation could have been obtained, although at the time such support was less available than it is today.

Quick action by Peace Corps staff, particularly in Tanzania, was also extremely important to the quality of the defense. Jack McPhee not only acted quickly but also made detailed notes on all his work in the early days. Arranging for Dr. Dockeray, taking photographs, getting Dr. McHugh involved, finding attorneys in Mwanza, and much more led to the impressive defense presented. U.S. ambassador to Tanzania John Burns cabled Jack Vaughn in September 1966 with high praise for the Peace Corps' management of the case: "From the very beginning handling of the Kinsey case reflected most sensitive judgment and performance on part of both PC/T [Peace Corps Tanzania] and PC/W [Peace Corps Washington] to whom belong the credit for the successful navigation of a course replete with pitfalls."[41]

Byron Georgiadis offered similar praise for the activities of Peace Corps officials in Tanzania, especially Paul Sack for "his perspicacity, energy and quick action soon after the unfortunate incident."[42] However, these actions must be viewed in light of the Peace Corps' professed position of "neutrality" on the case and the question of its responsibility to assist the prosecution to ensure that Peppy's life was not forgotten.

Despite Paul Sack's early concern that Bill might be guilty, he commented many years afterward that later information coupled with the testimony given at trial "removed all such doubt from me." In October 2011, Sack wrote to me that Byron Georgiadis told him that without the autopsy performed by Dr. Dockeray, he never could have won the case because the testimony of the government doctor was too damning. In the same letter, Sack reported on a conversation he had with Dr. Dockeray sometime after the trial. Dockeray told him "that he had tried to inflict on the skull of a dead person in the Nairobi morgue the same injuries that the prosecution claimed were inflicted on Peppy by the iron bar but was unable to do so."[43]

Although the Kinsey case may not have had "a lasting, adverse affect [sic] on the image of the Peace Corps in Tanzania," as suggested in the "Kinsey Trial in Retrospect" memo, only three years after the trial, in 1969, President Nyerere requested that the Peace Corps leave Tanzania. Not until 1979 would it be asked to return. Political issues around the Vietnam War and the U.S. role in the Congo were most likely the primary factors in the request to leave, although the memory of the Peace Corps trial and the embarrassing presentation by the prosecution would certainly not have helped.

Epilogue

When Peppy Kinsey's college roommate, Victoria Ferenbach, thought about Peppy's death, she had a fairly clear image in her mind of what might have happened on that high rock in Tanzania. She could see Peppy getting up and, as she often would, start to dance. Perhaps with the beer and the medication she had taken, she wasn't as careful of the edge of the rock as she should have been, and a dance move took her over. Speculation, but very much in keeping with the Peppy Victoria knew.[1] Of course, there is no way of knowing what actually happened on top of the rock. Did Peppy pass out or slip? Bill was facing away and told the court he couldn't see what happened. The prosecution claimed that no such fall took place.

Lives after Tanzania

Carroll Brewster returned to practice law in Connecticut and then entered academia, serving as president of Hollins University and then for many years as president of Hobart and Smith College.[2]

Byron Georgiadis returned to a successful legal practice in Nairobi. He died in 2010, and the lead item in his obituary described his involvement in the Kinsey case.[3]

Bill Kinsey returned to the United States and worked for PCDC for several months. He then entered graduate school, obtaining an M.A. in agricultural economics in 1968, an M.A in anthropology in 1971, and then a Ph.D. in 1978—all from Stanford University .[4]

Bill went on to become an expert on African land tenure and joined the School of Business and Economics faculty of the Free University of Amsterdam. In 2018, he was a senior research fellow of the Centre for Applied Social Sciences in Harare, Zimbabwe, and holds honorary appointments with the Centre for the Study of African Economies at the University of Oxford and the African Studies Centre at the University of Leiden. [5]

Tom McHugh returned to the United States and completed a surgical residency in Chicago. After that, he established a surgical and medical practice first in Chicago and then in Maine, where he stayed until his retirement.[6]

When Jack McPhee returned to the United States, he first worked for the Peace Corps, then with Volunteers for International Technical Assistance, and finally for the Department of Commerce in international trade, from which he retired in 2002.[7]

Judge Harold Platt continued his distinguished judicial career in East Africa and was eventually knighted. He became a judge of the High Court and Court of Appeal in Kenya from 1968 to 1989, judge of the Supreme Court of Uganda from 1989 to 1994, and chairman of the Uganda Law Reform Commission from 1994 to 2000.[8]

Paul Sack returned to the United States and worked for the Peace Corps as head of Program Planning for one and a half years in Washington, D.C. He then went back to San Francisco and resumed his real estate development career.[9]

Reflecting on the issues raised in the introduction, we can see how U.S. officials grappled with the complex nature of the case leading to Bill Kinsey's acquittal. Although missteps may have occurred along the way, in the end Peace Corps staff did their best to deal with the situation in a competent and even-handed manner. Despite Soviet claims to the contrary, the episode did not lead to a fracture of the U.S.-Tanzania relations, and Peace Corps officials could be seen as acting far differently from the "ugly American" so often portrayed in the literature of the era.

The Peace Corps

In his book *When the World Calls,* Stanley Meisler not only provides a list of impressive "returned volunteers" (volunteers who return to the United States after their service in another country) in government, journalism, academia, literature, and the arts but also addresses the question of the Peace Corps' impact. Meisler points out the difficulty of measuring the impact of a small group of volunteers on a country, in particular the impact of teachers. The Peace Corps has attempted to quantify some of its accomplishments, but without much success. Meisler cites data given in the Peace Corps annual report for 2008: "7750 Volunteers had worked with 2.1 million people, helped train 126,000 teachers, health workers, and other service providers, and assisted 24,000 government agencies and nongovernmental organizations throughout the world."[10] Similar statistics can be found in later reports. However, much of the assessment of Peace Corps success comes from anecdotal accounts. Volunteer Judy Guskin, a teacher in the Philippines, says, "Like most Peace Corps Volunteers . . . we affected the lives of a few individuals. For them, we thought we made a difference."[11] As far back as 2009, volunteers were bringing technological change to villages in Africa. By that time in many African countries, the people had by-passed phone landlines, which were largely nonexistent anyway, and cellphones had become ubiquitous. In Namibia, two volunteers developed software "that provides health information through cellphone based text messaging." Not only is preposted health information available online, but questions may be asked and answered by volunteers.[12]

Some commentators observe that the Peace Corps' greatest impact derives from the returned volunteers, who have become leaders in the many fields mentioned earlier and who provide a rich resource of people who have lived and worked in developing countries. These same returned volunteers often provide ongoing support for activities in their former host countries. Many of them belong to associations related to the countries where they served—for instance, Friends of Nigeria, Friends of Tanzania, Amigos de Bolivia y Peru, Friends of Malaysia, and others.[13] These organizations often raise money for projects in their associated countries. For example, in 2016 Friends of Tanzania funded eight projects in Tanzania totaling $25,137, plus member-designated projects totaling $28,489. Since its founding, this organization has made similar grants to fund and support a wide assortment of Tanzania projects.[14]

Of course, the Peace Corps has its critics as well. In 2008, a former Peace Corps director in Cameroon, Robert Strauss, authored an attack on the Peace Corps in *Foreign Policy* magazine. He concluded that people in the host countries rarely knew that the volunteers were from America, let alone in the Peace Corps; that the recruits were not particularly capable; that the size of programs in particular countries was largely random; that the Peace Corps is not a development organization; and much more. "Today," he commented, "the Peace Corps remains a Peter Pan organization, afraid to grow up, yet also afraid to question the thinking of its founding fathers."[15] Karen Rothmyer, a former volunteer, offered similar criticism in *The Nation* magazine in 2011 and concluded that perhaps the Peace Corps has outlasted its usefulness.[16]

Despite such criticism, the Peace Corps has developed a firm focus on important goals in the developing world and in America. As set forth in the budget request to Congress in 2018, the Peace Corps' three strategic goals are: (1) "building local capacity," (2) "sharing America with the World," and (3) "bringing the world back home." Among the global initiatives aimed at achieving such goals are (1) battling HIV/AIDS, (2) helping achieve food security, and (3) working on malaria prevention. To measure its success in reaching its goals, the Peace Corps has developed a comprehensive set of strategic objectives:

1. Volunteer well-being
2. Service opportunities of choice
3. Development of impact
4. Cross-cultural understanding
5. Continuation of service
6. Diversity and inclusion
7. Site development
8. Training
9. Development of a high-performing learning organization
10. Global connectivity
11. Measurement for results[17]

Such a well-developed planning and evaluation system allows the Peace Corps to respond to much of the criticism that has been directed at it.

At the time of the Kinsey case, female volunteers were a substantial part, although not a majority, of the volunteer population. In the following years, women would eventually become a majority of volunteers; by 2017, 62 percent of volunteers were women. As the change in composition took place, many questions were raised about the protection afforded to these women in foreign countries. The Peace Corps was perceived to have ignored rapes, sexual assaults, and harassment claims until the early 2000s, when volunteers began to raise such issues in the press, with Congress, and with the Peace Corps.[18] It was claimed that the Peace Corps was more interested in its image than in protecting women volunteers. Female volunteers' health has also been a subject of controversy. The initial policy adopted by Sargent Shriver that women could give birth in their assigned country was later changed to require termination of service if a woman became pregnant. In 2013, the policy was changed again to allow women to continue serving while pregnant, although the prohibition instituted in 1979 on "covering abortion even in cases of rape, incest or life endangerment" continued.[19] Despite the relaxing of the rule, the Peace Corps' expressed policy suggests that a pregnant woman may have little choice: "Pregnancy is treated in the same manner as other Volunteer health conditions that require medical attention. Given the circumstances under which Volunteers live and work in Peace Corps countries, it is rare that the Peace Corps' medical standards for continued service during pregnancy can be met."[20]

The Kinsey trial took place at a time when the Peace Corps was at the height of its popularity. In 1964, when the Kinseys entered training, the Peace Corps received the largest number of applications ever, 45,653. At the time of the trial in 1966, the largest number of volunteers ever were serving overseas, 15,556.[21] In recent years, the number serving has been approximately 7,000 each year.

In the end, Bill was found not guilty, and the Peace Corps could continue its activities largely unscathed and would become the most lasting legacy of the Kennedy presidency, a legacy perhaps best exemplified in a story from the time of President Kennedy's funeral. Jackie Kennedy had asked Sargent Shriver, director of the Peace Corps at the time, to oversee all the arrangements for the funeral. One of his duties was to greet the heads of state, the largest such gathering ever, which he did by giving each one a card for the funeral mass. The first to be welcomed was Haile Selassie, the emperor of Ethiopia. Shriver handed him a card and said, "Your Majesty, I want this card to be a memorial of President Kennedy, who loved your country very much." Selassie was crying and replied, "President Kennedy needs no memorial in our country because he has three hundred of his children working there today."[22] As of 2017, more than 230,000 "of his children" had served in the Peace Corps.[23]

The Peace Corps continues to have broad support throughout the United States, as shown by the positive comments relayed in the introduction. The late Ambassador Joseph Wilson offers one of the most ringing endorsements of the Peace Corps volunteers' work: "The Peace Corps is an ambassador's dream because of the Volunteers' impact on the lives of the people in villages where Americans are rarely seen. Volunteers are the human face of our country and consistently represent our values superbly."[24] Or as Lee Rieffel has written for the Brookings Institution, "The Peace Corps is one of the smallest instruments of the foreign policy tool kit. It is a 'boutique agency' with a superb reputation."[25]

The ongoing popularity of the Kennedy presidency and its linkage to the Peace Corps may derive from the famous quote from his inaugural address: "Ask not what your country can do for you—ask what you can do for your country." The Peace Corps has manifestly embodied that ideal.

Acknowledgments

Many Tanzanian Peace Corps officials offered me great support, allowing me to interview them, sharing documents, and reviewing and commenting on the manuscript. In particular, I must thank Jack McPhee, Dr. Tom McHugh, and Paul Sack. Similarly, Tony Essaye and Bill Josephson of Peace Corps Washington provided important insights, documents, and comments on the manuscript.

Returned Peace Corps volunteers provided time and effort in reviewing and commenting on the manuscript as well as sharing letters and other documents. I thank Barbara Boyle, Aileen Dower, Phil Ellison, Pam Engle Ellison, Donn Fry, Delores Ledbetter, Sharon Moore, John Oliver, Rick Seifert, John and Barbara Ratigan, David Rudenstine, Joe Winkelman, and Dwight Yates.

Peppy's sister, Charlotte Hawes, has been generous with her time, documents, and memories of her family.

Betty and Dan Clemmer, part of the Teachers for East African Program, shared memories, letters, and in particular Betty's memories of Peppy at Mount Holyoke.

Without John Coyne and his role as the institutional memory of the Peace Corps, this book would not have happened. It was his early FOIA request to the Peace Corps that opened access to so many essential historic documents. When I obtained the files of the case from Dick and Joan Richter, I knew I had the basis for an important history.

Peppy's college friends Vicky Simons Ferenbach and Susie Stevens Sullivan provided important insights in letters and interviews, complementing information provided by Peppy's other college friends Betty Clemmer and Barbara Ratigan.

Byron Georgiadis's son Nicholas, who now lives near me in Washington State, has been a great resource on all things related to his father.

Many staff members at the National Archives, Peace Corps headquarters, and the John F. Kennedy Library were generous with their time and knowledge.

Bruce Johnson at Davis Wright Tremaine LLP provided clear and comprehensive advice on all things legal.

A silent source of inspiration for many years has been Jim Read at the School of Oriental and African studies, London University, who originally asked me to write this story.

My editor at the University Press of Kentucky, Natalie O'Neal, her colleagues at the press, especially David Cobb, director of Editorial, Design, and Production, and copy editor Annie Barva have given me great support, guidance, and manuscript improvement in so many ways. My gratitude is deep and profound.

Last, to Barbara Ogle, editor, typist, sounding board, reviewer, researcher, muse, and to Ada Reid-Watson, proofreader extraordinaire, I give my deepest thanks.

Dramatis Personae

Gail Bagley	American Assessor at trial
Vance Barron	Peace Corps volunteer (PCV) friend of the Kinseys (father with same name)
Mark Bomani	Tanzanian attorney general
Paul Bomani	Tanzanian minister of economic affairs and development planning
Chester Bowles	American undersecretary of state
Carroll Brewster	Bill's American attorney
Richard Brooke-Edwards	son of Lady Marion Chesham and trial attendee
John Burns	American ambassador to Tanzania
Marion Chesham	Tanzanian legislator
Nancy Churchill	PCV nurse in Mwanza
Betty Clemmer	Peppy's college dorm mate, wife of Dan Clemmer
Dan Clemmer	American Teachers for East Africa teacher
Peter Clifford	head and neck specialist from Nairobi
John Coyne	Peace Corps official and author
Dr. Datar	regional medical officer in Mwanza
Charlotte Dennett	Peppy's mother
Raymond Dennett	Peppy's father
Tyler Dennett	Peppy's grandfather
Gerald Dockeray	Nairobi pathologist, expert witness
Marianne Dunn	PCV teacher, friend of Peppy
Ededen Effiwat	Tanzanian state attorney, prosecutor
Ann Ellison	PCV teacher, wife of Phil

255

Phil Ellison	PCV teacher, husband of Ann
Pam Engle Ellison	PCV in Mwanza
Anthony Essaye	Peace Corps deputy general counsel
Victoria Ferenbach	longtime friend of Peppy
Byron Georgiadis	Bill Kinsey's lead trial counsel
D. J. Gumbo	district magistrate
Elizabeth Harris	Peace Corps official in Washington, D.C.
Humbi Sayuda	witness
Norm Hummon	Tanzania Peace Corps deputy director
C. F. Ijumba	deputy director, Tanzania CID
William Josephson	Peace Corps general counsel
David Kadane	PCV attorney
Peter Kateti	assistant superintendent of police, prosecutor at PI
Rashide Kawawa	vice president of Tanzania
Martin Kifunta	police inspector, CID
Barrington King	American vice council in Tanganyika
Bill Kinsey	PCV teacher, defendant
Peppy Kinsey	PCV teacher, wife of Bill Kinsey
Bill Kinsey Sr.	father of Bill Kinsey
Delores Ledbetter	PCV
Father Robert Lefebvre	Maryknoll priest at Sayusayu
Father Charles Liberatore	priest in Maswa
M. M. J. S. Lukumbuzya	Tanzania ambassador to United States
Charlotte Lyles	PCV secretary in Mwanza
Padre Masunzu	trial witness
Tom McHugh	Peace Corps doctor, witness
Dr. McMahon	British doctor in Mwanza
Jack McPhee	Peace Corps regional director, Mwanza
Sandy McPhee	wife of Jack McPhee
Philip Mganga	Tanzanian assistant medical officer
Vinno Mhaisker	Tanzanian magistrate at the preliminary inquiry
Jim Morrissey	Peace Corps doctor in Dar es Salaam
Fred Mugobi	Tanzanian assessor at trial
B. Mulokozi	Tanzania foreign-affairs secretary
Julius Nyerere	president of Tanzania
John Oliver	PCV, author's housemate
Mr. Parekh	law partner of Gurbachan Singh

Leon Parker — Peace Corps staff member in Dar es Salaam
Harold Platt — trial judge
Bob Poole — Peace Corps director, Kenya
Tom Quimby — associate Peace Corps director for Africa
James Read — acting dean, University of Dar es Salaam Law School
Dick Richter — Peace Corps deputy director, Kenya
Joan Richter — Dick Richter's wife
Corporal Silashi — policeman in Maswa
Paul Sack — Peace Corps director, Tanzania
Gurbachan Singh — Bill Kinsey's Mwanza attorney
Sargent Shriver — former Peace Corps director
Charlotte Staelin — Peppy's sister
A. S. Swai — justice of the peace in Maswa
Virgi Natha Taank — Tanzanian photographer hired by the Peace Corps
Venerable Taylor — Anglican archdeacon in Dar es Salaam
Sargeant Thomas — policeman in Maswa
Jack Vaughn — Peace Corps director
Maganda Vilindo — trial witness

Notes

Abbreviations

JC   John Coyne Papers, Peace Corps files
NA   National Archives, Washington, D.C.
PC   Peace Corps
PI   Preliminary Inquiry
PR   Peter Reid files of Peace Corps files
RG   Record Group

Prologue

1. Charlotte Staelin Hawes, "Sisters," unpublished, unpaginated account of Peppy's life, copy in author's collection; Victoria Ferenbach to author, September 25, 2018.

Introduction

1. Norm Hummon, memo to file, April 2, 1966, Peace Corps (PC) files, John Coyne Peace Corps Papers (hereafter JC), author's collection; John Oliver to author, November 15, 2009; Jack McPhee, log, March 29, 1966, PC files, JC.

2. Anthony Essaye to William Josephson, memo, April 11, 1966, PC files, JC; Paul Sack, memo to file, March 31, 1966, PC files, JC.

3. Stanley Meisler, *When the World Calls: The Inside Story of the Peace Corps and Its First Fifty Years* (Boston: Beacon Press, 2011), 38–44.

4. Larry J. Sabato, *The Kennedy Half Century: The Presidency, Assassination, and Lasting Legacy of John F. Kennedy* (New York: Bloomsbury, 2013), 406–8.

5. Arthur M. Schlesinger, *A Thousand Days: John F. Kennedy in the White House* (Boston: Hough Mifflin; Cambridge: Riverside Press, 1965), 713.

6. Robert Dallek, *An Unfinished Life: John F. Kennedy 1917—1963* (New York: Little Brown, 2004), 708.

7. Harris Wofford, *Of Kennedys and Kings: Making Sense of the Sixties* (Pittsburg: University of Pittsburg Press, 1980), 243.

8. Schlesinger, *A Thousand Days,* 605.

9. Dallek, *An Unfinished Life,* 340.

10. Wofford, *Of Kennedys and Kings,* 245.

11. Lex Rieffel, *Reconsidering the Peace Corps,* policy brief (Washington, D.C.: Brookings Institution, December 2003), at https://www.brookings.edu/research/reconsidering-the-peace-corps/.

12. "Peace Corps," John F. Kennedy Library, n.d., at https://www.jfklibrary.org/JFK/JFK-in-History/Peace-Corps.aspx.

13. Meisler, *When the World Calls,* xi.

1. A Volunteer Is Dead

1. This account is based largely on the contemporaneous log kept by Jack McPhee, various dates, PC files, JC.

2. Jack McPhee, discussion with the author, May 21, 2012.

3. Peace Corps, *First Annual Peace Corps Report, 30 June 1962* (Washington, D.C.: Peace Corps, 1962), at http://peacecorpsonline.org/historyofthepeacecorps/annualreports/1ST_1962.PDF.

4. Dr. Tom McHugh, discussion with the author, February 25, 2012; Paul Sack, memo to file, March 28–31, 1966, PC files, JC.

5. Paul Sack, discussion with the author, March 18, 2012.

6. Tom McHugh, résumé, Tom McHugh files, author's collection.

7. PCDSM to PCDC, Cable no. 331, March 28, 1966, Record Group (RG) 84, Embassy Dar es Salaam AID 14 Kinsey Case, National Archives (NA), Washington, D.C.

8. PCDC to PCDSM, Cable no. 870, March 29, 1966, RG 84, NA.

9. Father Robert Lefebvre, discussion with the author, September 12, 2011.

10. This account is based largely on McPhee's log, various dates, PC files, JC.

11. Philip Mganga, AMO, "Report on Post Mortem Examination," March 20, 1966, PC files, JC; McHugh to Essaye, report, n.d., McHugh files; Philip Mganga, testimony at the preliminary inquiry in Maswa, May 5, 1966, PC files, JC.

12. Dr. James Morrissey, "Running Commentary," March 29, 1966, PC files, JC.

13. Sack, discussion with the author, August 14, 2015; "David Kadane," obituary, *New York Times,* April 18, 1981.

14. Morrissey, "Running Commentary," March 29, 1966; McPhee log.

15. This summary is based on "Report from Justice of the Peace," March 29, 1966, McHugh files.

2. A Lovely, Creative Woman and an All-American Boy from the South

1. Melissa Stanger, "The 50 Most Expensive Private High Schools in America," *Business Insider*, September 20, 2012, http://www.businessinsider.com/most-expensive-private -schools-2012-9.

2. Mount Holyoke College, "A Detailed History," n.d., at https://www.mtholyoke.edu /about/history/detailed.

3. *Llamarada*, yearbook, 1964, Mount Holyoke College, South Hadley, Mass.; Betty Clemmer, discussion with the author, September 6, 2009; Barbara Ratigan, discussion with the author, October 4, 2012 (Barbara was a Mount Holyoke classmate of Peppy's and a Peace Corps volunteer in Tanzania).

4. The following articles and websites provide general information about the Dennett and Woodall families: Williams College, "Williams History—Presidents—Dennett, Tyler (1882 – 1949)," n.d., at https://specialcollections.williams.edu/williams-history/presidents /dennett-tyler/; "Famous Philips Academy Alumni," Ranker, n.d., at https://www.ranker .com/list/famous-phillips-academy-alumni-and-students/reference; "Raymond Dennett," Prabook, n.d., https://prabook.com/web/raymond.dennett/1049079; "A Centennial Chronicle," American-Scandinavian Foundation, n.d., at http://www.amscan.org/app/uploads /2015/10/SR.Summer11_CentennialChronicle-Part-2.pdf; "Paid Death Notice: Deaths Dennett, Charlotte Woodall," *New York Times*, November 8, 2000, at https://www.nytimes .com/2000/11/08/classified/paid-notice-deaths-dennett-charlotte-woodall.htmlNovember 2000; Peter Heck, "Farewell to Colchester Farm CSA," *Chestertown Spy*, November 30, 2017, at https://chestertownspy.org/2017/11/30/farewell-to-colchester-farm-csa/; "Audrey Dennett," obituary, *Brattleboro Reformer*, September 5, 2009, at http://m.legacy.com/obituaries /brattleboro/obituary.aspx?n=audrey-dennett&pid=132307571&referrer=0&preview= false; "Delmarva People You Know," *Wilmington Sunday Morning Star*, June 12, 1938, at https://news.google.com/newspapers?Id=OQtKAAAAIBAJ&sjid=PyENAAAAIBAJ&pg =416,4901456&output=html text.

5. United States Peace Corps, "Peverley Kinsey Peace Corps Assessment 1964," PC files, JC.

6. Hawes, "Sisters."

7. Victoria Ferenbach, discussion with the author, November 30, 2012.

8. Randolph-Macon Academy, "About," n.d., at http://www.rma.edu.

9. Washington and Lee University, "The Honor System," n.d., at https://www.wlu.edu /about-wandl/history-and-traditions/our-traditions/the-honor-system.

10. Washington and Lee University, "A Brief History," n.d., at https://www.wlu.edu /about-wandl/history-and-traditions/a-brief-history.

11. "Virginia: College Will Remove Confederate Flags," *New York Times*, July 9, 2014.

12. *Calyx*, yearbook, 1964, Washington and Lee University, Lexington, Va.; "Bill H. Kinsey, Sr.," obituary, *Washington Daily News* (Washington, N.C.), February 2006, http://www .ncgenweb.us/beaufort/obits/obitsk.htm; Mrs. Bill H. Kinsey Sr. to Carroll Brewster, July 5, 1966, PC files, JC.

13. United States Peace Corps, *Peace Corps Biographies,* 56, author's collection. This pamphlet is a directory of the people who participated in the Tanganyika training program at Syracuse University.

3. A Tale of Three Cities

1. Regional Commission, Government of Tanzania, *Mwanza, 10 Tears of Progress in Mwanza Region* (Mwanza, Tanzania: Lake Printing Works, 1964).

2. S. J. K. Baker, "The East African Environment," in *History of East Africa,* ed. Roland Oliver and Gervase Mathew (Oxford: Clarendon Press, 1963), 1; Charles Meeks, *Brief Authority: A Memoir of Colonial Administration in Tanganyika,* ed. Innes Meeks (London: Radcliffe Press, 2011), 57, 69–77; E. P. Sagerson, "The Geology of East Africa," in *Handbook of Natural Resources of East Africa,* ed. E. W. Russell (Nairobi, Kenya: D. A. Hawkins in association with East African Literature Bureau, 1962), 52, rainfall map insert.

3. Father Robert Lefebrve, discussion with the author, September 12, 2011.

4. *See Dar es Salaam* (Dar es Salaam, Tanzania: Shell Oil, 1964); John Iliffe, *A Modern History of Tanganyika* (Cambridge: Cambridge University Press, 1979), 384–93, 400–404.

4. Government Officials Clarify the Situation

1. The details of this conversation with Director Ijumba come from PCDSM to PCDC, Cable no. 345, March 29, 1966, RG 84, NA; Norm Hummon, memo to file, March 29, 1966, PC files, JC.

2. Morrissey, memo to file, March 29, 1966, PC files, JC.

3. McHugh, discussion with the author, February 25, 2012.

4. McHugh, dictated report, March 29, 1966, McHugh files.

5. Sack, memo to file, March 28, 1966, PC files, JC.

6. This account is based largely on McPhee's log, various dates, PC files, JC.

7. The details of the state of Peppy's body at the time of McHugh's examination come from "McHugh Dictated Report of Superficial Examination of Mrs. Peverley Dennett Kinsey," March 29, 1966, McHugh files.

8. McHugh to Peace Corps Medical Division, memo, April 15, 1966, McHugh files; Dr. Tom McHugh, memo to file, n.d., PC files, JC; Essaye to Josephson, April 11, 1966, PC files, JC.

9. Richard (Dick) Richter, discussion with the author, January 12, 2012.

10. McHugh to author, October 1, 2016, author's collection.

11. The postmortem was not titled, signed, or dated, but it was accompanied by a copy of the handwritten version of the postmortem, PC files, JC.

12. Postmortem, PC files, JC.

13. Postmortem, PC files, JC.

14. PCDSM to PCDC, Cable no. 37, April 3, 1966, RG 84, NA.

5. Peace Corps Officials Visit Scene, Bail Is Sought, Peppy's Body Is Flown to Dar es Salaam

1. "Memorandum of Information Accumulated at Maswa–Mwanza by Paul Sack, 29–30 March 1966," PC files, JC.

2. McPhee log, March 30, 1966, PC files, JC; John Oliver, "Recollections of 1966 and Bill Kinsey Trial," memo to the author, November 15, 2009; Jack Vaughn to [name redacted, but possibly Reverend Vance Barron], May 25, 1966, PC files, JC.

3. Author's recollection.

4. Essaye to Josephson, April 11, 1966, PC files, JC; PCDSM to PCDC, Cable no. 156, April 13, 1966, RG 84, NA.

5. Sack, memo, March 31, 1966, PC files, JC.

6. McHugh to Essaye, April 14, 1966, PC files, JC.

7. The details of the trip to transport the body come from McHugh, discussion with the author, February 25, 2012.

8. PCDC to PCDSM, Cable no. 917, March 30, 1966, RG 84, NA.

9. PCDC to PCDSM, Cable no. 967, March 30, 1966, RG 84, NA.

10. PCDSM to PCDC, Cable no. 355, March 30, 1966, RG 84, NA.

11. Sack, memo to file, March 31, 1966, PC files, JC.

12. PCDSM to PCDC, Cable no. 374, March 31, 1966, RG 84, NA.

13. Tony Essaye, discussion with the author, June 3, 2010.

6. Life in Prison for Bill

1. McHugh to Peace Corps Medical Division, memo, April 15, 1966, McHugh files.

2. McPhee, memo to file, April 12, 1966, PC files, JC; PCDSM to PCDC, Cable no. 171, April 14, 1966, RG 84, NA; PCDSM to PCDC, Cable no. 243, April 20, 1966, RG 84, NA; McHugh, memo to file, April 22, 1966, McHugh files.

3. PCDSM to PCDC, Cable no. 207, April 16, 1966, RG 84, NA; PCDSM to PCDC, Cable no. 243, April 20, 1966, RG 84, NA; McHugh, memo to file, April 22, 1966, McHugh files.

4. PCDSM to PCDC, Cable no. 195, April 15, 1966, RG 84, NA.

5. PCDSM to PCDC, Cable no. 225, April 18, 1966, RG 84, NA.

6. McHugh, memo to file, April 22, 1966, McHugh files; Vincent J. D'andrea to McHugh, May 3, 1966, McHugh files.

7. PCDSM to PCDC, Cable no. 77, April 6, 1966, RG 84, NA.

8. McPhee, memo to file, April 29, 1966, PC files, JC; PCDSM to PCDC, Cable no. 386, April 30, 1966, RG 84, NA; PCDSM to PCDC, Cable no. 69, May 9, 1966, RG 84, NA.

9. Phil and Ann Ellison to parents, April 30, 1966, author's collection.

10. PCDSM to PCDC, Cable no. 277, May 7, 1966, RG 84, NA.

11. Sack to volunteers, May 27, 1966, PC files, JC.

12. PCDSM TO PCDC, Cable no. 321, June 7, 1966, PC files, JC.

13. PCDSM TO PCDC, Cable no. 321, June 7, 1966, PC files, JC.

14. PCDSM to PCDC, Cable no. 91, July 13, 1966, PC files, JC; PCDSM to PCDC, Cable no. 148, July 19, 1966, PC files, JC; Sack to Essaye, July 19, 1966, PC files, JC; PCDSM to PCDC, Cable no. 81, July 7, 1966, RG 84, NA.

15. Sack to Dr. and Mrs. Kinsey, July 19, 1966, PC files, JC.

16. PCDSM to PCDC, Cable no. 420, August 9, 1966, PC files, JC; PCDSM to PCDC, Cable no. 607, August 22, 1966, PC files, JC; PCDSM to PCDC, Cable no. 143, July 20, 1966, RG 84, NA.

17. Betty Clemmer, discussion with the author, September 16, 2009.

7. The Peace Corps and Tanzania

1. Meisler, *When the World Calls,* 5, 9, 21.

2. Philip Muehlenbeck, *Betting on the Africans: John F. Kennedy's Courting of African Nationalist Leaders* (New York: Oxford University Press, 2012), 112.

3. Muehlenbeck, *Betting on the Africans,* 98.

4. Charles Stuart Kennedy, "Interview with Barrington King," April 18, 1990, Frontline Diplomacy Oral History Collection, Library of Congress, at https://www.loc.gov/item /mfdipbib000616/.

5. Coates Redmon, *Come as You Are: The Peace Corps Story* (New York: Harcourt Brace Jovanovich, 1986), 36; Gerald T. Rice, *The Bold Experiment: JFK's Peace Corps* (Notre Dame, Ind.: University of Notre Dame Press, 1985), 94–96.

6. Redmon, *Come as You Are,* 95–96.

7. Quoted in Redmon, *Come as You Are,* 96–97.

8. Redmon, *Come as You Are,* 113.

9. Redmon, *Come as You Are,* 221.

10. Rice, *The Bold Experiment,* 126–27.

11. Rice, *The Bold Experiment,* 126–27.

12. Rice, *The Bold Experiment,* 127.

13. Elizabeth Pleck, *Domestic Tyranny: The Making of American Social Policy against Family Violence from Colonial Times to the Present* (Urbana: University of Illinois Press, 2004), xxvi, 196; Violence against Women Act of 1994, Pub. L. 103-322, Title IV, sec. 40001–703 of the Violent Crime Control and Law Enforcement Act, H. R. 3355.

14. Sam Frizell, "Peace Corps Report Says 1 in 5 Volunteers Are [*sic*] Sexually Assaulted," *Time,* November 30, 2015, at http://time.com/4129299/peace-corps-volunteers-sexual-assault/.

15. Peter Duignan and L. H. Gann, *The United States and Africa: A History* (New York: Cambridge University Press, 1984), 206, 217, 220–21.

16. Rice, *The Bold Experiment,* 174; Elizabeth Cobbs Hoffman, *All You Need Is Love: The Peace Corps and the Spirit of the 1960s* (1998; paperback reprint, Cambridge, Mass.: Harvard University Press, 2000), 133.

17. Richard Burton, *The Lake Regions of Africa* (1860; reprint, Mineola, N.Y.: Dover, 1995) 367; Greg Garrett, "Relocating Burton: Public and Private Writings on Africa," *Journal of African Writing,* no. 2 (1997): 70–79.

18. Iliffe, *A Modern History of Tanganyika,* 247.

19. Iliffe, *A Modern History of Tanganyika,* 123, 261–62.

20. Kenneth Ingham, "Tanganyika: The Mandate and Cameron, 1919—1931," in *History of East Africa,* 2 vols., ed. Vincent Harlow, E. M. Chilver, and Alison Smith (Oxford: Clarendon Press, 1965), 543–55.

21. Iliffe, *A Modern History of Tanganyika,* 464–67; Guy Hunter, *The New Societies of Tropical Africa* (New York: Praeger, 1964), 113; J. S. R. Cole and W. N. Denison, *Tanganyika: The Development of Its Laws and Constitution* (London: Stevens & Sons, 1964), 233; "Paul Bomani," in *Dictionary of African Biography,* ed. Emmanuel K. Akyeampong and Henry Louis Gates Jr. (New York: Oxford University Press, 2012), 484–85.

22. William Edgett Smith, *We Must Run While They Walk: A Portrait of Africa's Julius Nyerere* (New York: Random House, 1971), 44, 50, 53, 55.

23. At the time of the Kinsey trial, Bomani was the minister of economic affairs and development planning (*Tanganyika Directory 1964* [Dar es Salaam: Government of Tanzania, 1965], author's collection).

24. A. J. Hughes, *East Africa: The Search for Unity; Kenya, Tanganyika, Uganda, and Zanzibar* (Baltimore: Penguin Books, 1963), 71–73; Smith, *We Must Run While They Walk,* 83; Cole and Denison, *Tanganyika,* 47–48.

25. Smith, *We Must Run While They Walk,* 83.

26. Alistair Ross, "Introduction to the Chesham Papers," 1975, Bothwick Institute, University of York.

27. Hughes, *East Africa,* 77.

28. Kennedy, "Interview with Barrington King," quoting the head of the British administration.

29. Hughes, *East Africa,* 86–92.

30. Hughes, *East Africa,* 90; Smith, *We Must Run While They Walk,* 99, 116.

31. Hughes, *East Africa,* 77.

32. Smith, *We Must Run While They Walk,* 103–6; Hughes, *East Africa,* 246.

33. Smith, *We Must Run While They Walk,* 149–66; Julius Nyerere, *Freedom and Unity* (Dar es Salaam, Tanzania: Oxford University Press, 1966), 298.

34. The information in this paragraph and the preceding two paragraphs comes from Smith, *We Must Run While They Walk,* 190–201. According to John Ratigan, longtime Foreign Service officer, on a telephone that was tapped one of the officials spoke of having necessary "ammunition" to convince the State Department. The word *ammunition* was misunderstood, and the U.S. officials were expelled (John Ratigan, discussion with the author, November 17, 2018).

35. Julius Nyerere, *Freedom and Socialism* (Dar es Salaam, Tanzania: Oxford University Press 1968), 45–46.

36. Quoted in C. Payne Lucas and Kevin Lowther, "The Experience: Africa," in *Making a Difference: The Peace Corps at Twenty-Five,* ed. Milton Viorst (New York: Wiedenfeld & Nicholson, 1986), 108–9.

37. Quoted in Nyerere, *Freedom and Socialism,* 137.

38. John Ndembwike, *Life in Tanzania Today and since the Sixties* (Dar es Salaam, Tanzania: Continental Press, 2010), 92–97.

8. Peace Corps Officials Assess the Situation and Plan Future Action

1. PCDSM to PCDC, Cable no. 6, April 1, 1966, RG 84, NA.

2. PCDC to PCDSM, Cable no. 12, April 1, 1966, RG 84, NA. Cables sent on one date could be received on a second date. The receiving date is usually the one found on the document.

3. PCDC to PCDSM, Cable no. 45, April 1, 1966, RG 84, NA.

4. PCDC to PCDSM, Cable no. 50, April 2, 1966, RG 84, NA.

5. PCDC to PCDSM, Cable no. 43, April 2, 1966, RG 84, NA.

6. Sack to volunteers, April 1, 1966, PC files, author's collection (these PC files are hereafter referred to as "PC files, PR [Peter Reid]" to distinguish them from the John Coyne, JC, files).

7. Sack to volunteers, April 6, 1966, PC files, PR.

8. PCDSM to PCDC, Cable no. 30, April 2, 1966, RG, NA.

9. Norm Hummon, memo to file, April 2, 1966, PC files, JC.

10. Hummon, memo to file, April 2, 1966, PC files, JC.

11. PCDSM to PCDC, Cable no. 34, April 3, 1966, RG 84, NA.

12. PCDSM to PCDC, Cable no. 35, April 3, 1966, RG 84, NA.

13. PCDC to PCDSM, Cable no. 85, April 3, 1966, RG 84, NA.

14. PCDSM to PCDC, Cable no. 36, April 4, 1966, RG 84, NA.

15. PCDSM to PCDC, Cable no. 156, April 13, 1966, PC files, JC; McPhee log, April 12, 1966, PC files, JC.

16. Donna Hamilton, former U.S. State Department consular officer, discussion with the author, May 13, 2008.

17. PCDC to PCDSM, Cable no. 978, March 31, 1966, RG 84, NA.

18. Norm Hummon, "Report on Preparation and Evacuation of Remains," undated but attached to Hummon, memo to file, April 2, 1966, PC files, JC.

19. PCDC to PCDSM, Cable no. 219, April 3, 1966, RG 84, NA.

20. PCDSM to PCDC, Cable no. 35, April 3, 1966; PCDC to PCDSM, Cable no. 85, April 3, 1966; PCDSM to PCDC, Cable no. 41, April 4, 1966; PCDSM to PCDC, Cable no. 77, April 6, 1966: all in RG 84, NA.

21. PCDSM to PCDC, Cable no. 41, April 4, 1966, RG 84, NA.

22. PCDSM to PCDC, Cable no. 77, April 6, 1966, RG 84, NA.

23. Consular Mortuary Certificate, dated April 3, 1966, PC files, JC.

24. PCDC to PCDSM, Cable no. 85, April 3, 1966; see also PCDSM to PCDC, Cable no. 77, April 6, 1966, RG 84, NA. I would later meet Jim Read at the School of Oriental and African Studies in London, where he was on the faculty. Read was planning to edit a book on interesting legal cases from the British Commonwealth and asked if I would write a chapter on the Kinsey trial. I agreed that I would, but nothing came of the book, and I put the issue aside until many years later. Read appears again in the case; his syllabus on criminal law in Tanzania was one of the documents I obtained from the Peace Corps. He was also a source for potential attorneys to be hired for Bill by the Kinseys.

25. PCDC to PCDSM, Cable no. 85, April 3, 1966, and PCDSM to PCDC, Cable no. 77, April 6, 1966, RG 84, NA.

26. PCDC to PCDSM, Cable no. 146, April 7, 1966, RG 84, NA.

27. PCDSM to PCDC, Cable no. 107, April 7, 1966, RG 84, NA.

28. PCDSM to PCDC, Cable no. 119, April 8, 1966, RG 84, NA.

29. PCDC to PCDSM, Cable no. 152, April 6, 1966, RG 84, NA.

30. John McPhee, "A Reporter at Large: Fifty-Two People on a Continent," *New Yorker,* March 5, 1966.

31. William Josephson to Jack Vaughn, Peace Corps director, "Defense of Tanzania Volunteer in a Murder Prosecution," April 7, 1966, PC files, JC.

32. PCDSM to PCDC, Cable no. 69, May 9, 1966, RG 84, NA.

9. Syracuse University Training and Marriage

1. Dean Clifford L. Winters to Peace Corps trainees, Syracuse University, June 22, 1964, author's collection.

2. Syracuse University, "[Peace Corps] Training Program Description," 1964, author's collection.

3. Syracuse University, "[Peace Corps] Training Program Description," 1964, author's collection.

4. Quoted in C. Payne Lucas and Kevin Lowther, *Keeping Kennedy's Promise: The Peace Corps Moment of Truth,* 2nd ed. (Baltimore: Peace Corps Online, 2002), iii.

5. Hoffman, *All You Need Is Love,* 170.

6. Jonathan Zimmerman, *Innocents Abroad: American Teachers in the American Century* (Cambridge, Mass.: Harvard University Press, 2006), 1–19, 181–210.

7. Meisler, *When the World Calls,* 33–34.

8. John Coyne, "A PCV Death in Tanzania," Peace Corps Worldwide, April 19, 2011, at http://peacecorpsworldwide.org/?s=Bill+Kinsey.

9. See, for example, John Coyne, "PCV Accused of Murdering His Wife," Peace Corps Worldwide, December 29, 2017, at http://peacecorpsworldwide.org/?s=Bill+Kinsey; John Coyne, "PCV Charged with Murder," Peace Corps Worldwide, April 19, 2011, at http://peacecorpsworldwide.org/?s=Bill+Kinsey.

10. Hawes, "Sisters."

11. Ferenbach, discussion with the author, November 30, 2012.

10. Peace Corps Training in Tanzania, Binza Upper Primary School

1. Donn Fry to author, May 16, 2012, author's collection.

2. Hawes, "Sisters."

3. Trish Daniels, conversation with the author, July 26, 2012.

4. Delores Ledbetter, conversation with the author, October 28, 2011.

5. Lucas and Lowther, "The Experience," 115.

6. Hawes, "Sisters."

7. Quoted in Hawes, "Sisters."

8. Hawes, "Sisters."

9. Phil and Ann Ellison to parents, January 15 and February 26, 1966, author's collection.

10. Phil and Ann Ellison to parents, January 15, 1966, author's collection, emphasis in original.

11. Phil and Ann Ellison to parents, February 4, 1966, author's collection.

12. Ann Ellison to parents, March 29, 1966, author's collection.

13. Phil and Ann Ellison to parents, April 1, 1966, author's collection.

14. Phil and Ann Ellison to parents, April 26, 1966, author's collection.

11. Friends of Peppy

1. Betty Clemmer, discussion with the author, September 6, 1966; Betty Clemmer to the author, April 30, 2012.

2. Betty Clemmer, discussion with the author, September 6, 1966; Betty Clemmer to the author, April 30, 2012.

3. "Teachers for East Africa and Teacher Education in East Africa Hold 40th Reunion," Teachers College, Columbia University, May 16, 2002, at http://www.tc.columbia.edu/news .htm?articleid=3773&pub=7&issue=72.

4. Betty Clemmer, discussion with the author, September 6, 1966; Betty Clemmer to the author, April 30, 2012.

5. Dan Clemmer to his parents, March 25, 1966, author's collection.

6. Dan Clemmer to his parents, April 3, 1966, author's collection.

7. Betty Clemmer, discussion with the author, September 6, 1966; Betty Clemmer to the author, April 30, 2012.

8. Details about the school where the Dowers taught and Aileen's interactions with Peppy come from Aileen Dower, conversations with the author, April 17, May 5, May 12, 2011.

12. The Peace Corps and Criminal Defense

1. Meisler, *When the World Calls*, 137.

2. Cole and Denison, *Tanganyika*, 119.

3. PCDC to PCDSM, Cable no. 97, April 4, 1966, RG 84, NA; PCDSM to PCDC, Cable no. 45, April 4, 1966, RG 84, NA.

4. Essaye to Sack, April 20, 1966, McHugh files.

5. PCDSM to PCDC, Cable no. 55, April 5, 1966, RG 84, NA.

6. PCDSM to PCDC, Cable no. 56, April 5, 1966, RG 84, NA.

7. See the Fried, Frank website at http://www.friedfrank.com.

8. Bill Josephson to Director [Jack Vaughn], "Procurement of Legal Services to Defend Tanzanian Volunteer on Murder Prosecution," memo, April 7, 1966, PC files, JC. See also

Josephson to Director, "Procurement of Legal Services to Defend Tanzanian Volunteer on Murder Prosecution," memo, April 14, 1966, PC files, JC; Bill Josephson to Director, "Use of Foreign Services Act Section 1031 Authority to Procure Legal Services to Defend Tanzania Volunteer in Murder Prosecution," memo, April 7, 1966, PC files, JC.

9. Josephson to Director, "Procurement of Legal Services to Defend Tanzanian Volunteer on Murder Prosecution."

10. Josephson to Director, "Procurement of Legal Services to Defend Tanzanian Volunteer on Murder Prosecution."

11. Josephson to Director, "Use of Foreign Services Act Section 1031."

12. Josephson to Director, "Use of Foreign Services Act Section 1031," emphasis added.

13. Josephson to Director, "Procurement of Legal Services to Defend Tanzanian Volunteer on Murder Prosecution."

14. Quoted in "Peace Corps Seeks Legal Aid Overseas," *New York Times,* May 16, 1966. Josephson's announcement received wide coverage in the American press, including the *Hartford Courant,* the *Washington Pennsylvania Observer,* the *Arizona Daily Star,* the *Baltimore Morning Sun,* the *Chicago Tribune,* the *Cleveland Plain Dealer,* and others (copies in PC files, PR).

15. General counsel internal memo, April 20, 1966, PC files, JC.

16. Peace Corps Act Amendments, Pub. L. 89-572; 80 Stat. 764.

17. See, for example, "Murder Trial Angers Peace Corps Volunteers," *Nairobi Sunday Nation,* May 15, 1966; "Peace Corps Seeks Legal Aid Overseas," *New York Times,* May 16, 1966; "Legal Aid Sought for Corpsman," *Arizona Daily Star,* May 16, 1966; "Peace Corps Seeks Funds for Lawyers," *Chicago Tribune,* May 16, 1966.

18. Bill Josephson to Director, "Defense of Tanzania Volunteer in Murder Prosecution," memo, April 7, 1966, PC files, JC; PCDC to PCDSM, Cable no. 278, April 9, 1966, RG 84, NA.

19. PCDSM to PCDC, Cable no. 269, April 21, 1966, RG 84, NA; PCDC to PCDSM, Cable no. 536, April 22, 1966, RG 84, NA.

13. The Preliminary Inquiry

1. PCDC to PCDSM, Cable no. 548, April 21, 1966, RG 84, NA; PCDSM to PCDC, Cable no. 334, April 27, 1966, RG 84, NA.

2. PCDSM to PCDC, Cable no. 12, May 3, 1966, RG 84, NA.

3. Gurbachan Singh to Byron Georgiadis, May 4, 1966, PC files, JC; Sack, memo to file, May 6, 1966, PC files, JC.

4. "Peace Corps Man Faces Trial," *Boston Globe,* May 8, 1966; "Peace Corps Man on Trial," *Salem Statesman* (Oregon), May 6, 1966.

5. Sack to Peace Corps volunteers, May 10, 1966, PC files, JC.

6. PCDSM to PCDC, Cable no. 69, May 9, 1966, RG 84, NA.

7. PCDC to PCDSM, Cable no. 2, May 1, 1966, PC files, JC.

8. Details of the PI come from *Republic v. Bill Haywood Kinsey,* unpublished transcript of the preliminary hearing before Coram V. D. Mhaisker, Criminal Case no. 85, 1966, Tanzania, author's collection, hereafter "PI transcript"; subsequent notes cite specific pages.

9. Martin Kifunta, testimony, PI transcript, 1–5; "Corps Volunteer Is Impassive at Hearing," *Pottstown Mercury,* May 7, 1966.

10. Kifunta, testimony, PI transcript, 1–5; Dennis Neald, "Peace Corps Man Tells of Wife's Death," *Nairobi Sunday Nation,* May 8, 1966. Although the article in the *Sunday Nation* reports that Mhaisker read these statements, I do not find any such language in the transcript.

11. A. S. Swai, testimony, PI transcript, 7.

12. PCDSM to PCDC, Cable nos. 68 and 69, May 9, 1966, RG 84, NA.

13. Mhaisker's legal opinion on the statement, PI transcript, 8–9.

14. Philip Mganga, testimony, PI transcript, 10–12; PCDSM to PCDC, Cable no. 68, May 9, 1966, RG 84, NA; Denis Neald, "Peace Corps Man Faces Trial," *Boston Globe,* May 8, 1966.

15. These witnesses' testimony is given in PI transcript, 10.

16. Summary and quotes from Maganda Vilindo's testimony are from Neald, "Peace Corps Man Faces Trial."

17. Padre Masunzu, testimony, PI transcript, 13.

18. PI transcript, 14; PCDSM to PCDC, Cable no. 69, May 9, 1966, RG 84, NA; Neald, "Peace Corps Man Faces Trial."

19. Essaye to Josephson, April 11, 1966, PC files, JC.

20. Roger Traynor, "Ground Lost and Found in Criminal Discovery," *New York University Law Review* 39, no. 2 (April 1964): 749–70.

21. PCDM to PCDC, Cable no. 69, May 9, 1966, RG 84, NA.

22. Copies of these newspaper articles can be found in PC files, PR.

23. PCDSM to PCDC, Cable no. 56, May 7, 1966, RG 84, NA; PCDC to PCDSM, Cable no. 317, May 14, 1966, RG 84, NA.

24. Carroll Brewster to Mr. and Mrs. Kinsey [Bill's parents], May 11, 1966, PC files, JC; Byron Georgiadis, lecture to the Kenya Society, London, May 29, 2007, author's collection, 9, 12.

25. "Byron Nikos Georgiadis," obituary, *Old Cambrian Society,* January 2010, at http://www.oldcambrians.com/obituary-georgiadis,byron.html.

26. "Lives Remembered," *Telegraph,* February 9, 2010, at http://www.telegraph.co.uk /news/obituaries/7198658/lives-remembered.html.

27. Peter Leftie, "Lawyers Mourn Kenya's 'Most Costly' Attorney," *Nairobi Daily Nation,* January 5, 2010, at http://www.nation.co.ke/news/1056–836628-ijy8w2z/index.html.

14. Peace Corps Faces Challenges

1. Sack to Tom Quimby, May 14, 1966, PC files, PR.

2. Sack to Will Lotter, May 14, 1966, PC files, PR.

3. Dennis Neald, "Murder Trial Angers Peace Corps Volunteers," *Nairobi Sunday Nation,* May 16, 1966.

4. Hawes, "Sisters."

5. Vance Barron to Jack Vaughn, May 16, 1966, PC files, JC, emphasis in original.

6. Vaughn to Barron, May 25, 1966, PC files, PR.

7. Vaughn to Barron, July 7, 1966, PC files, JC.

8. Sack to Quimby, May 20, 1966, RG 84, NA.

9. Request for Authorization of Official Travel, May 18, 1966, PC files, JC.

15. Tanzanian Criminal Law

1. H. F. Morris and James Read, *Indirect Rule and the Search for Justice: Essays in East African Legal History* (Oxford: Clarendon Press, 1972), 74–75.

2. Antony N. Allott, *New Essays in African Law* (London: Butterworths, 1970), 13–15.

3. Morris, *Indirect Rule,* 110–11.

4. Morris, *Indirect Rule,* 73, 76.

5. Quoted in Morris, *Indirect Rule,* 84.

6. Hughes, *East Africa,* 32.

7. Cole and Denison, *Tanganyika,* 82.

8. H. F. Morris, "A History of the Adoption of Codes of Criminal Law and Procedure in British Colonial Africa, 1876–1935," *Journal of African Law* 18, no. 1 (1974): 22.

9. Cole and Denison, *Tanganyika,* 25.

10. Cole and Denison, *Tanganyika,* 156, 238; E. Cotran, "Tanzania," in *Judicial and Legal Systems in Africa,* ed. Antony N. Allott (London: Butterworths, 1970), 147, 154–58.

11. Cole and Denison, *Tanganyika,* 156–57; Allott, *New Essays,* 267.

12. Cole and Denison, *Tanganyika,* 137; Morris, *Indirect Rule,* 188.

13. Cole and Denison, *Tanganyika,* 156.

14. Cole and Dennison, *Tanganyika,* 247, note number within quotation and citation omitted.

15. Cole and Denison, *Tanganyika,* 247; Essaye to Josephson, April 11, 1966, reporting on the death penalty.

16. Cole and Denison, *Tanganyika,* 5.

16. McHugh and Singh Re-create the Scene of Peppy's Death

1. The description of McHugh and Singh's re-creation in this chapter comes from an undated memo by Tom McHugh, which he wrote on his visit to Impala Hill around May 30, 1966, McHugh files.

2. Georgiadis, lecture, 2007, 8.

17. Trial Preparation after the Preliminary Inquiry

1. Sack, conversation with the author, April 10, 2010.

2. McHugh to Brewster, June 21, 1966, McHugh files.

3. Hoffman, *All You Need Is Love,* 127.

4. Essaye to Singh, May 20, 1966, PC files, JC.

5. Brewster to McHugh, May 27, 1966, McHugh files.

6. McHugh to Essaye, April 14, 1966, PC files, JC.

7. Brewster to Byron Georgiadis, August 21, 1966, PC files, JC.

8. Brewster to Georgiadis, June 8, 1966; Brewster to McHugh, June 14, 1966; McHugh to Brewster, June 21, 1966: all in McHugh files.

9. Robert Selker to Brewster, July 8, 1966, McHugh files. "Enovid" and "Othonovum" were brand names for the birth-control medication Mestranol.

10. Mrs. Kinsey to Brewster, July 5, 1966, PC files, JC; PCDC to PCDSM, Cable no. 75, July 6, 1966, RG 84, NA; PCDC to PCDSM, Cable no. 143, July 18, 1966, RG 84, NA; PCDSM to PCDC, Cable no. 176, July 20, 1966, RG 84, NA.

11. Everett Jordan to Frank Weitzel, 1966, PC files, JC, mentioned in Weitzel to Jordan, June 22, 1966, PC files, JC; Jordan to J. William Fulbright, June 24, 1966, PC files, JC.

12. Sack to Essaye, July 4, 1966, PC files, JC.

13. PCDC to PCDSM, Cable no. 216, August 11, 1966, RG 84, NA; PCDSM to PCDC, Cable no. 470, August 12, 1966, RG 84, NA.

14. "Kennedy in Dar Warns of SA Danger," *Dar es Salaam Standard,* June 10, 1966; "'World Must Do Much More for Africa,'" *Dar es Salaam Standard,* June 11, 1966.

15. Sack to Essaye, July 20, 1966, PC files, JC.

16. Sack to Thomas Page, June 1, 1966, PC files, PR.

17. PCDSM to PCDC, Cable no. 149, July 19, 1966, PC files, JC.

18. Hoffman, *All You Need Is Love,* 54.

19. Page to Vaughn, July 30, 1966, PC files, JC.

20. PCDC to PCDSM, Cable no. 130, August 6, 1966, RG 84, NA; PCDSM to all American embassies in Africa with Peace Corps programs, Cable no. 415, August 8, 1966, RG 84, NA; Sack to Peace Corps volunteers, August 9, 1966, PC files, JC.

21. Vaughn to Sack, August 4, 1966, PC files, JC.

22. PCDSM to PCDC, Cable no. 631, August 24, 1966, RG 84, NA.

23. Essaye to Singh, August 2, 1966, PC files, JC.

24. Sack to Vaughn, August 23, 1966, PC files, JC.

25. PCDSM to PCDC, Cable no. 261, May 26, 1966, RG 84, NA.

26. PCDSM to PCDC, Cable no. 176, July 20, 1966; PCDSM to PCDC, Cable no. 262, July 26, 1966; PCDSM to PCDC, Cable no. 300, July 29, 1966; PCDSM to PCDC, Cable no. 369, August 4, 1966: all in RG 84, NA.

27. PCDSM to PCDC, Cable no. 369, August 4, 1966, RG 84, NA; McHugh to Brewster, telegram, August 8, 1966, PC files, JC.

28. Sack to Peace Corps volunteers, August 9, 1966, PC files, PR.

29. PCDSM to PCDC, Cable no. 362, June 30, 1966, RG 84, NA; PCDSM to PCDC, Cable no. 492, August 13, 1966, RG 84, NA.

30. Brewster to Georgiadis, August 21, 1966, PC files, JC; PC Nairobi to PCDC, Cable no. 824, August 17, 1966, RG 84, NA; PCDSM to PC Nairobi, Cable no. 540, August 17, 1966, RG 84, NA; PCDC to PCDSM, Cable no. 31039, August 18, 1966, RG 84, NA.

31. Brewster to Bill Kinsey, July 14, 1966, McHugh files.

32. PC Nairobi to PCDSM and PCDC, Cable no. 16118, August 17, 1966, PC files, JC.

33. Georgiadis, lecture, 2007, 4.

34. PCDC to PCDSM, Cable no. 592, August 26, 1966, RG 84, NA.

35. Georgiadis, lecture, 2.

36. Emails to the author from Tony Essaye, Paul Sack, and Tom McHugh, January 29, 30, 31, 2018, respectively, author's files.

18. Medical Analysis by Dr. Tom McHugh

1. McHugh, conversation with the author, September 7, 2013.

2. Noted in Brewster to Georgiadis, August 21, 1966, PC files, JC.

3. [Tom McHugh], "Statement of Personal Relationship with Mr. & Mrs. Kinsey," undated and unsigned but obviously prepared by McHugh and written in July or August 1966, McHugh files.

4. [Tom McHugh], "Evaluation of Drugs—Relation to Unconscious Episode," undated and unsigned but obviously prepared by McHugh and written in July or August 1966, McHugh files.

5. [Tom McHugh], "Injuries," undated and unsigned but obviously prepared by McHugh and written in July or August 1966, McHugh files, emphasis apparently supplied in pen by McHugh at a later date.

6. [Tom McHugh], "Fractures—Cause and Effect—Intra-cranial Bleeding," 1–6, undated and unsigned but obviously prepared by McHugh and written in July or August 1966, McHugh files.

7. [McHugh], "Fractures," 6–18.

8. Richard Patterson, *Lawyers Medical Encyclopedia of Personal Injuries and Allied Specialties,* 5th ed. (Charlottesville, Va.: Michie Company, Lexus/Nexus, 2005), 32–35; Randy Hanslick and Michael Graham, eds., *Forensic Pathology in Criminal Cases,* 2nd ed. (Charlottesville, Va.: Lexis, 2001); *Medical Dictionary* (Springfield, Mass.: Merriam-Webster, 2005).

9. Tom McHugh, "Statement of Personality Assessment of Bill Haywood Kinsey," August 15, 1966, McHugh files.

10. Georgiadis, lecture, 2007, 10, 19.

19. The Trial Begins in Mwanza

1. Richard Brooke-Edwards, "A Fourth Freedom," *Transition Magazine: An International Review,* no. 34 (1968): 5–16.

2. Lindsay Butler to author, July 28, 2015; Alistair Ross to author, July 12, 2015.

3. PCDSM to PCDC, Cable no. 665, August 26, 1966, RG 84, NA; Tony Essaye, notes taken during the trial, 1–2, PC files, JC; Georgiadis, lecture, 11.

4. Essaye trial notes, 1–2, PC files, JC; Georgiadis, lecture, 10.

5. PCDSM to PCDC, Cable no. 696, August 29, 1966, RG 84, NA; Eric Stevenson to Jack Vaughn, August 8, 1966, PC files, JC.

6. Sean Rippington, archivist, St. Peter's College, to author, March 10, 2014; PCDSM to PCDC, Cable no. 665, August 26, 1966, RG 84, NA; "Commissioners' Biographies, Uganda Law Reform Commission," 2005, at http://www.ulrc.go.ug/about_ULRC/commissioners_& staff.PHP (no longer available online, copy available in author's collection).

7. Essaye trial notes, 1, PC files, JC; PCDSM to PCDC, Cable no. 492, August 13, 1966, RG 84, NA; PCDSM to PCDC, Cable no. 665, August 26, 1966, RG 84, NA; PCDSM to PCDC, Cable no. 680, August 27, 1966, RG 84, NA; PCDSM to PCDC, Cable no. 690, August 27, 1966, RG 84, NA; PCDSM to PCDC, Cable no. 384, June 30, 1966, RG 84, NA; Cole and Denison, *Tanganyika,* 156.

8. Gail Bagley, discussion with the author, February 6, 2012.

9. "Murder Trial Hears Kinsey Diary Extract," *Dar es Salaam Standard,* August 27, 1966.

10. Tom Shactman, *Airlift to America: How Barack Obama, Sr., John F. Kennedy, Tom Mboya, and 800 East African Students Changed Their World and Ours* (New York: St. Martin's Press, 2009), 5–96.

11. Shactman, *Airlift to America,* 7.

12. Shactman, *Airlift to America,* 151–61.

13. F. B. Mugobi to the president of the African American Students Foundation, April 5, 1961, Tanzania Correspondence file no. 15, African American Students Foundation Archive, Michigan State University, East Lansing.

20. Trial Day One

1. Gail Bagley, discussions with the author, February 6 and 25, 2012; "Peace Corps Murder Trial Today," *Dar es Salaam Standard,* August 26, 1966.

2. "Peace Corps Murder Trial Today," *Nairobi Daily Nation,* August 27, 1966; Tony Essaye, trial notes, 1, PC files, JC; PCDSM to PCDC, Cable no. 665, August 26, 1966, RG 84, NA.

3. Essaye, trial notes, 1–2.

4. McHugh, discussion with the author, May 17, 2010; McHugh comments on manuscript draft, July 26, 2014.

5. Georgiadis, lecture, 2007, 13, 17; "Murder Court Hears Kinsey Diary Extract," *Dar es Salaam Standard,* August 27, 1966; "Peace Corps Murder Trial"; Essaye, trial notes, 1.

6. "Murder Court Hears Kinsey Diary Extract"; "Peace Corps Murder Trial.".

7. Philip Mganga, testimony, PI transcript, May 5, 1966, PC files, JC, 11. This quote and others from the PI transcript are given here on the assumption that the statement at the trial would be essentially the same as the statement made at the PI.

8. Georgiadis, lecture, 7.

9. Mganga, testimony, PI transcript, 11.

10. Mganga, testimony, PI transcript, 11.

11. The cross-examination of Mganga is pieced together from the following sources: Essaye, trial notes, 2, 3; "Murder Court Hears Kinsey Diary Extract"; "Peace Corps Murder Trial"; PCDSM to PCDC, Cable no. 665, August 26, 1966, RG 84, NA; Judge H. G. Platt, "Unpublished Decision in the Case of *The Republic v. Bill Haywood Kinsey*," Criminal Sessions Case No. 65 of 1966 [Tanzania], September 19, 1966; Mganga, testimony, PI transcript, 11; "Peace Corps Put on a Spot," *New York Sunday News*, November 20, 1966.

12. Tom McHugh, "Comments on the Testimony of Dr. Mganga Government Witness Number One," August 26, 1966, McHugh files.

13. Essaye, trial notes, 2, 3; "Murder Court Hears Kinsey Diary Extract"; "Peace Corps Murder Trial"; PCDSM to PCDC, Cable no. 665, August 26, 1966, RG 84, NA; Platt, "Unpublished Decision," September 19, 1966; Mganga, testimony, PI transcript, 11.

14. United Press International report, 37-TD10337AED, August 26, 1966, PC files, JC; PCDSM to PCDC, Cable no. 65, August 26, 1966, PC files, JC.

15. "'Most Peace Corps Members of CIA,'" *Dar es Salaam Standard*, December 29, 1964, reporting on the article in the *University Echo*.

16. "When Ambassadors Had Rhythm," *New York Times*, June 29, 2008.

21. Trial Day Two

1. Essaye, trial notes, 5.

2. This transcript was apparently prepared contemporaneously by Peace Corps staff and is in the McHugh files.

3. Essaye, trial notes, 4–8; "Kinsey Had Bloodstains on Clothes Says Witness," *Nairobi Sunday News*, August 28, 1966; "Police Testify in Peace Corps Teacher Death," *Philadelphia Bulletin*, August 28, 1966.

4. Essaye, trial notes, 7.

22. Trial Day Three

1. Essaye, trial notes, 30; Platt, "Unpublished Decision," 2–5.

2. Essaye, trial notes, 5.

3. Quoted in "Kinsey Court Hears Alleged Diary Notes," *Dar es Salaam Standard*, August 30, 1966; Platt, "Unpublished Decision," 10.

4. PCDSM to PCDC, Cable no. 715, August 30, 1966, PC files, JC. In his trial notes, Tony Essaye calls this dereliction "quite unbelievable" (7).

5. Quoted in "Kinsey Court Hears Alleged Diary Notes," *Dar es Salaam Standard*, August 30, 1966.

6. PCDSM to PCDC, Cable no. 700, August 29, 1966, RG 84, NA.

7. "Kinsey Court Hears Alleged Diary Notes"; Essaye, trial notes, 7.

8. Essaye, trial notes, 7.

9. Georgiadis, lecture, 2007, 11.

23. Trial Day Four

1. Wright Morris, *Ceremony in Lone Tree* (New York: New American Library of World Literature, 1962).

2. "Mwanza Court Told Kinsey Diary Was a Fiction," *Nairobi Daily Nation,* August 31, 1966; "Dramatic Turn in Kinsey Murder Trial," *Dar es Salaam Standard,* August 31, 1966.

3. "Mwanza Court Told Kinsey Diary Was a Fiction"; "Dramatic Turn in Kinsey Murder Trial"; Essaye, trial notes, 7; PCDSM to PCDC, Cable no. 692, September 1, 1966, RG 84, NA.

4. Quoted in "Dramatic Turn in Kinsey Murder Trial."

5. "Mwanza Court Told Kinsey Diary Was a Fiction"; "Dramatic Turn in Kinsey Murder Trial"; Essaye, trial notes, 7, 8.

6. "Mwanza Court Told Kinsey Diary Was a Fiction"; "Dramatic Turn in Kinsey Murder Trial"; Essaye, trial notes, 7, 8.

7. Quoted in "Dramatic Turn in Kinsey Murder Trial."

8. Platt, "Unpublished Decision," 6.

9. Platt, "Unpublished Decision," 5–6.

10. Platt, "Unpublished Decision," 5.

24. The Peace Corps Book Locker

1. Molly Guptell Manning, *When Books Went to War: The Stories That Helped Us Win World War II* (New York: Houghton Mifflin Harcourt, 2014).

2. Quoted in John Coyne, "The Fabulous Peace Corps Book Locker, Part 1," n.d., Peace Corps Worldwide, at https://peacecorpsworldwide.org/the-fabulous-peace-corps-book -locker-part-i/.

3. Peter Orner, "American Oddness, in All Its Glory," *New York Times,* July 19, 2019.

25. Trial Day Five

1. Essaye, trial notes, 10; "I Saw a Fight on Hill, Says Witness," *Dar es Salaam Standard,* September 1, 1966; "Kinsey Beat Wife on Head, Witness Tells Court," *Nairobi Daily Nation,* September 1, 1966.

2. Maganda Vilindo, testimony, included in Platt, "Unpublished Decision," 7.

3. Essaye, trial notes, 10; "I Saw Fight on Hill, Says Witness"; "Kinsey Beat Wife on Head, Witness Tells Court"; Platt, "Unpublished Decision," 7.

4. Platt, "Unpublished Decision," 7; Essaye, trial notes, 10.

5. "Kinsey Beat Wife on Head, Witness Tells Court."

6. "I Saw Fight on Hill, Says Witness"; Essaye, trial notes, 7.

7. Essaye, trial notes, 13; Platt, "Unpublished Decision," 11.

8. Essaye, trial notes, 13; Platt, "Unpublished Decision," 11.

9. Judge Alex Kozinski, "Criminal Law 2.0," *Georgetown Law Journal: Annual Review of Criminal Procedure* 44 (2015): iii.

26. Trial Day Six

1. Padre Masunzu, testimony, summary and quotation from Essaye, trial notes, 14.

2. Masunzu, testimony, summary from Essaye, trial notes, 14.

3. Essaye, trial notes, 14, 15; Platt, "Unpublished Decision," 7, 8.

4. Essaye, trial notes, 14, 15; Platt, "Unpublished Decision," 7, 8.

5. "I Loved My Wife, Kinsey Tells Court," *Nairobi Daily Nation,* September 2, 1966; PCDSM to PCDC, Cable no. 753, September 1, 1966, PC files, JC.

6. Dr. Barbara Ann Hoching and Laura Leigh Manville, "What of the Right to Silence: Still Supporting the Presumption of Innocence or a Growing Legal Fiction," *Macquerie Law Journal* 1, no. 1 (2001), at http://www.austlii.edu.au/au/journals/MqLawJl/2001/3.html.

7. Quoted in "I Loved My Wife, Kinsey Tells Court," *Nairobi Daily Nation.*

8. Barbara Boyle, discussion with the author, December 5, 2011.

9. Essaye, trial notes, 16; "I Loved My Wife, Kinsey Tells Court," *Dar es Salaam Standard,* September 2, 1966; PCDSM to PCDC, Cable no. 767, September 2, 1966, PC files, PR.

10. Quoted in "I Loved My Wife, Kinsey Tells Court," *Dar es Salaam Standard.*

11. PCDSM to PCDC, Cable no. 450, September 1, 1966, PC files, JC; PCDSM to PCDC, Cable no. 753, September 1, 1966, PC files, JC.

12. Bill Kinsey, testimony, summarized from "I Loved My Wife, Kinsey Tells Court," *Dar es Salaam Standard,* and "I Loved My Wife, Kinsey Tells Court," *Nairobi Daily Nation.*

27. Trial Day Seven

1. "Wife's Dying Word Was My Name—Kinsey," *Dar es Salaam Standard,* September 3, 1966.

2. "Kinsey Tells Court of Wife's 20 ft. Fall," *Nairobi Daily Nation,* September 3, 1966.

3. Bill Kinsey, testimony, summarized from Platt, "Unpublished Decision," 9.

4. "Wife's Dying Word Was My Name—Kinsey"; "Kinsey Tells Court of Wife's 20 ft. Fall."

5. Essaye, trial notes, 16–19.

6. "Kinsey Tells Court of Wife's 20 ft. Fall."

7. Essaye, trial notes, 19–20; PCDSM to PCDC, Cable no. 785, September 3, 1966, PC files, JC; Paul Sack to Singh and Parekh, Advocates, March 31, 1966, PC files, JC.

8. PCDC to PCDSM, Cable no. 34, September 2, 1966, RG 84, NA.

28. Trial Day Eight

1. "Mystery Move in Trial," *Dar es Salaam Sunday News,* September 4, 1966.

2. Associated Press report, September 3, 1966, PC files, JC, capitalization in the original.

3. Pam Engle Ellison, discussion with the author, November 19, 2011. Pam Engle subsequently remarried, and her name became "Pam Ellison," which led to some confusion as I was seeking to interview Ann and Phil Ellison.

4. Ann Ellison to parents, March 29, April 1, July 9, 1966, author's collection; Phil Ellison, discussions with the author, April 17, May 19, June 25, and August 15, 2013, May 9, 2014.

5. Tanzania Criminal Code, sec. 151; Cole and Dennison, *Tanganyika,* 158.

6. Phil Ellison, discussions with the author, April 17 and May 29, 2013; Pam Engle Ellison, discussion with the author, November 19, 2011.

7. Phil Ellison, discussions with the author, April 17 and May 29, 2013; Pam Engle Ellison, discussion with the author, November 19, 2011.

8. Phil and Ann Ellison to parents, August 21, 1966, author's collection.

29. Trial Day Nine

1. The account of this charge by the prosecution and the defense's response comes from "Legal Clash at Mwanza; BULLYING CHARGE DENIED," *Nairobi Daily Nation,* September 5, 1966; PCDSM to PCDC, Cable no. 102, September 6, 1966, RG 84, NA; Essaye, trial notes, 21.

2. PCDSM to PCDC, Cable no. 792, September 4, 1966, PC files, JC.

3. Georgiadis, lecture, 2007, 14; Essaye, trial notes, 21.

4. Georgiadis, lecture, 2007, 14.

5. Sack, conversation with the author, April 2010.

6. Hawes, "Sisters."

7. See, for instance, "Before Venezuela, US Had Long Involvement in Latin America," Associated Press, January 25, 2019, at https://apnews.com/2ded14659982426c9b255282773 4be83; Saeed Nahali Dehghan and Richard Norton-Taylor, "CIA Admits Role in 1953 Iranian Coup," *Guardian,* August 19, 2013, at https://www.theguardian.com/world/2013 /aug/19/cia-admits-role-1953-iranian-coup.

8. Quoted in PCDSM to PCDC, Cable no. 792, September 4, 1966, PC files, JC.

9. Essaye, trial notes, 21; Platt, "Unpublished Decision," 14.

10. The description of Dr. Dockeray in the witness stand comes from my recollection of him.

11. Dockeray, postmortem report, PC files, JC; Platt, "Unpublished Decision," 14–16; "Doctor Refutes Weapon Claim," *Norfolk Virginian-Pilot,* September 5, 1966, PC files, PR.

30. Trial Day Ten

1. Dr. Dockeray, testimony, summary gleaned from Platt, "Unpublished Decision," 14, 15; Dockeray, postmortem report, PC files, JC, 1–5.

2. "Injuries Bear Out Kinsey's Evidence of Fall—Doctor," *Nairobi Daily Nation,* September 6, 1966.

3. Dockeray, testimony, summary from Essaye, trial notes, 22, 23, and "Injuries Bear Out Kinsey's Evidence of Fall—Doctor."

4. Dockeray, testimony, summary from Essaye, trial notes, 22, 23, and "Injuries Bear Out Kinsey's Evidence of Fall—Doctor." It should be noted, however, that in Dockeray's

postmortem report, the following findings were given: "There was an abrasion 2" x ½ inch over the right ulna extending from just below the elbow to halfway down the forearm. This abrasion showed a 'skid-mark' appearance," and "There was a bruise on the back of the left forearm just below the elbow ½ inch in diameter and another above the elbow ½ inch in diameter" (see chapter 4).

5. Author's recollection.

6. Dockeray, testimony, summary and quotations from Essaye, trial notes, 23–24, and "Injuries Bear Out Kinsey's Evidence of Fall—Doctor."

7. Dale Peterson, *Jane Goodall: The Woman Who Redefined Man* (New York: Houghton Mifflin, 2006), 424, 425.

8. Quoted in "Doctor Tells of Kinsey's Distress," *Dar es Salaam Standard,* September 6, 1966.

9. The description of and quotations from McHugh's testimony in this and subsequent paragraphs come from Platt, "Unpublished Decision," 20, and "Doctor Tells of Kinsey's Distress."

31. Trial Day Eleven

1. "Court to Visit Death Scene," *Dar es Salaam Standard,* September 7, 1966.

2. Dr. Tom McHugh, testimony, summary and quotations gleaned from Essaye, trial notes, 23, and Platt, "Unpublished Decision," 17.

3. As given in Essaye, trial notes, 25.

4. Essaye, trial notes, 24.

5. Peter Clifford, testimony, summary gleaned from Essaye, trial notes, 24, and "Court to Visit Death Scene."

6. Essaye, trial notes, 25; Platt, "Unpublished Decision," 18.

7. PCDSM to PCDC, Cable no. 809, September 7, 1966, PC files, JC.

8. Georgiadis, lecture, 2007, 17.

32. Trial Day Twelve

1. Marianne Dunn, testimony, summary and quotations gleaned from Platt, "Unpublished Decision," 10, 20; Essaye, trial notes, 26; "Mother of Dead Girl Speaks for Kinsey," *Dar es Salaam Standard,* September 8, 1966; "Kinseys Never Had a Cross Word—Mother-in-Law," *Nairobi Daily Nation,* September 8, 1966.

2. Platt, "Unpublished Decision," 10, 20.

3. PC Nairobi to PCDC, Cable no. 416, August 19, 1966, RG 84, NA; "Mother of Dead Bride Testifies in Defense of Peace Corps Man," *Philadelphia Bulletin,* September 7, 1966.

4. Charlotte Dennett, testimony, summary based on and quotations from "Kinseys Never Had a Cross Word, Mother-in-Law."

5. Charlotte Dennett, testimony, quotations from "Kinseys Never Had a Cross Word, Mother-in-Law."

6. "Kinseys Never Had a Cross Word, Mother-in-Law"; Essaye, trial notes, 26; Platt, "Unpublished Decision," 10; "Mother of Dead Girl Speaks for Kinsey"; "Mother of Dead Bride Testifies in Defense of Peace Corps Man."

7. PCDC to PCDSM, Cable no. 157, September 8, 1966, PC files, JC.

8. Paul Sack, testimony, gleaned from PCDSM to PCDC, Cable no. 829, September 8, 1966, PC files, JC.

9. PCDC to PCDSM, Cable no. 122, September 7, 1966, RG 84, NA.

33. Trial Day Thirteen

1. PCDSM to PCDC, Cable no. 836, September 8, 1966, RG 84, NA; Essaye, trial notes, 26.

2. "Corpsman Returned to Scene of Death," *Palm Beach Post,* September 9, 1966, at https://palmbeachpost.newspapers.com/search/#query=Impala+Hill&ymd=1966-09-09; see also "Kinsey Court at Death Scene," *Dar es Salaam Standard,* September 9, 1966.

3. "Corpsman Returned to Scene of Death."

4. "Kinsey Court at Death Scene"; "Murder Trial Goes to Death Scene," *Nairobi Daily Nation,* September 9, 1966; "Corpsman Returned to Scene of Death."

34. Trial Day Fourteen

1. PCDSM to PCDC, Cable no. 847, September 9, 1966, RG 84, NA.

2. Georgiadis's summing up has been gathered and quoted from PCDSM to PCDC, Cable no. 847, September 9, 1966, RG 84, NA; "Prosecution a 'Damp Squib'— Georgiadis," *Dar es Salaam Standard,* September 10, 1966; Essaye, trial notes, 26; and "Murder Probe Was Inadequate—Defense," *Nairobi Daily Nation,* September 10, 1966. *Damp squib* is primarily a British a reference to a nineteenth-century mining explosive called a "squib" that would not detonate, so the phrase is used to describe something that does not work properly.

3. Effiwat's arguments are summarized and quoted from "Prosecution a 'Damp Squib— Georgiadis"; "Murder Probe Was Inadequate—Defense"; Essaye, trial notes, 26–28; Platt, "Unpublished Decision," 19; "Lawyer Raps [sic] Case against U.S. Corpsman," *Philadelphia Evening Bulletin,* September 9, 1966; PCDSM to PCDC, Cable no. 855, September 9, 1966, RG 84, NA; PCDSM to PCDC, Cable no. 847, September 9, 1966, RG 84, NA; "Kinsey: Final Pleas," *Nairobi Sunday Nation,* September 11, 1966.

4. PCDSM to PCDC, Cable no. 855, September 9, 1966, RG 84, NA.

35. Trial Day Fifteen

1. Essaye, trial notes, 29; "Kinsey Case Summing-up Today," *Nairobi Daily Nation,* September 12, 1966.

2. "Unexpected Adjournment by Kinsey Trial Judge," *Dar es Salaam Sunday News,* September 10, 1966; PCDSM to PCDC, Cable no. 857, September 10, 1966, PC files, PR.

3. PCDSM to PCDC, Cable no. 836, September 8, 1966, RG 84, NA.

4. PCDSM to PCDC, Cable no. 836, September 8, 1966; PCDSM to PCDC, Cable no. 855, September 9, 1966; PCDC to PCDSM, Cable no. 159, September 9, 1966; PCDC to PCDSM, Cable no. 224, September 11, 1966; PCDSM to PCDC, Cable no. 882, September 13, 1966; PCDC to PCDSM, Cable no. 242, September 13, 1966: all in RG 84, NA.

36. Trial Day Sixteen

1. Essaye, trial notes, 29; "Assessors Say Kinsey Is Not Guilty of Killing His Wife," *Nairobi Daily Nation,* September 13, 1966; "Kinsey Not Guilty, Say Assessors," *Dar es Salaam Standard,* September 13, 1966.

2. Summarized from Essaye, trial notes, 29; PCDSM to PCDC, Cable no. 952, September 12, 1966, PC files, JC.

3. Summarized from Essaye, trial notes, 30.

4. Summarized from Essaye, trial notes, 31.

5. Summarized from Essaye, trial notes, 31

6. Summarized from Essaye, trial notes, 31.

7. Summarized from Essaye, trial notes, 32, 33.

8. Summarized from Essaye, trial notes, 33; PCDSM to PCDC, Cable no. 879, September 12, 1966, PC files, JC.

9. Summarized from "Assessors Say Kinsey Is Not Guilty of Killing His Wife"; "Kinsey Not Guilty, Say Assessors"; Essaye, trial notes, 33.

10. Summarized from "Assessors Say Kinsey Is Not Guilty of Killing His Wife"; "Kinsey Not Guilty, Say Assessors"; Essaye, trial notes, 33; "Tanzania Jury Asks Judge to Free U.S. Man," *Philadelphia Bulletin,* September 13, 1966.

11. Gail Bagley, discussion with the author, February 6, 2012.

12. PCDSM to PCDC, Cable no. 927, September 16, 1966, RG 84, NA.

13. Associated Press report, September 16, 1966, PC files, JC.

14. PCDC to PCDSM, Cable no. 242, September 13, 1966, RG 84, NA.

15. PCDSM to PCDC, Cable no. 952, September 12, 1966, PC files, JC.

37. Trial Day Seventeen

1. "Kinsey Verdict on Monday," *Nairobi Daily Nation,* September 17, 1966.

2. PCDSM to PCDC, Cable no. 915, September 15, 1966, RG 84, NA.

3. PCDSM to PCDC, Cable no. 927, September 16, 1966, RG 84, NA.

4. PCDC to PCDSM, Cable no. 341, September 17, 1966, RG 84, NA; PCDSM to PCDC, Cable no. 942, September 17, 1966, RG 84, NA.

38. Trial Day Eighteen

The epigraph is from Tanzania Criminal Code, sec. 170, 171, quoted in Cole and Dennison, *Tanganyika,* 157.

1. "High Court Acquits Kinsey of Murder Charge," *Dar es Salaam Standard,* September 20, 1966; "Kinsey Acquitted of Murder," *Nairobi Daily Nation,* September 20, 1966.
2. Platt, "Unpublished Decision," 1, 2.
3. Phil and Ann Ellison to parents, September 17, 1966, author's collection; Platt, "Unpublished Decision," 2.
4. Platt, "Unpublished Decision," 3–4.
5. Platt, "Unpublished Decision," 4.
6. Platt, "Unpublished Decision," 4–6.
7. Platt, "Unpublished Decision," 3, 6.
8. Quoted in Platt, "Unpublished Decision," 7.
9. Platt, "Unpublished Decision," 5–8.
10. Platt, "Unpublished Decision," 9.
11. Platt, "Unpublished Decision," 9.
12. Platt, "Unpublished Decision," 10.
13. Platt, "Unpublished Decision," 10–11.
14. Platt, "Unpublished Decision," 13.
15. Platt, "Unpublished Decision," 14.
16. Platt, "Unpublished Decision," 15.
17. Platt, "Unpublished Decision," 16.
18. Platt, "Unpublished Decision," 18.
19. Platt, "Unpublished Decision," 19–21.
20. Platt, "Unpublished Decision," 22.
21. Sack, discussion with the author, April 10, 2010; PCDSM to PCDC, Cable no. 975, September 21, 1966, RG 84, NA.
22. PCDSM to PCDC, Cable no. 947, September 19, 1966, RG 84, NA.

Conclusion

1. Anthony Essaye, discussion with the author, June 3, 2010.
2. Essaye, discussion with the author, May 18, 2012.
3. As paraphrased in James Curran to John Burns, September 20, 1966, RG 84, NA.
4. Richard Richter, discussion with the author, January 12, 2012.
5. PCDSM to PCDC, Cable no. 975, September 21, 1966, RG 84, NA.
6. Sack to Bill Kinsey, October 19, 1966, McHugh files.
7. PCDSM to PCDC, Cable no. 975, September 21, 1966, RG 84, NA.
8. Sack to Kinsey, October 19, 1966, McHugh files.
9. Essaye to Sack, October 25, 1966, McHugh files.

10. McHugh to Brewster, October 18, 1966, McHugh files.

11. Platt, "Unpublished Decision," 2.

12. "The Kinsey Trial in Retrospect," undated and unattributed memo, RG 84, NA.

13. Phil and Ann Ellison to parents, September 17, 1966, author's collection.

14. See PCDSM to PCDC, Cable no. 345, March 29, 1966, RG 84, NA; Hummon, memo to file, March 29, 1966, PC files, JC; Sack, memo to file, March 31, 1966, PC files, JC.

15. McHugh to Brewster, October 18, 1966.

16. Brewster to Michael Sharlott, December 16, 1966, McHugh files.

17. Georgiadis, lecture, 2007, 5, 8, emphasis in original.

18. Georgiadis, lecture, 2007, 11.

19. Gerald Uelman, *Lessons from the Trial: The People v. O. J. Simpson* (Kansas City, Ks.: Andrews and McMeel, 1996), 62–63.

20. Uelman, *Lessons from the Trial,* 115, 166–77.

21. "Tanzania: In Another Country," *Newsweek,* October 3, 1966.

22. Sack to Vaughn, October 7, 1966, McHugh files.

23. The summary and quotations in the next six paragraphs come from "The Kinsey Trial in Retrospect."

24. Italics added here.

25. PCDSM to PCDC, Cable no. 975, September 21, 1966, RG 84, NA.

26. See "American in Tanzania Freed in Wife's Death," *New York Times,* September 21, 1966; "Trials: A Grudging Acquittal," *Time,* September 30, 1966; and "Tanzania: In Another Country."

27. "Trials: The Peace Corps Murder Case," *Time,* September 16, 1966.

28. Ruth Reynolds, "The Peace Corps Put on a Spot," *New York Sunday News,* November 20, 1966.

29. Georgiadis, lecture, 2007, 17.

30. Philip Weiss, *American Taboo: A Murder in the Peace Corps* (New York: Harper Collins, 2004), 182.

31. Meisler, W*hen the World Calls,* 138.

32. John Coyne, "A PCV Death in Tanzania," Peace Corps Worldwide, September 9, 2009, at http://peacecorpsworldwide.org/in-tanzania/, which includes William Edington's comment, posted April 3, 2010.

33. Dick Slama, comment in response to Coyne, "A PCV Death in Tanzania," posted September 11, 2016.

34. Peppy Kinsey to Susie Stevens (Sullivan), December 28, 1964, author's collection.

35. Peppy Kinsey to Stevens (Sullivan), March 13, 1965, author's collection.

36. Peppy Kinsey to Stevens (Sullivan), March 13, 1965, author's collection.

37. Peppy Kinsey to Stevens (Sullivan), August 30, 1965, author's collection, emphasis in original.

38. Peppy Kinsey to Stevens (Sullivan), November 1965 (no day provided), emphasis in original, author's collection.

39. Peppy Kinsey to Stevens (Sullivan), January 29, 1966, author's collection.

40. Georgiadis, lecture, 2007, 2.

41. U.S. embassy, Dar es Salaam, to PCDC, Cable no. 1033, September 26, 1966, RG 84, NA.

42. Georgiadis to Vaughn, October 12, 1966, McHugh files.

43. Sack to author, October 7, 1966, author's collection.

Epilogue

1. Ferenbach, discussion with the author, November 30, 2012.

2. "1982–1991: Carol Worcester Brewster," Hollins University Presidents, Hollins University, 1975, at https://digitalcommons.hollins.edu/presidents/6/; "Carol W. Brewster," Past Presidents, Hobart and William Smith Colleges, n.d., http://www.hws.edu/about/pastpresidents.aspx

3. "Lawyers Mourn Kenya's 'Most Costly' Attorney," *Nairobi Daily Nation,* May 1, 2010.

4. National Student Clearinghouse, at http://www.studentclearinghouse.org.

5. For examples of Kinsey's work, see Bill H. Kinsey, "Zimbabwe's Land Reform Program: Underinvestment in Post-conflict Tranformation," *World Development* 32, no. 2 (2004): 1669–96, at https://sarpn.org/documents/d0001133/P1249-Kinsey_Zim_Land_Reform_2004.pdf, and "Space and Time: A Long-Term Perspective on Land Reform from Zimbabwe's Experience," seminar, Africa Studies Centre, Leiden, May 24, 2018, at https://www.ascleiden.nl/news/seminar-bill-kinsey-space-and-time-long-term-perspective-land-reform-zimbabwes-experience.

6. McHugh, conversation with the author, August 29, 2014.

7. Jack McPhee to author, May 22, 2012, author's files.

8. Uganda Law Commission, report on commissioners' biographies, undated, at http://www.ulrc.go.ug/about_commissioners_&staff.php; no longer online, copy in author's files.

9. Sack, discussion with the author, March 18, 2012.

10. Meisler, *When the World Calls,* 221.

11. Quoted in Meisler, *When the World Calls,* 222.

12. See "Notes from the Field," *Peace Corps Times,* no. 3 (2009), at https://files.peacecorps.gov/multimedia/pdf/media/PCTimes2009_03.pdf.

13. See the National Peace Corps Association website at https://www.peacecorpsconnect.org.

14. See Friends of Tanzania, n.d., at https://www.fotanzania.org.

15. Robert Strauss, "Think Again: The Peace Corps," *Foreign Policy,* April 22, 2008, at https://foreignpolicy.com/author/robert-l-strauss/.

16. Karen Rothmyer, "The Peace Corps at 50: Remnant of a Bygone Era?" *The Nation,* March 21, 2011, at https://www.thenation.com/article/peace-corps-50-remnant-bygone-era/.

17. Peace Corps, *The Peace Corps Fiscal Year 2018 Congressional Budget Justification* (Washington, D.C.: Peace Corps, 2018), at https://files.peacecorps.gov/documents/open-government/peacecorps_cbj_2018.pdf.

18. Peace Corps Office of Inspector General, *Final Report: The Peace Corps' Sexual Assault Risk Reduction and Response Program* (Washington, D.C.: Peace Corps, November 2016), at https://files.peacecorps.gov/documents/inspector-general/Final_Evaluation_Report _on_the_Peace_Corps_Sexual_Assault_Risk_Reduction_and_Response_Program.pdf.

19. "Peace Corps Ends Discriminatory Pregnancy Policy," *Rewire News,* December 19, 2013, at https://rewire.news/article/2013/12/19/peace-corps-ends-discriminatory-pregnancy -policy/.

20. Peace Corps, "Women's Health Information," n.d., at https://www.peacecorps.gov /volunteer/health-and-safety/medical-care-during-service/#women.

21. Hoffman, *All You Need Is Love,* 230.

22. Mark Shriver, *A Good Man: Rediscovering My Father, Sargent Shriver* (New York: Holt, 2012), 12.

23. Peace Corps, *The Peace Corps Fiscal Year 2018 Congressional Budget Justification.*

24. Joseph Wilson, *The Politics of Truth: Inside the Lies That Led to War and Betrayed My Wife's CIA Identity. A Diplomat's Memoir* (New York: Avalon, 2004), 190.

25. Rieffel, *Reconsidering the Peace Corps,* 1.

Bibliography

Allott, Antony N., ed. *Judicial and Legal Systems in Africa.* London: Butterworths, 1970.
————. *New Essays in African Law.* London: Butterworths, 1970.
Ashabranner, Brent. *A Moment in History: The First Ten Years of the Peace Corps.* New York: Doubleday, 1971.
Baker, S. J. K. "The East African Environment." In *History of East Africa,* edited by Roland Oliver and Gervase Matthew. Oxford: Oxford University Press, 1963.
Bjerk, Paul. *Julius Nyerere.* Athens: Ohio University Press, 2017.
Bowles, Chester. *Promises to Keep: My Years in Public Life, 1941–1969.* New York: Harper & Row, 1971.
Brennan, James R. *TAIFA: Making Nation and Race in Urban Tanzania.* Athens: Ohio University Press, 2012.
Brooke-Edwards, Richard. "A Fourth Freedom." *Transition Magazine: An International Review,* no. 34 (1968): 5–16.
Buchert, Lene. *Education in the Development of Tanzania: 1919–90.* London: James Currey, 1994.
Bugliosi, Vincent. *Outrage: The Five Reasons Why O. J. Simpson Got Away with Murder.* New York: Norton, 1996.
Burrill, Emily S., Richard L. Roberts, and Elizabeth Thornberry, eds. *Domestic Violence and the Law in Colonial and Postcolonial Africa.* Athens: Ohio University Press, 2010.
Burton, Richard. *The Lake Regions of Central Africa.* 1860. Reprint. Mineola, N.Y.: Dover, 1995.
Calyx. Washington and Lee yearbook, 1964.
Cole, J. S. R., and W. N. Denison. *Tanganyika: The Development of Its Laws and Constitution.* London: Stevens & Sons, 1964.
Cotran, Eugene. "Tanzania." In *Judicial and Legal Systems in Africa,* edited by Antony N. Allott. London: Butterworths, 1970.
Dallek, Robert. *An Unfinished Life: John F. Kennedy 1917—1963.* New York: Little Brown, 2004.

Dennison, Harriet. *Leopards at My Door: Peace Corps, Tanzania, 1966–1967.* Portland, Ore.: Powell's Espresso Book Machine, 2013.

Duignan, Peter, and L. H. Gann. *The United States and Africa: A History.* New York: Cambridge University Press, 1984.

Garrett, Greg. "Relocating Burton: Public and Private Writings on Africa." *Journal of African Writing,* no. 2 (1997): 70–79.

Georgadis, Byron. Lecture given at the Kenya Society, London, May 29, 2007. Copy in author's collection.

Hanslick, Randy, and Michael Graham, eds. *Forensic Pathology in Criminal Cases.* 2nd ed. Charlottesville, Va.: Lexis, 2001.

Harlow, Vincent, E. M. Chilver, and Alison Smith. *History of East Africa.* 2 vols. Oxford: Clarendon Press, 1965.

Hatch, John. *Two African Statesmen: Kaunda of Zambia and Nyerere of Tanzania.* London: Secker & Warburg, 1976.

Hawes, Charlotte. "Sisters." Unpublished manuscript, n.d. Copy in author's collection.

Hickman, G. M., and W. H. G. Dickens. *The Lands and Peoples of East Africa: A School Certificate Geography.* London: Longmans, Green, 1960.

Hoching, Dr. Barbara, and Laura Leigh Manville. "What of the Right to Silence: Still Supporting the Presumption of Innocence or a Growing Legal Fiction." *Macquerie Law Journal* 1, no. 1 (2001). At http://www.austlii.edu.au/au/journals/MqLawJl/2001/3.html.

Hoffman, Elizabeth Cobbs. *All You Need Is Love: The Peace Corps and the Spirit of the 1960s.* 1998. Paperback reprint. Cambridge, Mass.: Harvard University Press, 2000.

Hughes, A. J. *East Africa: The Search for Unity; Kenya, Tanganyika, Uganda, and Zanzibar.* Baltimore: Penguin Books, 1963.

Hunter, Guy. *The New Societies of Tropical Africa.* New York: Praeger, 1964.

Iliffe, John. *A Modern History of Tanganyika.* Cambridge: Cambridge University Press, 1979.

Ingham, Kenneth. "Tanganyika: The Mandate and Cameron, 1919–1931." In *History of East Africa,* 2 vols., edited by Vincent Harlow, E. M. Chilver, and Alison Smith. Oxford: Clarendon Press, 1965.

James, R. W. *Land Tenure and Policy in Tanzania.* Toronto: University of Toronto Press, 1971.

Kennedy, Charles Stewart. "Interview with Barrington King." April 18, 1990. Frontline Diplomacy Oral History Collection, Library of Congress. At http://www.loc.gov/item/mfdipbib000616/.

Kozinski, Judge Alex. "Criminal Law 2.0." *Georgetown Law Journal: Annual Review of Criminal Procedure* 44 (2015): iii–xliv.

Latham, Michael E. *Modernization as Ideology: American Social Science and "Nation Building" in the Kennedy Era.* Chapel Hill: University of North Carolina Press, 2000.

Leavitt, Leonard. *An African Season.* New York: Simon and Schuster, 1966.

Legal and Human Rights Center. *Tanzania Human Rights Report 2008.* Dar es Salaam, Tanzania: Legal and Human Rights Center, 2008. At https://2009-2017.state.gov/j/drl/rls/hrrpt/2008/af/119028.htm.

Llamarada. Yearbook, Mount Holyoke University, South Hadley, Mass., 1964.

Lucas, C. Payne, and Kevin Lowther. "The Experience: Africa." In *Making a Difference: The Peace Corps at Twenty-Five,* edited by Milton Viorst. New York: Weidenfeld & Nicholson, 1986.

———. *Keeping Kennedy's Promise: The Peace Corps Moment of Truth.* 2nd ed. Baltimore: PeaceCorpsonline.org, 2002.

Maddox, Gregory H., and James L. Giblin, eds. *In Search of a Nation: Histories of Authority and Dissidence in Tanzania.* Oxford: James Currey, 2005.

Manning, Molly Guptil. *When Books Went to War: The Stories That Helped Us Win World War II.* New York: Houghton Mifflin Harcourt, 2014.

McPhee, John. "A Reporter at Large: Fifty-Two People on a Continent." *New Yorker,* March 5, 1966.

Medical Dictionary. Springfield, Mass.: Merriam-Webster, 2005.

Meeks, Charles. *Brief Authority: A Memoir of Colonial Administration in Tanganyika.* Edited by Innes Meeks. London: Radcliffe Press, 2011.

Meisler, Stanley. *When the World Calls: The Inside Story of the Peace Corps and Its First Fifty Years.* Boston: Beacon Press, 2011.

Morris, H. F. "A History of the Adoption of Codes of Criminal Law and Procedure in British Colonial Africa, 1876–1935." *Journal of African Law* 18, no. 1 (1974): 6–23.

Morris, H. F., and James Read. *Indirect Rule and the Search for Justice: Essays in East African Legal History.* Oxford: Clarendon Press, 1972.

Morris, Wright. *Ceremony in Lone Tree.* New York: New American Library of World Literature, 1962.

Muehlenbeck, Philip. *Betting on the Africans: John F. Kennedy's Courting of African Nationalist Leaders.* New York: Oxford University Press, 2012.

Ndembwike, John. *Life in Tanzania Today and since the Sixties.* Dar es Salaam, Tanzania: Continental Press, 2010.

Nyerere, Julius K. *Freedom and Socialism.* Dar es Salaam, Tanzania: Oxford University Press, 1968.

———. *Freedom and Unity.* Dar es Salaam, Tanzania: Oxford University Press, 1966.

Oliver, Roland, and Mathew Gervase, eds. *History of East Africa.* London: Oxford University Press, 1963.

Patterson, Richard. *Lawyers Medical Encyclopedia of Personal Injuries and Allied Specialties.* 5th ed. Charlottesville, Va.: Michie Company, Lexus/Nexus, 2005.

"Paul Bomani." In *Dictionary of African Biography*, edited by Emmanuel K. Akyeampoeg and Henry Louis Gates Jr. New York: Oxford University Press, 2012.

Peace Corps. *First Annual Peace Corps Report, June 30, 1962.* Washington, D.C.: Peace Corps, 1962. At http://www.peacecorpsonline.org/historyofthepeacecorps/annualreports/1ST_1962.PDF.

———. *The Peace Corps Fiscal Year 2018 Congressional Budget Justification.* Washington, D.C.: Peace Corps, 2018. At https://files.peacecorps.gov/documents/open-government/peacecorps_cbj_2018.pdf.

Peace Corps Office of Inspector General. *Final Report: The Peace Corps' Sexual Assault Risk Reduction and Response Program.* Washington, D.C.: Peace Corps, November 2016. At https://files.peacecorps.gov/documents/inspector-general/Final_Evaluation_Report _on_the_Peace_Corps_Sexual_Assault_Risk_Reduction_and_Response_Program .pdf.

Peterson, Dale. *Jane Goodall: The Woman Who Redefined Man.* New York: Houghton Mifflin, 2006.

Platt, Judge H. G. "Unpublished Decision in the Case of *The Republic v. Bill Haywood Kinsey.* Criminal Sessions Case No. 65 of 1966 [Tanzania]." September 19, 1966. Copy in the author's collection.

Pleck, Elizabeth. *Domestic Tyranny: The Making of American Social Policy against Family Violence from Colonial Times to the Present.* Urbana: University of Illinois Press, 2004.

Pratt, R. Cranford. *The Critical Phase in Tanzania 1945–1968: Nyerere and the Emergence of a Socialist Strategy.* Cambridge: Cambridge University Press, 1976.

Read, James. "Criminal Law Materials." Faculty of Law, University College, Dar es Salaam. Tanzania, 1966.

Redmon, Coates. *Come as You Are: The Peace Corps Story.* New York: Harcourt Brace Jovanovich, 1986.

Republic v. Bill Haywood Kinsey. Unpublished transcript of the preliminary hearing before Coram V. D. Mhaisker. Criminal Case no. 85, 1966, Tanzania. Peace Corps files obtained by John Coyne. Copy in the author's collection.

Rice, Gerald T. *The Bold Experiment: JFK's Peace Corps.* Notre Dame, Ind.: University of Notre Dame Press, 1985.

Rieffel, Lex. *Reconsidering the Peace Corps.* Policy brief. Washington, D.C.: Brookings Institution, December 2003. At https://www.brookings.edu/research/reconsidering-the -peace-corps/.

Rotberg, Robert J. *Africa and Its Explorers.* Cambridge, Mass.: Harvard University Press, 1970.

Rothmyer, Karen. "The Peace Corps at 50: Remnant of a Bygone Era?" *The Nation,* March 21, 2011. At https://www.thenation.com/article/peace-corps-50-remnant-bygone-era/.

Rubin, Neville, and Eugene Cotran, eds. *Readings in African Law.* Vol. 2. London: Frank Cass, 1970.

Russell, E. W. *The Natural Resources of East Africa.* Nairobi, Kenya: East African Literature Bureau, 1962.

Sabato, Larry J. *The Kennedy Half Century: The Presidency, Assassination, and Lasting Legacy of John F. Kennedy.* New York: Bloomsbury, 2013.

Sagerson, E. P. "The Geology of East Africa." In *Handbook of Natural Resources of East Africa,* edited by E. W. Russell. Nairobi, Kenya: D. A. Hawkins in association with East African Literature Bureau, 1962.

Schlesinger, Arthur M. *A Thousand Days: John F. Kennedy in the White House.* Boston: Hough Mifflin; Cambridge: Riverside Press, 1965.

Schwarz, Karen. *What You Can Do for Your Country: Inside the Peace Corps, a Thirty Year History.* New York: Anchor Books Doubleday, 1991.

See Dar es Salaam. Dar es Salaam, Tanzania: Shell Oil, 1964.

Shachtman, Tom. *Airlift to America: How Barack Obama, Sr., John F. Kennedy, Tom Mboya, and 800 East African Students Changed Their World and Ours.* New York: St. Martin's Press, 2009.

Shriver, Mark. *A Good Man: Rediscovering My Father, Sargent Shriver.* New York: Holt, 2012.

Smith, William Edgett. *We Must Run While They Walk: A Portrait of Africa's Julius Nyerere.* New York: Random House, 1971.

Steinberg, S. H., ed. *The Statesman's Yearbook 1964–1965.* New York: St. Martin's Press, 1964.

Strauss, Robert. "Think Again: The Peace Corps." *Foreign Policy,* April 22, 2008. At https://foreignpolicy.com/author/robert-l-strauss/.

Tanganyika Directory. Dar es Salaam: Government of the United Republic of Tanzania, 1965. Copy in the author's collection.

Tanganyika Guide. Dar es Salaam, Tanzania: n.p., 1948. Copy in the author's collection.

Toobin, Jeffrey. *The Run of His Life: The People v. O. J. Simpson.* New York: Random House, 1996.

Traynor, Roger. "Ground Lost and Found in Criminal Discovery." *New York University Law Review* 39, no. 2 (April 1964): 749–70.

Turner, Barry, ed. *The Statesman's Year Book 2012.* New York: Macmillan, 2011.

Uelman, Gerald F. *Lessons from the Trial: The People v. O. J. Simpson.* Kansas City, Ks.: Andrews and McMeel, 1996.

Viorst, Milton, ed. *Making a Difference: The Peace Corps at Twenty-Five.* New York: Weidenfeld & Nicolson, 1986.

Weiss, Philip. *American Taboo: A Murder in the Peace Corps.* New York: Harper Collins, 2004.

Wilson, Joseph C. *The Politics of Truth: Inside the Lies That Led to War and Betrayed My Wife's CIA Identity. A Diplomat's Memoir.* New York: Avalon, 2004.

Wofford, Harris. *Of Kennedys and Kings: Making Sense of the Sixties.* Pittsburg: University of Pittsburg Press, 1980.

Zimmerman, Jonathan. *Innocents Abroad: American Teachers in the American Century.* Cambridge, Mass.: Harvard University Press, 2006.

Index